302.542 G00
W/C

To Stanley Cohen

Moral Panics

The Social Construction of Deviance

Erich Goode and
Nachman Ben-Yehuda

BLACKWELL
Oxford UK & Cambridge USA

First published in USA 1994
Reprinted 1995, 1996, 1997, 1999, 2001, 2002

Blackwell Publishers Inc
350 Main Street
Malden, Massachusetts 02148, USA

Blackwell Publishers Ltd
108 Cowley Road
Oxford OX4 1JF, UK

Library of Congress Cataloging in Publication Data
Goode, Erich.
Moral panics: the social construction of deviance/Erich Goode and
Nachman Ben-Yehuda
p. cm.
Includes bibliographical references and index.
ISBN 0–631–18904–1 (alk. paper) — ISBN 0–631–18905–X (pbk)
1. Deviant behaviour. 2. Social problems. 3. Moral conditions.
I. Ben-Yehuda, Nachman. II. Title.
HM291.G647   1994   93–48397
302.5'42—dc20   CIP

British Library Cataloguing in Publication Data
A CIP catalogue record for this book is available from the British Library

Typeset in 11 on 13pt Plantin
by Best-set Typesetter Ltd, Hong Kong
Printed and bound in Great Britain
by T. J. International Ltd, Padstow, Cornwall

This book is printed on acid-free paper.

CONTENTS

PREFACE AND ACKNOWLEDGMENTS

Contemplating the folly of collective action has preoccupied countless social observers for millennia. This book is no mere debunking exercise, however. Much seemingly unreasonable behavior makes sense if viewed through a particular conceptual lens. To counter the classic "Why?" question – why do so many of us become fearful of and concerned by seeming threats that are less harmful or dangerous than others? – we offer the "Why not?" question; to most of us, such fears and concerns make a great deal of sense. Rationality is bounded by culture, and what seems unreasonable and irrational within one cultural framework is distinctly reasonable and rational in another. Yes, beliefs and actions that offer striking departures from empirical reality – what is widely recognized to be true – generally demand an explanation. But by what rules do we establish empirical truth? What cultural framework informs us that one assertion is true and another false? Even when we admit the empirical truth or falsity of certain versions of events in the material world, why does one set of events stir our fear and concern, while another does not? Here we establish that this question cannot be answered with fact or logic, with a rational assessment of risk or danger. Again, the "Why?" question; and once again, the "Why not?" question.

The senior author lives in a suburb of New York City, a municipality some friends, acquaintances, and colleagues refuse to venture into. Why? Robbery, murder, violence, crime. The statistics on crime reveal roughly 1.2 million robberies in the United States each year – relatively few of which result in physical harm – and about 25,000 murders. Goodness, the rationalist would argue, your odds of being injured in a household accident or being killed by a host of diseases are greater than being a victim of a serious crime. Why should such a low-odds threat – violent crime – deter one from engaging in pleasureable urban activities? To many of us who live with the fear of urban crime, the rationalist's position seems inane and meaningless.

x Preface and Acknowledgments

The junior author lives in Israel; political violence figures heavily in the fears and concerns of Israelis (and foreigners who have loved ones in, or are contemplating visiting, Israel), especially since the Palestinian uprising, or Intifada, began in December 1987. Many Jews have begun avoiding going into predominantly Palestinian areas, such as the Old City of Jerusalem, East Jerusalem, and the occupied territories – the West Bank and Gaza. Those who do so are warned by their peers: why expose yourself to such danger? they ask. Yet, the number of individuals who have been killed in Israel and the territories by political violence in the past six years is under a thousand souls, of whom perhaps 200 were Jews killed by Arab terrorists. The chances of dying in an automobile accident is far greater. Why the exaggerated fear? What makes one threat more fearful than another, more prodigious source of danger and death?

The subject of this book is fears and concerns such as these. Again, while they seem exaggerated from a strictly rational or empirical perspective, they make sense when viewed through the lives of the people experiencing them. They should not be dismissed as unreasonable, irrational or pathological. At the same time, an investigation of such seemingly unreasonable fears and concerns should not degenerate into an apology for them. Some fears spawn harmful policy, and rationalizing them may help to neutralize political forces working to nullify that harm. In short, these fears and conerns are part and parcel of the human condition, an expression of human frailty. We are all subject to them; all societies are wracked by them. An investigation of their bases and dynamics will help illuminate the bases and dynamics of society generally. It is a pity they have not been subject to the systematic study they deserve. This book represents a step in correcting that deficiency.

We would like to thank Stan Cohen, Mimi Ajzenstadt, and Menachem Horowitz for their valuable assistance and advice. In addition, the senior author would like to thank the Lady Davis Fellowship Trust for granting him a visiting professorship at the Hebrew University of Jerusalem for the spring semester of 1993, which made it possible for this book to be written. The office staff of the Department of Sociology at Hebrew University, too, must be thanked for their generous assistance. He would also like to thank his wife, Barbara Weinstein, for her encouragement and assistance. He would like to thank too the Council for International Exchange of Scholars for having the good sense to award her a Fulbright Lectureship, which made our stay in Israel a geat deal more comfortable than would otherwise have been the case.

The second author would like to thank Etti Ben-Yehuda for her continuous support love and encouragement, and Tzach and Guy for their patience and love.

Some pages and chapters of this book were borrowed or adapted from several of the authors' previously published works. Parts of the Prologue, "A Representative Moral Panic: Satanic Ritual Abuse," and Chapters 7 and 8, were borrowed or adapted from Erich Goode, *Collective Behavior* (Harcourt Brace Jovanovich, 1992), pp. 50–2, 55, 337–42, 434–40, and passim. A few pages of "The Prohibition Movement, 1900–1920" and Chapter 12 were borrowed or adapted from Erich Goode, *Drugs in American Society* (4th edn) (McGraw-Hill, 1993), pp. 166–7, 48–57. In addition, Erich Goode, "The American Drug Panic of the 1980s: Social Construction or Objective Threat?" *Violence, Aggression and Terrorism*, 3(4) (1989), pp. 327–44, has been incorporated into Chapter 12. Chapter 4 was adapted, and the section, "A Representative Moral Panic: LSD in the 1960s," borrowed, from Erich Goode, *Deviant Behavior* (4th edn) (Prentice-Hall, 1994). Chapter 10 is adapted from Nachman Ben-Yehuda, "The European Witch Craze of the 14th to 17th Centuries: A Sociologist's Perspective," *The American Journal of Sociology*, 86(1) (1980), pp. 1–31, and *Deviance and Moral Boundaries: Witchcraft, the Occult, Science Fiction, and Scientists* (University of Chicago Press, 1985), pp. 23–73. Chapter 11 is adapted from Nachman Ben-Yehuda, "The Sociology of Moral Panics: Toward a New Synthesis," *The Sociological Quarterly* (published by JAI Press Inc.), 27(4) (1986), pp. 495–513, and *The Politics and Morality of Deviance: Moral Panics, Drug Abuse, Deviant Science, and Reversed Stigmatization* (State University of New York Press, 1990), pp. 97–133. Permission to use or reprint this material is gratefully acknowledged.

PROLOGUE

Views on the rationality of collective action have swung back and forth over the centuries. The eighteenth century has been characterized as the Age of Reason; leading intellectuals argued that men and women acted out of strictly rationalistic principles – they were motivated to seek pleasure and avoid pain. Cesare Beccaria (1738–94) held that the state should administer punishment to wrongdoers just sufficiently painful to counterbalance the pleasure they would derive from committing criminal acts (Gibbons, 1992, p. 16). Being rational, most of us will seek to avoid pain by not committing crimes.

But by some time in the nineteenth century, something of an age of unreason was upon us. In 1841, Charles Mackay (1814–89), a Scottish poet, journalist, and song-writer, published a book entitled *Memoirs of Extraordinary Popular Delusions*. (In a later edition, he changed its title.) In it, Mackay described such phenomena as the Crusades, prophecies, astrology, fortune-telling, the witch mania of Renaissance Europe, belief in haunted houses, popular admiration for thieves and bandits, political and religious control of hair and beard styles, and "tulipomania," or the economic craze that gripped the Netherlands in the seventeenth century, which entailed buying and selling tulip bulbs at incredibly high and, supposedly, inflated prices. Mackay argued that nations, "like individuals, have their whims and their peculiarities, their seasons of excitement and recklessness, when they care not what they do." Whole communities, he asserted, "suddenly fix their minds upon one object, and go mad in its pursuit; millions of people become simultaneously impressed with one delusion, and run after it, until their attention is caught by some new folly more captivating than the first" (1932, p. xix).

These views were echoed half a century later in the writing of Gustave LeBon (1841–1931). In *The Crowd*, published in 1895, LeBon argued that when people assemble in gatherings, they lose their individual characteristics and become transformed into a homogeneous, irrational mob, whose members are characterized by stupidity (1982,

p. 9), suggestibility (p. 10), impulsivity and "irresistible impetuosity" (p. 11), babarism (p. 12), "irritability, incapacity to reason, the absence of judgment and of the critical spirit, the exaggeration of the senti-ment" (p. 16), credulity (pp. 20ff), and intolerance (p. 37). Members of the crowd are like a hypnotized individual in the hands of a hypno-tist. "The conscious personality has entirely vanished; will and discern-ment are lost" (p. 11). In a crowd, every member is like "an automaton who has ceased to be guided by his will" (p. 12). The individual in a crowd has become someone who "descends several rungs in the ladder of civilisation," a "creature acting by instinct" (p. 12).

The views of Mackay and LeBon found a later, somewhat more sophisticated, expression in the work of Robert Park (1864–1944) and Herbert Blumer (1900–87), who argued that irrational, even destruc-tive behavior could be generated by means of a mechanism Blumer referred to as social "contagion" (Park, 1972; Blumer, 1939, 1969), whereby "discomfort, frustration, insecurity and . . . alienation or loneliness" are communicated from one individual to another, thus generating "social unrest," a widespread feeling in the form of "vague apprehensions, alarm, fears, insecurity, eagerness, or aroused pugnacity" (Blumer, 1969, pp. 72, 73).

But during the 1960s and 1970s, the pendulum swung back in the "rationalist" direction. Rational calculus or game theory (Berk, 1974) argued that, in engaging in collective actions that attempt to attain a specific goal, people tend to weigh the costs and benefits of their behavior in a careful, rational, calculating fashion; they arrive at a course of action that maximizes their reward and minimizes their cost.

The "resource mobilization" perspective (McCarthy and Zald, 1973; Zald and McCarthy, 1987) argued that social movements are successful to the extent that movement entrepreneurs and strategists can marshall talent, skill, knowledge, money, media time and attention, connections with the rich and powerful – in short, resources – and focus them on a particular issue or condition.

A cadre of sociologists examined crowd behavior and found that the traditional "irrationalist" approach was empirically in error; human gatherings do not typically act in the frenzied, destructive, irrational fashion described by Mackay, LeBon, Park, and Blumer. Instead, crowds assemble and disperse according to ordinary, everyday physi-cal, social, and contextual factors and contingencies, such as employ-ment, childcare, and the lay-out of public squares and streets; very few members of any crowd engage in the irrational behavior posited by our quartet of early theorists (McPhail and Miller, 1973; Miller, 1985; McPhail, 1991).

And the study of disasters, too, manifested this pendulum shift to a more rational and less self-destructive view of human action: It has shown that, in the face of disaster, most people do not engage in the barbaric, selfish, unthinking, emotional, and the often self-destructive behavior depicted in the media; rather, they tend to act in a relatively calm, rational, and even altrustic fashion. In fact, these researchers argue, one of the most important features of disaster-related behavior is the impact that rationally-instituted and administered bureaucratic organizations have on the process of coping with disaster-generated havoc (Barton, 1969; Dynes, 1970).

And yet, it must be admitted, while much collective action is appropriate to the task, goal, challenge, or threat at hand, not all of it can be characterized as completely rational. Erroneous beliefs purportedly accounting for the events of the day are often held, and strategy may be pursued which seems almost designed to defeat self-professed goals. In a crisis, enemies may be designated who pose no concrete threat whatsoever; not uncommonly, fear arises over nonexistent conditions; major, serious, life-threatening problems are sometimes ignored; harmful behavior may be tolerated. While much, possibly most, collective action does fit the rationalistic model, some of it – at times, in specific locales, seemingly, all of it – does not. No one wishes to return to the bizarre and fantastical theories of LeBon and his ilk, yet events of interest to us all simply cannot be accounted for by means of the strictly rationalistic model.

How are we then to account for seemingly irrational behavior when it does occur? At least two explanations have been offered.

First, extreme or radical relativity can, in effect, define rationality out of existence; no objective standard exists, this perspective holds, by which one assertion, belief, or view can be regarded as more, or less, rational, true, or effective. There is no "ontologically privileged" position from which the concrete, literal truth of assertions, or the effectiveness or ineffectiveness of specific goal-directed actions, may be determined (Aronson, 1984; Kitsuse and Schneider, 1989; Kitsuse and Spector, 1973; Spector and Kitsuse, 1977; Woolgar and Pawluch, 1985; Ibarra and Kitsuse, 1993).

And second, the less powerful members of a society may hold views or pursue policies which may subvert their own interests, but which may serve the interests of the more powerful members of the society. In the latter case, the supposedly irrational behavior under scrutiny may be quite rational for the segments, categories, or classes of the society who command society's resources, but irrational for those who don't realize they are being manipulated and exploited (Hall et al., 1978; Reinarman and Levine, 1989; Zatz, 1987; Levine and Reinarman, 1988).

Our dissatisfaction with these recent developments – the strictly rationalist perspective, radical relativism, and the assumption that elites dominate social institutions to the extent that they can control or dictate human consciousness and behavior – led to the writing of this book. We see these perspectives as incapable of understanding some of the more fascinating and revealing episodes of collective action in human history. Such episodes, we contend, can be regarded as a test for theories of human behavior in general. In these episodes, people have become intensely concerned about a particular issue or perceived threat – which, as measured by concrete indicators, turns out not to be especially damaging – and have assembled, and taken action, to remedy the problem; yet, somehow, at a later point in time, they lost interest in the issue or threat, often turning their attention to other matters. These episodes have been referred to as *moral panics*.

The Canudos Massacre: Brazil, 1893–7

For twenty years, a religious mystic who came to be known as Antonio Conselheiro wandered the northeast backlands of Brazil, "preaching against ungodly behavior and rebuilding rural churches and cemeteries that had fallen into disrepair in the forbidding, semiarid interior" (Levine, 1992, p. 2). In 1893, Conselheiro led a pious group of disciples into an inaccessible mountain valley in Bahia; there, on the site of an abandoned ranch, he founded a religious community – Canudos. Thousands were attracted to it, drawn "by Conselheiro's charismatic madness. He promised only sacrifice and hard work and asked residents to live according to God's commandments and await the coming of the Millennium, when would come redemption, the Day of Judgment" (p. 2). Conselheiro's vision was that the weak would inherit the earth; the order of nature itself would be overturned, with rainfall blessing the customarily arid region, ushering in an era of agricultural abundance. Within two years the settlement became the second largest city in the state of Bahia; at its height, Canudos's population was more than a tenth of that of the city of São Paulo at the time (p. 2).

Landowners did not take kindly to the loss of their labor-force; they demanded government intervention. The Catholic church, struggling against what it saw as heterodoxy, apostasy, and the influence of Afro-Brazilian cults, likewise demanded immediate action. The army dispatched soldiers to capture Conselheiro. The task proved to be far more formidable than any official had dreamed. The first three assaults were repulsed by tenacious resistance from Conselheiro's followers. The campaign stretched out over two years. Finally, in October 1897, Canudos was encircled by 8,000 troops serving under three generals and Brazil's Minister of War, and was bombarded into submission by heavy artillery. The repression of the community had been violent and bloody. Thousands of Conselheiro's followers were killed; the captured survivors numbered only in the hundreds. The wounded were drawn and quartered or "hacked to pieces limb by limb" (p. 190). Soldier "killed children by smashing their skulls against trees" (p. 190). Conselheiro's head was cut off and displayed on a pike. (It turns out that he had already died two weeks before the final assault, probably of dysentery.) All 5,000 houses in the settlement were "smashed, leveled and burned" (p. 190); the grounds of Canudos were torched and dynamited. "The army systematically eradicated the remaining traces of the holy city as if it had housed the devil incarnate" (p. 190).

The resistance of Canudos had generated a crisis in Brazilian society:

> Highlighted by the universal fascination with stories about crazed religious fanatics, the Canudos conflict flooded the press, invading not only editorials, columns, and news dispatches, but even feature stories and humor. For the first time in Brazil, newspapers were used to create a sense of public panic. Canudos accounts appeared daily, almost always on the front page; indeed, the story was the first ever to receive daily coverage in the Brazilian press. More than a dozen major newspapers sent war correspondents to the front and ran daily columns reporting events . . . Something about Canudos provoked anxiety, which would be soothed only by evidence that Canudos had been destroyed. (Levine, 1992, p. 24)

In order to understand the intensity of the public concern in Brazil in the 1890s over the existence of a religious community consisting of a few thousand souls who, as far as anyone could tell, were not violating any of the country's criminal statutes, it is necessary to turn the calendar back a century and examine the events of the time. The abolition of slavery had been achieved in Brazil in 1888; the monarchy had been overthrown in 1889. A standard, uniform system of weights and measures had been introduced, and the Portuguese language was being standardized on a nationwide basis by decree. Brazil, it seemed, was poised on the very brink of modernity. By forming a fanatical, millennial community, Conselheiro was defying government authority, which was attempting to extend its reach into every hamlet in Brazil. Indeed, Canudos rejected the very civilizing process itself; the millenarians threatened to plunge Brazilian society back into a state of darkness and superstition. The backlanders had defied "the progressive and modern benefits of civilized life" (p. 155). "Urban Brazilians were proud of their material and political accomplishments and felt only shame at the dark, primitive world of the hinterlands" (p. 155). Only one possible solution to the challenge posed by Canudos existed: The movement must be crushed, the community obliterated, and Conselheiro and his followers exterminated.

The Boys of Boise

On November 2, 1955, the citizens of Boise, Idaho, woke up to a headline in *The Idaho Daily Statesman*, which read: "Three Boise Men Admit Sex Charges." Charles Brokaw, a freight worker, Ralph Cooper, a shoe-store employee, and Vernon Cassel, a clothing-store clerk, were charged, the newspaper story said, with "infamous crimes against nature" (Gerassi, 1966, p. 1), which referred to various homosexual practices. An investigation "was being launched" into allegations of "immoral acts involving teen-age boys" (p. 1). Although the authorities "had barely scratched the surface," the article continued, there was incomplete evidence that similar acts were committed by other adults against about a hundred boys (p. 2). That day, conversation in Boise revolved around the arrests and their disturbing implications. Was it possible that "a vast secret organization of perverts" had been operating in Boise and that "every kid in high school" had been corrupted (p. 3)? Citizens called the (then, only) high school, police headquarters, the *Statesman* – and one another – "stressing the acute seriousness of the whole matter" (p. 3).

On the next day, November 3, in an editorial entitled "Crush the Monster," the *Statesman* demanded that the "whole sordid situation" be "completely cleared up, and the premises thoroughly cleaned and disinfected" (p. 4). Such an editorial "was bound to generate panic, and it did" (p. 4). However, when the *Statesman* called for all agencies to "crush the monster," one thing was certain: "there was no such thing" (p. 5). Three "rather unimportant, unassuming, unpolitical individuals had been arrested for doing something either infamous or lewd with some minors," and a probate-court officer claimed that some other adults had done the same thing with as many as a hundred teenagers. "On that kind of evidence, most newspapers would only demand more information" (p. 5).

A week later, one of the defendants, Ralph Cooper – who had a long record of arrests and convictions – received an astounding life sentence for his crimes. (He was released after nine years.) The other two men received 15-year sentences. Four days after Cooper's imprisonment, Joe Moore, vice-president of the Idaho First National Bank, was arrested on felony charges of committing, once again, an "infamous crime against nature" (p. 12). Another *Statesman* editorial appeared the next day which warned Boise parents "to keep an eye on the whereabouts" of their children" because "a number of boys have been victimized by these perverts . . . No matter what is required, this sordid mess must be removed from this community" (p. 13).

Men who stopped to talk to adolescent boys, men who paused to look at football practice, even men "who were not good, kind, obedient husbands," were denounced (pp. 13–14). The county's prosecuting attorney, Blaine Evans, became a local hero. He vowed to "eliminate" all homosexuals from Boise. Though this sort of talk made the town's citizens alarmed, at least, they reasoned, "something was being done" about the problem (p. 13). On the morning of November 15, a young teacher, an admitted homosexual, while eating his breakfast of eggs, toast, and coffee and reading his morning *Statesman*, came upon the news item of Moore's arrest, accompanied by Blaine's promise to "eliminate" all homosexuals. He never finished his breakfast. "He jumped up from his seat, pulled out his suitcases, packed as fast as he could, got into his car, and drove straight to San Francisco, never even bothering to call up the school to let it be known that he would be absent. The cold eggs, coffee and toast remained on his table for two days before someone from his school came by to see what had happened" (p. 14).

On December 2, Charles Herbert Gordon, an interior decorator, pled guilty to "lewd and lascivious conduct," and was sentenced to 15 years' imprisonment. On December 11, a dozen men, some prominent citizens, were arrested on homosexual charges. On December 12, the scandal reached national proportions; *Time* magazine ran a story claiming that "a widespread homosexual underworld that involved some of Boise's most prominent men and had preyed on hundreds of teen-age boys for the past decade" (p. ix). On December 19, a curfew was established in Boise for minors age 16 and younger. On December 22, the Boise City Council called for the conviction and sentencing of all arrested homosexuals. On December 23, five homosexuals were sentenced to periods ranging from six months to ten years. In April, the mayor announced that nearly 1,500 persons had been interviewed concerning the investigation. Over the next year, the arrests and sentences continued; by January 1957, the scandal was regarded as having come to an end (pp. xv–xviii).

Why the panic over homosexuality in Boise in 1955 and 1956? Why the ludicrous and almost literally impossible assertion that a "ring" or "organization" of adult men were preying on scores, possibly hundreds, of local boys? Was the issue homosexuality in the first place? And *to whom* was it an issue?

One journalist (Gerassi, 1966) claimed that the investigation which launched the panic was undertaken by the city's power elite, the "Boise gang," a circle of rich, powerful, and conservative executives, entrepreneurs, and politicians, to discredit City Hall – "which was then in the hands of a fairly decent, reformist administration" (p. 21) – and one council member in particular whose son had been involved in the homosexual activity under investigation. In addition, the intention was to flush out and discredit a member of that powerful inner circle, a man referred to publicly as the "Queen." The irony of the scandal was that the individuals who were the real target of the scandal were never named, while the unintended victims, many humble and power-less, were punished. Moreover, not all of the individuals who were named had sex with underage minors; several, in fact, engaged in homosexual acts with consenting adults (though still a crime in the state of Idaho in 1955). Even those who technically violated the state's laws against sex with minors were involved in activity with a small number of 15-, 16-, and 17-year-old juvenile delinquents and male prostitutes who hustled adult homosexuals for pay and en-gaged in blackmail against them. The Boise sex scandal proved to be a proverbial "tempest in a teapot."

When questioned a decade later, the prosecuting attorney responsi-ble for the cases defended his role in investigating and arresting homo-sexuals: we had to get "these guys," he said, "because they strike at the core of society, I mean the family and the family unit. And when you get these guys crawling around the streets, you've got to prosecute to save the family" (p. 25). When asked why such a fuss was made at this particular time and why the sentences at this time were so harsh, he replied, "I guess we didn't know that there were so many of them in the community. You know, when it's going on in the basement of the Public Library, and in the hotels, and these guys are soliciting business all over town, you've got to do something about it, don't you?" (p. 24). A Boise Valley farmer put the matter even more simply; when inter-viewed ten years after the scandal, he said: "We grow them tough out here . . . and that's the way we want to grow them. None of this hanky-panky and city stuff for us. Our kids have to be men, just like their forefathers . . . There's no room for these queers. We don't want them. They should be run out of the state" (p. 129).

Rumor in Orléans, France, May 1969

In May 1969, in Orléans, France, a rumor began to spread to the effect that six women's dress shops in town were involved in what was referred to at the time as the "white slave traffic." Young women, it was said, were forcibly drugged by injection while trying on dresses in fitting-rooms, and spirited away under the cover of darkness to foreign locales and forced into prostitution. All six of the shops that were the focus of the rumor were owned by Jews. At one stage of the develop-ment of this rumor, it was claimed that all the shops were connected by means of underground tunnels that met in a main sewer which flowed into the Loire River, where a boat (in one version, a submarine) picked up its "cargo," again, under the cloak of darkness (Morin, 1971).

Of course, no women were drugged or abducted, and none dis-appeared from Orléans. The story was – it hardly needs to be stated –

a complete invention, a rumor utterly lacking in substance. Why did it arise where and when it did? Fantastic stories of the enforced prostitution of young women, especially in exotic foreign locales, has been a theme in western literature for well over two centuries. But why Orléans and why 1969?

Early in 1969, a French translation of a supposedly journalistic book, entitled *Sex Slavery*, was published. One of the stories in this book detailed an attempted clothing-store fitting-room abduction by means of a drug injection. In the second week of May 1969, a translation of the attempted fitting-room kidnapping account appeared in a French magazine, *Noir et Blanc* under the title, "White Slavery Tricks." No source was attributed, the event was said to have occurred "not long ago," and erotic photographs accompanied the article. The rumor in Orléans began to circulate the week after the magazine hit the newsstands; clearly, the *Noir et Blanc* article had launched the rumor.

Still, *Noir et Blanc* was a national magazine, sold all over France. Why did the white slavery story crop up in Orléans and not throughout the country? A second event almost certainly provided another catalyst. On May 10, a new department of a boutique celebrated its opening. Called "The Dungeon," its fitting-rooms were located in a cellar; the decor was mysterious, medieval, and dungeon-like. (Significantly, no rumors circulated about "The Dungeon," whose owner was *not* Jewish.) Thus, while the article in *Noir et Blanc* provided the "script," the opening of "The Dungeon" provided the "appropriate stage-setting" (Morin, 1971, p. 22). Both events acted as catalysts in launching the white slavery rumor in Orléans in May 1969.

But why were Jewish boutique owners selected as the perpetrators of this nefarious activity? More specifically, the rumor did *not* circulate about elderly Jews with foreign accents or recent Jewish immigrants from North Africa. "It concentrated exclusively on a group of shopowners who had nothing exotic about them, who looked just like anyone else but through that very fact contrived to conceal the one mysterious difference which the whole world knew: their Jewishness" (Morin, 1971, p. 28). Thus, it was not so much the fact of their *difference* from the rest of the French population that was significant, but their *similarity*. They had assimilated into French society but they had remained different – and exotic – by virtue of being Jewish.

The rumor mobilized no police action, and not a single line in the press endorsed it. Indeed, the story was so fantastic and unbelievable that no mainstream organization or institution gave any credence to it whatsoever. However, to the story's true believers, these facts simply demonstrated its validity – they did not challenge it: "More and more girls were disappearing. Yet why was it that the police . . . somehow failed to arrest these white slavers?" Moreover, how can we "explain the total silence of the newspapers?" Anxiety and hysteria, "soon sought and found an . . . explanation. . . . Everyone had been bribed, bought – the police, the Prefect, the Press – *by the Jews*. The authorities had sold [out] and were now acting as agents for these hidden powers, operating from their underground hideout" (Morin, 1971, p. 28).

On May 30, after one store owner received anonymous phone calls – one requesting "fresh meat," another addresses in Tangier – representatives of the Jewish community got together and decided to take action. However, the police told them that nothing could be done until after the weekend, that is, after Monday, when the first round of the upcoming presidential elections took place. On Saturday, normally the week's biggest shopping day, crowds gathered outside several of the more centrally located shops, but very few customers entered them. The owners sensed hostile glances from members of the crowd. One heard, "Don't buy anything from the Jews," uttered outside his shop. On a bus, returning home that night, an assistant in one of the shops was told, "You work for the Jews – you must know all about it!" (Morin, 1971, p. 32). The night before, an assistant was dragged out of the store in which she worked by her husband, who shouted, "I'm not going to let you stay in this place a moment longer!" (p. 32). All the store owners felt threatened and apprehensive; they believed that elements in the community were beginning to mobilize against them.

On June 2, two local daily newspapers (one left of center, the other, right of center) vigorously denounced the rumor. Within ten days, statements were released by several parents' associations, several professional educational institutions, chambers of commerce, manufacturers' organizations, the local Communist Party, and the Bishop of Orléans. In short order, editorials and articles appeared in a number of prestigeous Paris newspapers and magazines, again, attacking the rumor and those who propagated it, emphasizing its anti-Semitic theme. White the principal rumor was quashed by this barrage of denunciation, nonetheless, the suspicion remained on the part of some Orléans residents that something fishy was going on. "Someone's hiding something from us" and "There's no smoke without fire" were two commonly heard phrases at the time (Morin, 1971, p. 40). A "mishmash of mini-myths" (p. 40), "subrumors" (p. 38), and "mini-rumors" (p. 42) continued to circulate in the wake of the collapse of the principal rumor. Some believed that "a German" (that is, a Nazi) was behind the fabrication in order to discredit the Jews; as evidence, the name of a German chain store was invoked. Perhaps the Jews started the whole thing, some said, to discredit competitors. Some blamed the communists. Or others, the left generally. Some retained portions of the rumor but discarded others. Some suspected even more sinister activities for which white slavery was only a cover story. "A purely fabulous tale turned into a historical pseudo-event, stirred up scandal, all but started a panic, then became a bizarre and shady enigma" (Morin, 1971, p. 43). Within a matter of two months, even the mini-rumors began to dissipate.*

Moral Panics

In each of these cases – the furor over Canudos in Brazil at the end of the nineteenth century, the fear and persecution of homosexuals in Boise, Idaho, in the 1950s, and the rumor that young women were being abducted from clothing stores in Orléans, France, in 1969 – we have a moral panic on our hands. In each, there is strong, widespread (although not necessarily universal) fear or concern that evil doings are afoot, that certain enemies of society are trying to harm some or all of the rest of us. In each of these three cases, this fear or concern is referred to by the author describing and analyzing it as a "panic" (Levine, 1992, p. 24; Gerassi, 1966, p. 4; Morin, 1971, p. 43). In each, evidence suggests, the fear or concern that was generated was all out of proportion to the threat that was, or seemed to be, posed by the behavior, or the supposed behavior, of some. In one case, the basis for the threat was completely nonexistent and in two, the basis existed, but the threat was, in all likelihood, imaginary. And in each case, the panic was not simply the product of the over-active imaginations of a number of unconnected individuals scattered around a city or a society. Rather, in each case, the fear and concern had a social foundation, a dynamic that revealed the inner workings of the society in which it took place.

While the moral panics concept is fairly recent, the concrete manifestations of moral panics have been described and analyzed for some time in a more or less implicit fashion. The development of the concept, however, has focused a spotlight on its causes, acompaniments, variations, and consequences. Having a specific concept to classify and capture the phenomena enables us to notice elements and dynamics

---

* Interestingly, to many residents, the fact that the rumor was widely denounced did not invalidate it; some retained a suspicion that it might nonetheless be true. In 1985, a similar "white slave traffic" rumor broke out in La Roche-sur-Yon, France. This suggests that "a good rumor never dies. It temporarily quiets down and, like a volcano, reawakens at some later date" (Kapferer, 1990, pp. 113, 114). During the course of the 1985 rumor episode, one woman who was interviewed stated: "Oh yeah, the Orléans rumor. Come to think of it, no one ever found out if it was true or false, that story about the girls who were kidnapped" (p. 114).

that we would have otherwise missed. The development of the moral panics concept did not, however, spring full-blown from the head of its creator.* Rather, it developed from earlier concepts, most notably the *moral crusade*.

---

*　Actually, the first published use of the term, "moral panic," to our knowledge, appeared not in 1972, with Stanley Cohen's book, *Folk Devils and Moral Panics*, but in the previous year, in 1971, in an essay by a friend and peer of Cohen's, Jock Young (1971b), in a book edited by Cohen. Young wrote that "moral panic over drug-taking results in the setting-up of drug squads" by police departments, which produces an increase in drug-related arrests. Thus it is Young, not Cohen, who has to be credited with the first published use of the term. (We would like to thank Mimi Ajzenstadt for pointing this fact out to us.) Cohen's earlier work (1967) looks at public, media, and official reactions to the Mods and Rockers, *minus* the actual term, "moral panic."

1

A PRELUDE TO MORAL PANICS: THREE MORAL CRUSADES

The Prohibition Movement, 1900–1920

Between the late eighteenth and the early nineteenth centuries, Americans drank considerably more than they do today; heavy alcohol consumption was "utilitarian . . . a normal part of personal and community habits" (Lender and Martin, 1987, p. 9). Beer and cider were common at mealtimes, with children often partaking; farmers typically took a jug to the fields with them, employers often gave their employees liquor on the job; and politicians "treated" the electorate to alcoholic beverages, including on election day at polling places. In 1790, when the first national census was taken, the per capita alcohol consumption for all Americans aged 15 and older was 5.8 gallons per year, considerably more than twice as high as it is today; by 1830, this had actually risen to 7.1 gallons. Said one observer in 1814, "the quantity of ardent spirits" consumed in the United States at the time "surpasses belief." In the early 1800s, drinking "had reached unparalleled levels." The notion that alcohol "was necessary for health remained firmly fixed. It was common to down a glass of whiskey or other spirits before breakfast . . . instead of taking coffee or tea . . . Even school children took their sip of whiskey, the morning and afternoon glasses being considered 'absolutely indispensable to man and boy.'" Distilled spirits "were a basic part of the diet – most people thought that whiskey was as essential as bread" (Lender and Martin, 1987, pp. 205, 46, 47, 53; Goode, 1993, p. 166).

In 1784, Benjamin Rush, a prominent Philadelphia physician, signer of the Declaration of Independence, and Surgeon General of the Continental Army, published a book entitled *An Enquiry into the Effects of Ardent Spirits on the Human Mind and Body*. Rush challenged the conventional wisdom that prevailed at the time that drinking alcohol was an unmixed good. Rush did not condemn drinking per se; his primary target was the consumption of hard liquor. "Consumed in quantity over the years," he wrote, distilled spirits "could destroy a person's health and even cause death." Rush was the first scientist or physician to label alcoholism a disease characterized by compulsion and progressively more serious stages. Although the book did not have an immediate impact on moderating drinking in the United States, it "had sown the seeds of reform movements to come." By the first quarter of the nineteenth century, the temperance movement had been launched; by 1830, temperance reform "constituted a burgenoning national movement," boasting 1.5 million members who proselytized righteously for their cause (Lender and Martin, 1987, p. 68; Goode, 1993, p. 167). At first, the temperance movement accepted drinking in moderation; by the end of the nineteenth century, however, its primary goal became a complete cessation of the consumption of all alcoholic beverages. In 1919, it accomplished its crowning achievement: the ratification of national alcohol Prohibition. In 1920, Prohibition outlawed the sale of all alcoholic beverages in the United States. To achieve this end, it was necessary for the temperance movement to create a *crisis* in American society, a crisis over the consumption of alcohol.

The movement toward Prohibition was not the "long-awaited outcropping of a slowly developing movement over 90 years of agitation. It was the result of a relatively short wave of political organization supported by the new enthusiasm of church members in evangelical congregations." At a convention of the Anti-Saloon League in 1913, celebrating the League's twentieth anniversiary, James Franklin Hanley, ex-governor of Indiana, declared the League's goal to be a total national prohibition on the manufacture, sale, import, export, and transport of "intoxicating liquor" to be used as a beverage. Echoed John Granville Wooley, a Prohibition Party candidate, "the crime of crimes . . . must go" (Kobler, 1973, p. 198). To that end, the Anti-Saloon League and the Women's Christian Temperance Union (WTCU) lobbied as perhaps no social movement had ever done in American history to outlaw the sale of alcoholic beverages. They buttonholed elected representatives, addressed meetings, gave speeches, prepared material for the press, organized petition drives, and distributed literature through churches, corporations, and labor unions. In 1909, the League printed over 100 million prohibitionst pamphlets and leaflets; in 1912, it had turned out a quarter of a *billion* printed book pages of prohibitionist literature a *month*.

The "wet" lobby did not take this threat lying down; in 1915 alone, 450 million pieces of anti-prohibitionist literature were distributed. However, the alcohol lobby's literature "so blatantly displayed self-interest that it was ineffective" (Sinclair, 1962, pp. 126, 131, 133). The prohibitionists even enlisted the help of infants and children; children marched near polling booths on election days, dressed in white, clutching American flags, carrying banners, and chanting slogans (Sinclair,

1962, p. 126). Congressman Richmond Pearson Hobson (a Democrat from Alabama) delivered a prohibitionist polemic entitled "The Great Destroyer"; he claimed that alcohol killed five times as many people as all of the wars ever fought, and that it was the cause of feeblemindedness and "sexual perversion" among women. A blatant racist, Hobson opined that, unless "the Great Destroyer" were itself destroyed, Asians ("the yellow peril") would overrun the earth. "Liquor will actually make a brute out of a Negro," Hobson pontificated, "causing him to commit unnatural crimes. The effect is the same on the white man, though . . . being further evolved, it takes longer to reduce him to the same level" (Kobler, 1973, p. 199).

Prior to 1900, give or take a few years, the dominant orientation of the temperance movement was a humanitarian reform of the behavior of the poor and the underprivileged; its dominant orientation was *assimilative reform* – that is, reform the drinker, make him sober. Before the turn of the century, drinking was seen as a curse of the downtrodden masses from which they must be saved by more enlightened folk – that is, the abstemious, teetotaling, respectable Christian middle class. The real enemy was seen by temperance reformers as the trafficking in alcohol, not its consumers, who were unable to help themselves. One sermon delivered in a church at the turn of the century illustrates this approach nicely:

> The liquor traffic is the most fiendish, corrupt, and hell-soaked institution that ever crawled out of the eternal pit. It is the open sore of this land . . . It takes the kind, loving husband and father, smothers every spark of love in his bosom, and transforms him into a heartless wretch, makes him steal the shoes from his starving babe's feet to find the price of a glass of liquor. It takes your sweet, innocent daughter, robs her of her virtue, and transforms her into a brazen, wanton harlot . . . The open saloon as an institution has its origin in hell, and it is manufacturing subjects to be sent back to hell. (quoted in Ray, 1978, p. 131)

However, after 1900, during the first two decades of the twentieth century, the temper of prohibitionists shifted from pity and compassion toward the drinker to one of righteous wrath, indignation, anger generated by behavior that was seen as "unworthy, base, or disgraceful" (Gusfield, 1955, p. 225). The movement had shifted from assimilative reform to *coercive reform*; the drinker was no longer to be saved but punished. Self-righteous anger became the dominant emotion of the prohibitionist movement; its activists saw the movement as a "lobby for the Lord." In short, in early twentieth-century agitation for national Prohibition, the temperance movement came to define drinking as an unmixed evil, and opponents of Prohibition were seen as "enemies to be conquered." Drinkers were seen not as unfortunate wretches to be helped so much as enemies of society who should be punished.

With the outbreak of the First World War in 1914, and especially after the official entry of the United States into the hostilities in 1917, a new element entered the conflict over Prohibition: patriotism. Since many breweries were established by German immigrants, and since the "wet" lobby was heavily represented by the beer interests, drinking and opposition to Prohibition became identified with the enemy. This concern was so strong that it continued for several years *after* the First World War. In 1919, in an annual report of the Women's Christian Temperance Union, the organization's president stated that Prohibition was a patriotic victory over the "un-American liquor traffic"; the sale of alcohol, she declared, has always been "of alien and autocratic origin" (Gusfield, 1963, p. 123). As late as 1927, one senator said at the annual conventional of the Women's Christian Temperance Union that to refuse to obey the law "is equivalent to treason" (Gusfield, 1963, p. 119).

In short, by the early part of the twentieth century, the temperance movement came to be motivated mainly by "hostility, hatred, and anger toward the enemy" (Gusfield, 1963, p. 111). Their anger was directed at evil men (for most of them were men) who engaged in harmful, evil deeds – first, purveyors of alcohol, then drinkers. These men were seen as devils, deviants – the enemy. In the first part of the twentieth century, a self-righteous panic was generated over the sale and consumption of alcohol. The enemy had to be defeated and the behavior eliminated. Only then would the Golden Age be ushered in. Said Billy Sunday, one of the most famous Christian preachers of all time, in a sermon on the passage of the eighteenth Amendment to an audience of 10,000 souls: "The reign of tears is over. The slums will soon be a memory. We will turn our prisons into factories and our jails into storehouses and corncribs. Men will walk upright now, women will smile, and children will laugh. Hell will be forever for rent" (Kobler, 1973, p. 12).

The Crusade for Anti-marijuana Legislation, the 1930s

In 1930, relatively few Americans smoked marijuana or even knew anyone who did. During that year, only 16 states had laws on the books which made the possession of marijuana a crime. Even in the states in which marijuana possession was against the law, "relatively lax enforcement of the existing . . . laws" prevailed (Becker, 1963, p. 137). When police officers noticed it at all, they usually "dismissed it as not warranting major attempts at enforcement"; enforcement was simply "not seriously undertaken" (p. 138). Although during the 1920s and into the early 1930s, some Americans began to notice marijuana use among some Mexican-Americans, they "did not express much concern about it" (p. 135). In short, circa 1930, the dominant public attitude toward marijuana use was apathy and indifference (p. 135).

Suddenly and dramatically, during the mid to late 1930s, all that changed. By 1937, every one of the then 48 states had passed a law outlawing marijuana possession; during that year, The Marihuana Tax Act, a federal anti-marijuana law, was passed. For the first time, Americans began to be arrested for marijuana possession and sale in large numbers. In addition, between the early and the late 1930s, scores of sensationalistic articles were published in national magazines, and hundreds appeared in local newspapers, on the supposedly damaging effects of this dangerous drug. Marijuana was dubbed in the press as the "killer weed," the "weed of madness," a "sex-crazing drug menace," the "burning weed of hell," a "gloomy monster of destruction." Journalists and propagandists allowed an almost unlimited reign to the lurid side of their imagination. Every conceivable evil was concocted concerning the effects of marijuana, the principal ones being insanity, sexual licence, and violence. A popular film was released in 1937 with the frightening title *Reefer Madness*, illustrating the "marijuana makes you go crazy, become sexually promiscuous, and want to kill people" theme.

Why this dramatic shift? How was it that a rarely used drug – its use, confined, for the most part, to a small proportion of urban Blacks, Mexican-Americans living in the Southwest, working-class whites, some jazz musicians and enthusiasts in New Orleans and elsewhere, and a few literary, bohemian, and demimonde figures – become criminalized in every jurisdiction in the country within the span of less than a decade? Why was marijuana the focus of numerous grossly exaggerated, inaccurate, and extremely sensationalistic articles in the national and local press? Did a medical study determine that the drug was harmful, that it represented a threat to body and mind? Did a survey reveal a sudden upsurge in use in the United States between the early and the mid 1930s? Did Americans begin to *notice* a dramatic increase in marijuana use in their communities?

Howard Becker (1963, pp. 135–46) argued that the passage of the marijuana laws was the result of the efforts of key moral entrepreneurs, specifically, officials in the Federal Bureau of Narcotics (FBN), who "perceived an area of wrongdoing that properly belonged in their jurisdiction and moved to put it there" (p. 138). The Bureau's thrust comprised two prongs. First, FBN officials worked directly with state legislatures – which included drawing up model legislation – to facilitate the passage of the state marijuana laws. And second, they provided "facts and figures" to the media which formed the basis for articles in national magazines (p. 138); "through the press and other communications media," the Bureau sought to generate "a favorable public attitude toward the proposed" law (p. 139). In a survey of articles published just before and after the passage of the Marihuana Tax Act, Becker (1963, p. 141) found that a majority made direct use of material provided by the Bureau. One of the most dramatic and sensationalstic of these articles was co-authored by none other than the head of the Federal Bureau of Narcotics, Harry Anslinger himself (1937).

In short, there was no sudden upsurge in marijuana use in the 1930s, and no newly discovered research findings which pointed to a previously unknown threat from the use of the drug. The "national menace" from marijuana claimed by FBN officials did not have a basis in fact. The Bureau created a crisis where no basis for it existed, and the campaign created a "new class of outsiders – marihuana users" (Becker, 1963, p. 145).

The Sexual Psychopath Laws, the 1930s to the 1950s

It is November 1949. The mutilated body of a small girl is found in a neighborhood in Los Angeles. The police are alerted, and a description of the crime and the suspect, one Fred Stroble, is relayed to nearby cities and counties; a blockade is set up along the Mexican border. Hotels, motels, bus stations, and bars are watched. Men matching the suspect's description are taken off public transportation and brought to police stations for questioning. The media broadcast details of a number of similar past crimes, some stretching back a quarter of a century. There is a sudden increase in the number of crimes involving young girls being molested reported to the police. The body of a drowned man is pulled from the Pacific Ocean; it is initially incorrectly reported as the suspect. After three days, Fred Stroble is spotted getting off a bus by a police officer, and he is apprehended and arrested. The arresting officer's photograph is printed in scores of newspapers across the country as the "capturer of the sex fiend." Details of the case and related cases continue to be presented in the news. The Los Angeles District Attorney secures a confession from Stroble, who then meets with assembled reporters; "with beads of sweat standing on his face and neck," he repeats a confession of his crimes to the press (Sutherland, 1950b, pp. 143–4).

Between 1937 and 1950, "sexual psychopath" laws were passed in a dozen American states and the District of Columbia. In each state, there is a pattern to the passage of these laws. The process begins with "a few serious sex crimes committed in quick succession" which are "given nationwide publicity." Articles appear in national magazines bearing titles such as "How Safe Is Your Daughter?", "What Can We Do About Sex Crimes?", and "Terror in Our Cities." Letters to the editor of local newpapers are published on the subject, demanding action. School superintendents remind teachers and principals to be on the lookout for men loitering around schoolyard; parent–teacher's associations sponsor mass meetings on the problem of sex offenders. The head of the Federal Bureau of Investigation calls for an all-out war against sex criminals. National leaders are quoted in the press concerning the most effective methods of controlling sex crimes. Victims of sex offenses, and relatives of victims, rise up and make public declarations which are dutifully reported in the media. Politicians demand that legislatures call special sessions to pass laws to deal with the problem. Communities are "thrown in a panic" about the danger that violent sexual psychopaths pose to women and children. Legislative committees are appointed, and recommendations are made. For the most part, very little debate or discussion takes place in state legislatures about the proposed bills and in most, yet another version of the "sexual psychopath" law is passed. In no location is either the fear, or the passage of the law, related to an increase in the incidence of sex crimes (Sutherland, 1950b, pp. 144–6, 1950a).

Moral Crusades and Moral Panics

In these three cases, a form of behavior – the consumption of alcohol, the sexual assault and molestation of children, and the use of marijuana – was defined as a major problem by certain officials, authorities, moral crusaders, and/or segments of the public. More than a social problem was generated and sustained in these cases, however, for the *intensity* of the concern that was aroused was greater for these behaviors than is usually the case for most social problems. In each case, some form of immoral wrongdoing – deviant behavior – was seen to be responsible for the problem. Some specific individuals were targeted as deviants – drinkers, child molesters, and marijuana users. In each case, the furor or intense concern that emerged over the issue in question subsided after a time: Public sentiment soured on Prohibition not long after it had been instituted; official, media, and public concern about marijuana faded by the early 1940s; and the sexual psychopath laws, once they were passed, were rarely applied.

These three cases represent examples of moral crusades. A moral crusade is not *necessarily* a moral panic, the subject of this book. The two concepts overlap, of course; there are both similarities and differences between crusades and panics. The campaign against and massacre of Canudos in Brazil in the 1890s and the hysteria over and persecution of homosexuals in Boise, Idaho, in the 1950s were both moral panics and moral crusades. On the other hand, the rumor in Orléans, France, in 1969 represented a case in which a moral panic broke out which did not become a moral crusade. On the other side of the coin, what is most noteworthy about the campaign against alcohol sale and consumption prior to (and even after) 1920, the campaign against marijuana in the 1930s, and the campaign to sercure the passage of the sexual psychopath laws between the 1930s and the 1950s, is that they are clearcut cases of moral crusades. The panic they generated is one of their interesting but secondary features. Activists used widespread (or local) concern over the behavior campaigned against in the service of their crusades.

The moral crusades concept implies that the activitists who are working to bring about change are motivated by moral, and not rational and protectionist, interests. Still, the two could coincide, as both Becker (1963, pp. 148–8) and Gusfield (1955, p. 223) emphasize; moreover, because of the nature of their moral positions, crusaders could very easily mistake the first for the second. Thus, calling a campaign a moral crusade does not *preclude* rational and protectionist interests as well. In contrast, the moral panics concept, as we shall see, implies a certain *disassociation* between protectionism and concern, that is, that concern and fear are not *strictly* a product of the magnitude of the threat, and therefore that the steps taken to protect the society from that threat may be somewhat misplaced. In addition, the notion of a crusade necessitates crusaders, or what Becker (1963, pp. 147ff) refers to as *moral entrepreneurs* – that is, organizers, activists, do-gooders, movement advocates who push for a given cause. Moral panics, in contrast, are often, even usually – but not *necessarily* – initiated by activists. To put things another way, the moral entrepreneur *creates* the crusade: no entrepreneur, no crusade. By definition, the latter is a direct product of the former. In contrast, the engineered, consciously created quality of the moral panic is an empirical, not a definitional, question. It may have been initiated anywhere – by crusaders, by the general public, by political or economic elites, by the media. For instance moral crusaders may have recognized an incipient panic and gotten on a bandwagon that was already in motion. The panic implies fairly widespread public concern – whereas the crusade does not – and that concern could have been triggered by a variety of sources. The moral panic is not *by definition* a conscious creation of activists; while the campaign against Canudos in Brazil in the 1890s and the furor over homosexuals in Boise, Idaho, in the 1950s were generated by elitist crusades, the rumor about "sexual slavery" in Orléans was more spontaneous and accompanied by no active crusade whatsoever.

Not one of these three cases of moral crusades, therefore, represents a perfect example of the moral panic. Gusfield is emphatic about the fact that the concern over the passage and enforcement of the Prohibition law represented a "symbolic crusade," that is, it was not primarily about drinking per se, but represented a conflict between two contrasting lifestyles and, specifically, their claim to be represented by or legitimated in the law: a sober, ascetic, abstemious, small-town, native-born, white-collar or farming, white Anglo-Saxon Protestant way of life, versus a more immigrant-derived, urban, Catholic, working class *or* a more cosmopolitan, hedonistic, college-educated, "new" middle-class way of life whose representatives had ceased to be tied to a local community. Hence, to the temperance movement, the enemy was as much a way of life as it was a specific form of behavior – drinking, that is.

And the marijuana panic of the 1930s was not covered extensively in the media; only a few dozen articles appeared on the subject in national magazines (Himmelstein, 1983), although those published in local newspapers were far more numerous and equally as lurid; thus, the concern over marijuana use in the 1930s may have been more a *local* and *regional* panic than a *national* panic (Bonnie and Whitebread, 1974). Moreover, the Marihuana Tax Act, and most of the state laws, were passed without much notice or fanfare. Some evidence even exists to suggest that the Federal Bureau of Narcotics did not generate the marijuana scare of the 1930s (Musto, 1987, pp. 210–29); instead, it may have been more of a grassroots concern than Becker's classic analysis suggests (Bonnie and Whitebread, 1970, 1974; Himmelstein, 1983).

And the sexual psychopath laws of the late 1930s and the 1940s represented a genuine, if misguided and unrealistic – and ultimately futile – effort to provide what some segments of the psychiatric profession regarded at the time as human, scientific treatment rather than punishment of the sex offender. Thus, although the concern over alcohol consumption in the first two decades of this century, marijuana in the 1930s, and sexual psychopathy in the 1940s, do not provide perfect examples of what we refer to today as moral panics, it was out of such concerns that our contemporary understanding of the moral panic grew.

2

ENTER MORAL PANICS

The place, Clacton, a small seaside resort community on England's eastern coast, one with an extremely limited range of facilities and amusements for young people. The time, Easter Sunday, 1964. The weather, cold and wet. Hundreds of adolescents and young adults are milling around on the streets and sidewalks, bored and irritated, seeking fun and adventure. A rumor – perhaps true, perhaps false – begins circulating that a bartender refused to serve several young people. A scuffle breaks out on the pavement; factions begin separating out. Youths on motorcycles and scooters roar up and down the street. A starter's pistol is fired into the air. The windows of a dance hall are smashed; some beach huts are destroyed. The damage – perhaps £500 in value, several times that in today's currency. The police, unaccustomed to such rowdiness, overreact by arresting nearly 100 young people, on charges ranging from "abusive behavior" to assaulting a police officer (Cohen, 1972, pp. 29ff).

Media Reaction

While not exactly raw material for a major story on youth violence, the seaside disturbances nonetheless touched off what can only be described as an orgy of sensationalistic news items. On Monday, the day after these events, every national newspaper with the exception of *The Times* ran a lead story on the Clacton disturbances. "Day of Terror by Scooter Groups" screamed the *Daily Telegraph*; claimed the *Daily Express*, "Youngsters Beat Up Town"; the *Daily Mirror* chimed in with, "Wild Ones Invade Seaside." On Tuesday, the press coverage was much the same. Editorials on the subject of youth violence began to appear. The Home Secretary was "urged" to take firm action to deal with the problem. Articles began to appear featuring interviews with Mods and Rockers, the two youth factions, current in Britain at the time, who were involved in the scuffles and the vandalism. The Mods (the term stood for "modernists") tended to be well-dressed, fashion-conscious teenagers and young adults who frequented discos, listened to the music of the Beatles, the Who, and the Rolling Stones, and, if they were on wheels, rode motorscooters. The Rockers tended to be tougher, more politically reactionary, more classically delinquent; they usually stemmed from a working-class background, and often rode motorbikes.

Theories were articulated in the press attempting to explain what was referred to as the mob violence. Accounts of police and court actions were reported; local residents were interviewed concerning the subject, their views widely publicized. The story was deemed so important that much of the press around the world covered the incidents, with major stories appearing in the United States, Canada, Australia, South Africa, and the European continent. *The New York Times* printed a large photograph of two adolescent girls accompanying its story. The Belgian newspapers captioned one photo "West Side Story on English Coast" (pp. 31ff). Youth fights and vandalism at resorts continued to be a major theme in the British press for some three years. Each time a disturbance broke out, much the same exaggerated, sensationalistic stories were repeated. But by the beginning of 1967, young Britishers no longer identified with the Mods or the Rockers, and the youth-violence angle gave way to other issues.

Enter Stanley Cohen

In 1964, Stanley Cohen was a graduate student at the University of London searching for a research topic for his dissertation. A South African who left his homeland for political reasons, a radical who was attracted to the causes and activities of underdogs and eager to critique the doings of the smug and powerful, Cohen found society's reaction to the exhuberant activities of rebellious youth both disturbing and intriguing.

To Cohen, a major issue was the "fundamentally inappropriate" reaction by much of society to certain relatively minor events and conditions. The press, especially, had created a horror story practically out of whole cloth. The seriousness of events were exaggerated and distorted – in terms of the number of young people involved, the nature of the violence committed, the amount of damage inflicted, and their impact on the community, not to mention the importance of the events to the society as a whole. Obviously false stories were repeated as true; unconfirmed rumors were taken as fresh evidence of further atrocities (Cohen, 1972, pp. 31ff). During such times of overheated and exaggerated sense of threat, the society generally, including the press and the police, reacted toward the designated behavior and its enactors in a process Cohen referred to as "community sensitization" (1967, p. 280). Once a class of behavior, and a category of deviants, are identified, extremely small deviations from the norm become noticed, commented on, judged, and reacted to. In the case, the Clacton disturbances, minor offenses, or even gatherings which might become offenses, were instantly the focus of press and police attention. The process of sensitization was summed up in a headline at the time which read: "Seaside Resorts Prepare for the Hooligans' Invasion" (1967, p. 281). Moreover, on more than one occasion, the over-zealousness of the police resulted in an escalation of the conflict, where, for instance, by insisting that the crowd "move along," some of "the more labile members" of a crowd were provoked to resist, blows were exchanged, which led to their arrest (1967, p. 281). To Cohen, the sensitization and escalation processes were central to the public's reaction to the Mods and Rockers.

Cohen launched the term *moral panic* as a means of characterizing the reactions of the media, the public, and agents of social control to the youthful disturbances. In a moral panic, Cohen wrote:

> A condition, episode, person or group of persons emerges to become defined as a threat to societal values and interests; its nature is presented in a stylized and stereotypical fashion by the mass media; the moral barricades are manned by editors, bishops, politicians and other right-thinking people; socially accredited experts pronounce their diagnoses and solutions; ways of coping are evolved or . . . resorted to; the condition then disappears, submerges or deteriorates and becomes more visible. Sometimes the subject of the panic is quite novel and at other times it is something which has been in existence long enough, but suddenly appears in the limelight. Sometimes the panic passes over and is forgotten, except in folklore and collective memory; at other times it has more serious and long-lasting repercussions and might produce such changes as those in legal and social policy or even in the way society conceives itself. (1972, p. 9)

Actors in the Drama of the Moral Panic

How is this panic expressed? How did Cohen know he had a panic on his hands after the 1964 Clacton disturbances? Cohen looked at the reaction of five segments of society: the press, the public, agents of social control, or law enforcement, lawmakers and politicians, and action groups.

The Press

The way the press handled the seaside events could be characterized by exaggerated attention, exaggerated events, distortion, and stereotyping

(1972, pp. 31–8). As we saw, newspapers "over-reported" the events; the scuffles and minor acts of vandalism that took place were accorded a place in the media far out of proportion to their importance. Not only was the focus of attention exaggerated, but the stories describing the events also exaggerated their seriousness. Phrases such as "riot," "orgy of destruction," scenes being "smeared with blood and violence," "battle," and a "screaming mob," were used regularly. If one boat was overturned, reports claimed that "boats" were overturned. One story claimed that, in one resort, the windows of "all" the dance halls by the beach were smashed, which was true – however, the town only had one dance hall, and some of its windows were smashed by youths (1972, pp. 32–3).

The stories also distorted the events and repeated obviously false stories. One youth told a judge that he would pay his fine with a £75 check. This was repeated as long as four years after the event, usually to show that the rebellious youths were affluent hordes whom "fines couldn't touch." In fact, the youth made this statement as a "pathetic gesture of bravado." He not only did not have the money, he didn't even have a bank account, and had never signed a check in his life (1972, p. 33). But because the tale confirmed a certain public image of the events and who perpetrated them, it was repeated and believed as true. Although myth-making characterizes all societies at all times, during times of the moral panic, the process is especially rapid, and a given myth is especially likely to be believed on relatively little evidence (1972, p. 33).

The youth violence and vandalism stories that ran in the British press between 1964 and 1967 tended to follow a stereotypical pattern. For the most part, they put together a composite picture, containing a number of central elements. It was almost as if a new story could be written simply by stitching these elements together. There was very little interest in what actually happened; what counted is how closely a news account conformed to the stereotype. The youths were depicted as being part of gangs, even though all of the youths involved were part of very loose assemblies rather tightly structured gangs. The seaside villages were said to have been victims of an "invasion from London," even though many – in all likelihood, most – were local youths or came from nearby towns and villages. Few stories omitted the fact that many of the offenders were on motorscooters or motorbikes, even though the overwhelming majority were on foot. Offenders were said to come from affluent families, even though those on whom data could be gathered lived in extremely modest economic circumstances. They were said to have come to the resorts deliberately to make trouble, even though, in reality, nearly all came merely hoping that there would be some trouble to watch. The offenses described in the press were nearly always violent ones, even though only a tenth of the offenders were charged with violent crimes; even most of the offenses that did take place entailed relatively trivial acts such as petty theft, threatening behavior, and obstruction. The financial loss to local businesses was said to have been drastic. If anything, the reverse was true: more people than usual came to the resorts to check out the action. In short, one indication that a moral panic is taking place is the stereotypical fashion in which the subject is treated in the press (1972, pp. 34–8).

The Public

Cohen's conception of moral panics includes the dimension of public concern. There must be some latent potential on the part of the public to react to a given issue to begin with, some raw material out of which a media campaign about a given issue can be built. The public may hold a more sophisticated view of the issue than the press (1972, pp. 65–70), but if the media is infused with hysteria about a particular issue or condition which does *not* generate public concern, then we do not have a moral panic on our hands. The media's exaggerated attention must touch something of a responsive chord in the general public. The disturbances that attracted so much attention broke out in the 1960s, at a time when much of the adult British public, with the Second World War and the postwar era deprivations still fresh on their minds, saw a younger generation growing up in affluence (they "never had it so good," was a common refrain), responding not with gratitude but with disdain, rebellion, and delinquency. The problem was that the younger generation had been coddled, indulged, treated with kid gloves; the solution – a tougher parental hand, stricter social control, harsher penalties for transgressions, stiffer fines and jail sentences. In short, the events at Clacton and other seaside communities were focused on and reacted to by much of the public as a symbol for some of the larger problems plaguing British society. The events themselves were not so important as what they seemed to represent. But in order to see these disturbances as central, it became necessary to exaggerate and distort their reality.

Law Enforcement

In addition to the press and the general public, the actions of the social (or "societal") control culture demonstrated that a moral panic was taking place in Britain in the mid 1960s over the Mods and Rockers (1972, pp. 85ff). In a moral panic, segments of the society are sensitized to trouble from certain quarters (1972, pp. 77ff); the society is said to be faced with a "clear and present danger" the signs of which it is so sharply attuned to. In no sector is this principle more clearly evident than in public attitudes about what the police and the courts – law enforcement – ought to be doing about the perceived threat. Ties between and among local police forces are established and strengthened, and those between the local and national levels of law enforcement are activated, in order to more effectively deal with the problems faced by the putative threat (1972, p. 86). Cohen calls this process *diffusion*.

Efforts are made by officers to broaden the scope of law enforcement and increase its intensity; punitive and overly zealous actions already taken are justified on the basis of the enormity of the threat the society faces (1972, pp. 86–7). Cohen refers to this as *escalation*. New methods of control are proposed both to legislators and to the police: stiffer sentences, expanded police powers, confiscating motorscooters and motorbikes, banning Mod clothing, cutting long hair on youths, drafting toublemakers into the military, and so on (1972, pp. 88–91). Some police practices, previously rarely used, that were called up to deal with unacceptable Mod and Rocker behavior included: riding suspicious youths out of town or to the railroad station; keeping crowds moving along; confiscating studded belts; keeping certain troublesome locations free of Mods and Rockers; verbally harassing adolescents, particularly in a crowd situation, to "show them up" and "deflate their egos" (1972, p. 95), making immediate (and often wrongful) arrests, and so on (1972, pp. 92–8). The thinking among agents of social control is that "new situations need new remedies"; a national problem called for a drastic solution, and often, this entailed suspending rights and liberties previously enjoyed.

Politicians and Legislators

Members of Parliament (MPs) "took an immediate and considerable interest in disturbances in their own constituencies" (p. 133). Stiffer penalties for youth offenses were called for. Local merchants were assured that "hooliganism" would not threaten their economic interests and would not be repeated. Statements by MPs were issued to the press; "Jail These Wild Ones – Call by MPs," ran one such story. A return to corporal punishment for hooliganism was called for by some. Meetings were held between MPs and local police chiefs, and summaries were sent to the Home Secretary. Suggestions were made by one MP that Britain revive non-military national service, such as construction or mining, as a punishment for hooliganism. A suggestion to raise the minimum driving age from 16 to 19 was introduced in the House of Lords. A Malicious Damage Bill was introduced and debated in the House of Commons only a month after the Clacton incident; in further debate on the Bill two months later, the seaside disturbances became the central imagery dominating the discussion. Though some politicians recognized that the concern was exaggerated, and had a moderating influence on the discussion, the dominant mood among politicians and legislators toward youth crime in the period following the initial incident was angry, self-righteous, vindictive, condemnatory, and punitive. Politicians and other groups alligned themselves against a devil and on the side of angels; the fact is, they picked an "easy target," one that "hardly existed." What counted was not the nature of the target but what side they were on and what they were against (1972, p. 138). Such symbolic allignments represent one defining quality of the moral panic.

Action Groups

At some point, moral panics generate appeals, campaigns, and finally, "fully fleged action groups" (p. 119) which arise to cope with the newly-existing threat. These are "moral entrepreneurs" (Becker, 1963, pp. 147ff) who believe that existing remedies are insufficient. Action groups can be seen as "germinal social movements" (Cohen, 1972, p. 120). Often, participants have something to gain personally from rallying against a problem, but this is not a necessary determinant. The Mods and the Rockers generated two local action groups, one of which proposed that convicted Mods and Rockers be subjected to a penal-style program of discipline and hard labor (1972, p. 121), and the other of which favored the reintroduction of a variety of harsher penalties, including whippings of young offenders with a birch rod (1972, p. 125). These action groups did not grow into social movements, nor did they survive the demise of the Mods and the Rockers.

There are two additional features that characterize moral panics, two developments that inform the observer that a society is in the grip of a moral panic: the creation of *folk devils* (1972, pp. 40ff) and the development of a *disaster mentality* (pp. 144ff).

Folk Devils

A folk devil is the personification of evil. Folk devils permit instant recognition; they are "unambiguously unfavorable symbols" (Turner and Surace, 1956, pp. 16–20; Cohen, 1972, p. 41), that is, stripped of all favorable characteristics and imparted with exclusively negative ones. In such a symbolization process, "images are made much sharper than reality" (Cohen, 1972, p. 43). While all folk devils are created out of some existing and recognizable elements, a full-scale *demonology* takes place by which the members of a new evil category are placed "in the gallery of contemporary folk devils" (p. 44). Once a category has been identified in the media as consisting of troublemakers, the supposed havoc-wreaking behavior of its members reported to the public, and their supposed stereotypical features litanized, the process of creating a new folk devil is complete; from then on, all mention of representatives of the new category revolves around their central, and exclusively negative, features. All moral panics, by their very nature, identify, denounce, and attempt to root out folk devils. A condition that generates such widespread public concern must have had a personal agent responsible for its inception and maintenance. Such evil does not arise by happenstance or out of thin air; there must be a circle of evil individuals who are engaged in undermining society as we know it. In short, folk devils are *deviants*; they are engaged in wrongdoing; their actions are harmful to society; they are selfish and evil; they must be stopped, their actions neutralized. Only an effort of substantial magnitude will permit us to return to normal.

The Disaster Analogy

And lastly, in moral panics, Cohen argues, preparations are taken very much like those taken before, during, and after a disaster, such as a hurricane, a volcano eruption, or an earthquake. As during disasters, in the moral panic, there are predictions of impending doom, a "warning phase," sensitization to cues of danger, coping mechanisms, frequent overreactions, the institutionalization of threat, rumors speculating about what is happening or will happen, false alarms, and, occasionally, mass delusion (1972, pp. 144–8). The perceived threat to, and subsequent reaction by, conventional society to the projected invasion of hordes of deviants and delinquents has many strong parallels with the steps taken before, during, and after a natural disaster.

The Contribution of the Moral Panics Concept

The concept of the moral panic expands our understanding of social structure, social process, and social change. It ties together concepts from a variety of disparate areas – deviance, crime, collective behavior, social problems, and social movements. Moral panics are likely to "clarify [the] normative contours" and "moral boundaries" of the society in which they occur, demonstrate that there are limits to how much diversity can be tolerated in a society. Focusing on moral panics emphasizes the fact that reactions to unconventional behavior do not arise solely as a consequence of a rational and realistic assessment of the concrete damage that the behavior in question is likely to inflict on the society. Without resorting to conspiratorial thinking, an investigation of the moral panic emphasizes that social reaction to a new and seemingly threatening phenomenon arise as a consequence of that phenomenon's real or supposed threat to certain "positions, statuses, interests, ideologies, and values" (Cohen, 1972, p. 191). The cast of characters Cohen located in the moral panic – the media, the general public, the agents of social control, lawmakers and politicians, and action groups – are distressed by a certain perceived threat for a reason. If all panics entailed a public reaction to a specific, clearly identifiable threat, the magnitude of which can be objectively assessed and readily agreed upon, then such reactions would require no explanation. On the other hand, if, as Cohen argues, the reaction is out of proportion to the threat, we are led to ask why it arises; the panic is problematic – it demands an explanation.

Why a moral panic over *this* supposed threat, but not *that*, potentially even more damaging, one? Why does *this* cast of characters become incensed by the threat the behavior supposedly poses, but not *that* cast of characters? Why a moral panic at this time, but not before or after? How and why do moral panics arise? How and why do they die out? What role do interests play in the moral panic? Are the dynamics of the moral panic different during different historical time periods, or different from one society to another? What does the moral panic tell us about how society is constituted, how it works, how it changes over time? Cohen's concept introduces the observer of society to a wide range of questions and potential explorations.

3

MORAL PANICS:
AN INTRODUCTION

At times, then, societies are gripped by moral panics. During the moral panic, the behavior of some of the members of a society is thought to be so problematic to others, the evil they do, or are thought to do, is felt to be so wounding to the substance and fabric of the body social, that serious steps must be taken to control the behavior, punish the perpetrators, and repair the damage. The threat this evil presumably poses is felt to represent a crisis for that society: something must be done about it, and that something must be done now; if steps are not taken immediately, or soon, we will suffer even graver consequences. The sentiment generated or stirred up by this threat can be referred to as a kind of fever; it can be characterized by heightened emotion, fear, dread, anxiety, hostility, and a strong feeling of righteousness. In a moral panic, a group or category engages, or is said to engage, in unacceptable, immoral behavior, presumably causes or is responsible for serious harmful consequences, and is therefore seen as a threat to the well-being, basic values, and interests of the society presumably threatened by them. These perpetrators or supposed perpetrators come to be regarded as the enemy – or an enemy – of society, "folk devils" (Cohen, 1972), deviants, outsiders, legitimate and deserving targets of self-righteous anger, hostility, and punishment.

The moral panic, then, is characterized by the feeling, held by a substantial number of the members of a given society, that evildoers pose a threat to the society and to the moral order as a consequence of their behavior and, therefore, "something should be done" about them and their behavior. A major focus of that "something" typically entails strengthening the social control apparatus of the society – tougher or renewed rules, more intense public hostility and condemnation, more laws, longer sentences, more police, more arrests, and more prison cells. If society has become morally lax, a revival of traditional values may be necessary; if innocent people are victimized by crime, a crackdown on offenders will do the trick; if the young and the morally weak, wavering, and questionable are dabbling (or might dabble) in evil, harmful deeds, they should be made aware of what they are doing and its consequences. A major cause of the problem is, some will say, society's weak and insufficient efforts to control the wrongdoing; a major solution is to strengthen those efforts. Not everyone gripped by the moral panic sees legislation and law enforcement as the solution to the problem, however. Even when there is widespread agreement that the problem exists, the proper solution will be argued about, fought over, and negotiated; eventually, some legal outcome, one way or the other, will be reached – that is, to legislate or not to legislate – as a result of interaction between and among contending parties. Nonetheless, the question of the appropriate social and legal control of the responsible parties *almost inevitably* accompanies the moral panic. And legislation and its enforcement are usually seen as only one step; for those for whom the behavior in question is seen as a threat, measures such as education, socialization, normative changes, prevention, "treatment," and "cures" will be suggested and debated.

It is almost axiomatic in the literature that moral panics arise in troubled times, during which a serious *threat* is sensed to the interests or values of the society as a whole or to segments of a society. What would cause the public, the press, politicians, and the police, to become seized with the idea that a relatively innocuous agent is dangerous and in need of control? At times, these actors are incapable of facing, or are unwilling to face, a very real and concrete threat whose recognition would be painful, inconvenient, or disruptive. Much of the moral panics literature is devoted to tracing out the underlying motives of the various actors on the moral panics stage. In the 1970s, British capitalism was threatened and beleaguered (it still is); to deflect attention away from this very real problem, authorities exaggerated the concrete threat posed to lawabiding citizens by muggers and other street crime (Hall et al., 1978). In Renaissance Europe, with the Catholic hierarchy facing challenges from secularism and the Protestant Reformation, witches were seized upon as a major subversive force, threatening Catholicism from within (Ben-Yehuda, 1980, 1985). Drug scares divert attention away from a society's most serious and pressing problems (Levine and Reinarman, 1988). Panics need not be hoked up or fabricated by cynical, manipulating agents scheming for their own advantage, however, indeed, some of the agents responsible for the moral panic actually *believe* their rhetoric concerning the locus of the problem or threat. The stress and anxiety is said to be *caused by* the putative threat, which would evaporate when the threat is removed. Moral panics arise, the literature tells us, during troubled, difficult, disturbing, threatening times, or to groups or categories who experience trouble, difficulty, disturbances in their lives.

Of course, we must be careful to avoid ad hoc explanations, of assuming beforehand that collective and social stress must automatically be present for moral panics to break out. Stress could be defined so broadly that all societies suffer from it. In principle, however, the hypothesis that moral panics are generated by social stress is testable. We suspect that the hypothesis will be supported more often than not, but that, if we define social stress as a dimension that is high in some societies and low in others, abundant numbers of cases of moral panics can be located in societies in which, according to our definition, stress is virtually lacking. We do not wish to pin all our hopes to a single hypothesis. At the same time, social and collective stress should be kept in mind as a hypothesis that has guided much of the literature on moral panics.

Indicators of the Moral Panic

What characterizes the moral panic? How do we know when a moral panic takes hold in a given society? The concept of the moral panic is defined by at least five crucial elements or criteria.

Concern

First, there must be a heightened level of *concern* over the behavior of a certain group or category and the consequences that that behavior presumably causes for the rest of the society. This concern should be manifested or measureable in concrete ways, through, for example, public opinion polls, public commentary in the form of media attention, proposed legislation, social movement activity, and so on. Best (1990, p. 160) distinguishes *concern* from *fear*. We agree. The concern felt by the public need not manifest itself in the form of fear, although both have at least one element in common: both are seen by those who feel them to be a reasonable response to what is regarded as a very real and palpable threat.

Hostility

Second, there must be an increased level of *hostility* toward the group or category regarded as engaging in the behavior in question. Members of this category are collectively designated as the enemy, or an enemy, of respectable society; their behavior is seen as harmful or threatening to the values, the interests, possibly the very existence, of the society, or at least a sizeable segment of that society. That is, not only must the condition, phenomenon, or behavior be seen as threatening, but a clearly identifiable group in or segment of the society must be seen as *responsible* for the threat. Thus, a division is made between "us" – good, decent, respectable folk – and "them" – deviants, bad guys, undesirables, outsiders, criminals, the underworld, disreputable folk – between "we" and "they". This dichotomization includes *stereotyping*: generating "folk devils" or villains and folk heroes in this morality play of evil versus good (Cohen, 1972, pp. 11–12). In a slightly less dramatic fashion, we can see a parallel between the stereotyping process in moral panics and the routine processing of criminal suspects: the suspicion of the police that a crime has been committed or is in progress is aroused in part on the basis of stereotypical characteristics possessed by a suspect, such as age, race, presumed socioeconomic characteristics, physical appearance, location, and so on (Barlow, 1993, pp. 358–61).

Consensus

Third, there must be substantial or widespread *agreement* or *consensus* – that is, at least a certain minimal measure of consensus in the society as a whole or in designated segments of the society – that the threat is real, serious, and caused by the wrongdoing group members and their behavior. This sentiment must be fairly widespread, although the proportion of the population who feels this way need not be universal or, indeed, even make up a literal majority. To put it another way: moral panics come in different sizes – some gripping the vast majority of the members of a given society at a given time, others creating concern only among certain of its groups or categories. At no exact point are we able to say that a panic exists; however, if the number is insubstantial, clearly, one does not. It should be stated that we will focus on some society-wide moral panics, but others we look at will be subcultural, local, or regional. Consensus that a problem exists and should be dealt with can grip the residents of a given group or community, but may be lacking in the society as a whole; this does not mean that a moral panic does not exist, only that there is group or regional variation in the eruption of moral panics. Some discussions (for instance Zatz, 1987) do not even posit widespread public concern as an essential defining element of the moral panic, while others (Hall et al., 1978) assume that public concern is little more than an expression of elite interests.

Is it possible to have a moral panic *in the absence of* strong public concern? The elitist conception of moral panics regards public concern as irrelevant, either ignoring it altogether or regarding it as epiphemenonal, virtually an automatic byproduct of a conspiracy "engineered" or "orchestrated" by the powers that be. The problem with this approach is that many campaigns motivated by elite interests and engineered by elite efforts fail to materialize or simply fizzle out. As we point out later in the book (chapter 9), the 1992 Republican presidential campaign in the United States was initially and substantially based on "family values" – with its attendant attacks on homosexuality, abortion, divorce, and other presumed Democratic-tolerated vices – a theme which failed to catch fire with the American voter. And, as we shall see in more detail in later in this chapter and in chapters 9 and 12, and the Epilogue, during the early 1970s, President Richard Nixon launched a campaign against drug abuse which failed to capture the American public's imagination beyond his presidency (although it did have extremely important long-range *institutional* consequences). In addition, the general public, or segments of the public, have interests of their own, and often become intensely concerned with issues that elites would just as soon be ignored – as we shall see, nuclear contamination and fears of satanism offer examples here. To sweep public concern under the rug as an irrelevant criterion of the moral panic is either to fail to recognize a key ingredient in this crucial process or to make a seriously mistaken assumption about its dynamics.

Still, it is important to remind ourselves that definitions of threat or crisis are rarely unopposed in a large, complex society. The question of whether or not a society is seriously threatened at a given time by a given agent or problem is typically debated, argued about, negotiated. To put the matter a bit differently, in some moral panics, the opposing voice is weak and unorganized, while in others, it is strong and united. During the 1900–20 pre-Prohibition period, as we saw, the threat that alcohol posed and the viability of a national ban on alcohol were fought over vigorously. The "dry" forces, however, were far more united, were fired by an unparalleled moral fervor (while the arguments of the "wet" forces were seen by much of the public as motivated by self-interest) and, during and after the First World War, could invoke patriotism in opposition to the enemy beer brewer's German origins (Gusfield, 1955, 1963; Sinclair, 1962; Kobler, 1973).

During the British moral panic of the 1980s that centered around threats to women and children, the forces who *resisted* defining some aspects of these threats as major in scope captured public attention and favor as often as the forces who saw these threats as major and necessitating drastic new measures to deal with them (Jenkins, 1992). On the other hand, one reason why marijuana was criminalized on the federal level and in most states of the United States was that there were few, or scattered, or weak, voices in opposition to the laws. In emphasizing that some measure of consensus is necessary to define a moral panic, we do not mean to convey the impression that a sense of panic seizes everyone, or a majority, in a society at a given time. However, while there is often – usually – disagreement concerning definitions of a condition as a threat, a substantial segment of the public must see threat in that condition for the concern to qualify as a moral panic.

Disproportionality

Fourth, there is the implicit assumption in the use of the term moral panic that there is a sense on the part of many members of the society that a more sizeable number of individuals are engaged in the behavior in question than actually are, and the threat, danger, or damage said to be caused by the behavior is far more substantial than, is incommensurate with and in fact is "above and beyond that which a realistic appraisal could sustain" (Davis and Stasz, 1990, p. 129). More colloquially, one criterion of the moral panic, to quote Jones, Gallagher, and McFalls (1989, p. 4), in a slightly different context, is that "objective molehills have been made into subjective mountains." The degree of public concern over the behavior itself, the problem it poses, or condition it creates is far greater than is true for comparable, even more damaging, actions. In short, the term moral panic conveys the implication that public concern is in excess of what is appropriate if concern were directly proportional to objective harm. In moral panics, the generation and dissemination of figures or numbers is extremely important – addicts, deaths, dollars, crimes, victims, injuries, illnesses – and most of the figures cited by moral panic "claims-makers" are wildly exaggerated. Clearly, in locating the moral panic, some measure of objective harm must be taken.

We want to be very careful about what we mean by the objective dimension because, as we saw in the Prologue, and as we shall see in chapter 6, a segment of contemporary social scientists (and humanists) – radical relativists or strict constructionists (Aronson, 1984; Kitsuse and Schneider, 1989; Woolgar and Pawluch, 1985) – wish to define the objective dimension out of existence. All views of reality are relative, they say, and equally subjective; there is no "ontologically privileged" position, no view of reality that can be taken as more authoritative or definitive than any other, no set of data or criteria that determine – with more validity than any other – what is true, valid, or accurate. As a consequence, they argue, there cannot be any such thing as a "panic," since we cannot determine the seriousness of the objective threat against which we may measure subjective concern – in short, disproportionality is an empty, meaningless concept. A claim of fire in a crowded theater is simply a claim, they say – whether an actual fire exists or not is both irrelevant and incapable of verification; what's important is how and why that claim comes to be made, and by whom. We are social scientists, they say; to examine the "objective dimension," located in other disciplines, is to be guilty of "ontological gerrymandering" (Woolgar and Pawluch, 1985), smuggling objectivist principles into a study of subjective claims.

We acknowledge that determining and assessing the objective dimension is often a tricky propostion. Scientists frequently draw conclusions from incomplete information. Many scientific studies are poorly conducted; the conclusions of many scientists which have been accepted as true by the scientific community have been shown to be, upon closer inspection, erroneous and invalid. Contrarily, all too often, conclusions eventually accepted as true were regarded as false for years because of factors completely or largely extraneous to the nature of the evidence. (See Ben-Yehuda, 1985, pp. 106–67, Ben-Yehuda, 1990a, pp. 181–219, for a discussion of some of these issues.) Occasionally, scientific fraud – "fudging," "cooking," or fabricating data, or plagiarizing the work of others – is revealed (Ben-Yehuda, 1985, pp. 168–207; Kilbourne and Kilbourne, 1983). All of this is quite true and worth reiterating. Moreover, all of these statements apply with equal force to medicine, the social sciences, and allied fields. In short, the same frailties to which ordinary men and women are subject also befall the expert; no statement by any scientist, expert, or knowledgeable figure should be regarded as definitive or <u>final</u>. All statements based on evidence are tentative; we can never know anything with absolute certainty. All statements, including those made by scientists, are constructions from a particular vantage point.

However, admitting that there are flaws in what is taken as some expert or scientific wisdom should not be stretched and twisted to reach the conclusion that what scientists and other experts say about the nature of the material and social world is untrue, or no more likely to be true than those made by the man and woman on the street. (For an insightful discussion of these and related issues, see Cole, 1993.) Even those who argue for the relativity of scientific, medical, and other expert truth in theory, *in practice* accept the fact that experts know more than the rest of us. (If they, or a loved one, needs an operation, do they seek the services of a respected surgeon – or the 10-year-old kid down the block with a rusty pocket knife in his hand?) The fact is, we place varying degrees of confidence in different statements. We can be almost completely confident that some propositions, accepted by all or almost all practicing natural or social scientists, medical figures or other experts, are true: the earth is round, not flat; species were generated over a period of billions of years through a process of evolution, and not in a single week through divine creation; the existence of the Holocaust – the systematic murder of millions of Jews and other ethnic groups by the Nazis during the 1930s and 1940s – is a verified historical fact, and is not a false claim hoked up by evil Zionists and their agents and dupes; and so on. Likewise, and more to the point of moral panics, we can have a great deal of confidence, given the nature of the evidence, that: LSD does not seriously damage chromosomes or cause birth defects; satanists are not kidnapping, abusing, torturing, and murdering tens of thousands of children every year in the United States and England; legal drug use is responsible for far more deaths than the abuse of illegal drugs; in 1982, not even close to half of Israeli high school students abused illegal drugs, nor do they do so now; in Renaissance Europe, hundreds of thousands of men and women did not literally consort with an actual, concrete devil; and so on.

In short, though we must be cautious, modest, and tentative about making statements concerning what is real and true about events in the material world, we nonetheless can be fairly confident that some statements are true and others are false. As Stephen Jay Gould says, "fact" does not imply "absolute certainty." Absolute certainty exists only in mathematics, logic, and theology. Any statements describing the material or empirical world must retain a measure of uncertainty, small though it may be, for statements regarded as facts. Natural and especially social scientists do not make a claim to eternal, perpetual truth. According to Gould, what is called a fact is that which has been "confirmed to such a degree it would be perverse to withhold provisional assent." He adds: "I suppose that apples might start to rise tomorrow [instead of fall], but the possibility does not merit equal time in physics classrooms" (1984, p. 255). We know the difference between claims and verified facts; the fact that we work with both does not distress us, nor cause us to experience a crisis of "ontological gerrymandering." We "smuggle" no objectivist assumptions into the study of subjective claims, but in order to apprehend and understand these claims, we have to make the – for us blatantly obvious – assumptions that the world is real, that we can know the world through our senses, and so on. Without these assumptions, even the strict relativist or constructionist would be put out of business.

It is only by knowing the empirical nature of a given threat that we are able to determine the degree of disproportionality. The concept of the moral panic *rests* on disproportionality. If we cannot determine disproportionality, we cannot conclude that a given episode of fear or concern represents a case of a moral panic. Again: we can only know disproportionality by assessing threat from existing empirical information. But, once again, to repeat: our knowledge of the material world is never definitive, never absolutely certain. We are permitted only *degrees* of confidence. Still, that may be enough, for some issues, to feel fairly certain that what we say is correct.

Volatility

And fifth, by their very nature, moral panics are *volatile*; they erupt fairly suddenly (although they may lie dormant or latent for long periods of time, and may reappear from time to time) and, nearly as suddenly, subside. Some moral panics may become *routinized* or *institutionalized*, that is, the moral concern about the target behavior results in, or remains in place in the form of, social movement organizations, legislation, enforcement practices, informal interpersonal norms or practices for punishing transgressors, after it has run its course. Others merely vanish, almost without trace; the legal, cultural, moral, and social fabric of the society after the panic is essentially no different from the way it was before; no new social control mechanisms are instituted as a consequence of its eruption. But, whether it has a long-term impact or not, the degree of hostility generated during a moral panic tends to be fairly limited temporally; the fever pitch that characterizes a society during the moral panic during its course is not typically sustainable over a long stretch of time. In that respect, it is similar to fashion, the fad, and the craze; the moral panic is, therefore, as we saw, a form of collective behavior.

To describe moral panics as volatile and relatively short-lived does not mean that they do not have structural or historical antecedents. The specific issue that generates a particular moral panic may have done so in the past, perhaps even the not-so-distant past. In fact, one or another moral panic which seems to have been sustained over a long period of time is almost certainly a conceptual grouping of a series of more or less discrete, more or less localized, more or less short-term panics. (For a detailed examination of a panic centered around an accusation of satanic ritual abuse at the local level – yet, at the same time, one that can be framed within the context of the more long-lasting national satanic ritual abuse panic – see Wright, 1993a, 1993b.) The Renaissance witch craze, for example, was not active during the entire period of its 200 to 300 years of existence. It flared up at one time and place and subsided, burst forth later in another location and died down, and so on. A heated, continent-wide, panic-like craze spanning nearly 300 years is simply not sustainable at a fever pitch.

For example, the American drug panic, which at first glance appears to stretch back over a century, upon closer inspection, turns out to be relatively local and time-delimited. One of the most remarkable features of note about the many drug panics that have seized American society over the past century is that, typically, later ones have been built upon earlier ones. That is, organizations and institutions are often established at one point in time and remain in place and help generate concern later on, at the appropriate time. In the early 1970s in the United States, heroin addiction received substantial attention from politicians, especially President Richard Nixon, and the media. But public concern about drug abuse remained at a fairly low level throughout most of the 1970s (at a time, ironically, when drug use was at historically high levels). President Nixon was instrumental in establishing a number of organizations and institutions that played a role during later, more fevered and fearful times, which helped to focus and intensify the drug panic of the late 1980s.

Between 1969 and 1974, the federal budget devoted to all aspects of drug abuse increased nearly *ten times* (Goldberg, 1980, p. 25). In June 1971, Nixon declared an "all-out global war on international drug trafficking" (p. 37). In 1972, Congress passed the Drug Abuse Office and Treatment Act, centralizing the federal drug effort and expanding its budget (p. 40). In 1974, the National Institute on Drug Abuse (NIDA) was established (p. 45); one of the most important federal agencies which deals with drug abuse, it sponsors drug-related research, gathers and publishes drug abuse data, and publishes and disseminates anti-drug literature. President Nixon's effort to generate a moral panic was partly successful: largely as a result of his speeches and institutional initiatives, by February 1973, according to a Gallup Poll, fully 20 percent of the American public regarded drug abuse as the number one problem facing the country at that time. However, after Nixon left office (in disgrace, in 1974), the initiative fizzled out; between the mid and the late 1970s, a negligible proportion of Americans (in the 2–3 percent range) saw drug abuse as the nation's most important problem. More important, however, Nixon created a number of institutional mechanisms during his administration that remained in place, to serve their role at a more opportune moment. Thus, although Nixon's crusade against drugs had a short-lived impact *as a moral panic*, it paved the way for later, even more intense drug panics.

We believe that these criteria spell out a more or less definable, measureable social phenomenon. Certain social concerns may come to mind, but which lack one or more of these defining characteristics. Certainly the American public is fearful of and concerned about AIDS. But is their concern disproportionate to the threat posed, or harm caused, by the disease? Certainly not if we measure that threat or harm by number of years of working life (that is, before the age of 65) lost to the disease. In this sense, the seriousness of AIDS ranks above heart disease, on the same level with cancer, and only slightly below accidents; by this measure, AIDS is one of the three leading causes of death in the United States, and in the rest of the world as well (Eckholm, 1992).

Some threatening or supposedly threatening conditions which qualify according to the criterion of disproportionality lack the "folk devil" element – for instance, the swine flu scare that took place in the United States in the 1970s. At the same time, often, parties who are accused of keeping a supposed threat which is lacking in a folk devil hidden from the public may themselves become designated as deviants or folk devils.

Other supposed threats do not attract sufficient fear or concern felt by any substantial social group to qualify as a moral panic – that is, the criterion of consensus is lacking. Making a somewhat different point, Spector and Kitsuse (1977, pp. 80–1) mention the case of a student who seemed inordinately concerned about the number of reflector panels on the back of post office trucks; expressing "outrage," he accused various parties of being responsible for "waste, poor planning, and excess" (p. 80). Unless and until this student's outrage is shared by substantial numbers of individuals, in our view, it cannot qualify as a moral panic.

Likewise, if a given fear is a more or less constant and abiding element in a society, it lacks the element of volatility; according to this criterion, therefore, it does not qualify as a moral panic. As we saw, however, volatility is a matter of degree. Some panics burst forth and disappear within a fairly delimited period of time. The LSD scare was confined almost exclusively to the late 1960s. (Will it make a comeback on the same scale? We doubt it.) However, more broadly, one or another drug scare has burst forth and subsided on the American landscape for over a century. The satanic witch craze gripped Europe for nearly three centuries. The fact that certain concerns are long-lasting does not mean that they are not panics, however, since the intensity of these concerns, both locally and society-wide, waxes and wanes over time.

In short, the concept, moral panic, does *not* define a concern over a given issue or putative threat about which a given cynical observer is unsympathetic, or feels is morally or ideologically inappropriate. (At least one of the authors is intensely concerned about a threat – nuclear contamination – about which the experts claim public concern is excessive. And one of us has argued that concern over illegal drug use may have some objective foundation.) The moral panic is a phenomenon – given its broad and sprawling nature – that can be located and measured in a farily unbiased fashion. It does not matter whether we sympathize with the concern or not. What is important is that the concern locates a "folk devil," is shared, is out of synch with the measureable seriousness of the condition that generates it, and varies in intensity over time. As we shall see, if that concern is focused exclusively on moral or symbolic issues as ends in themselves, it cannot be regarded as a moral panic. The point that the moral panics concept is scientifically defensible, and not an invidious, ideologically motivated term of debunking, needs to be stressed in the strongest possible fashion.

The Locus of Moral Panics

We must never lose sight of the fact that fear and concern are expressed in specific actions taken, beliefs held, or sentiments felt *by specific individuals* in a society or community. *Who* is "panicked" by the condition in question? Some moral panics are widespread in that they grip substantial numbers of the members of a given society; others are more geographically localized, or characterize only representatives of specific categories, groups, or segments of the society. *To whom* is the panic "a panic"? is an ongoing question that demands an answer. We would be naive to assume that panics somehow suffuse the society as a whole to the extent that all the members of a given society are obsessed about the issue, and they are obsessed about it all the time. While some of the actions taken as a result of a moral panic are society-wide in their impact or implications – federal laws, for instance – they are always the product of what specific individuals or members of specific groups do. There may be intense disagreement in a given society about whether or not a given condition or issue represents a valid cause for concern. As Jenkins (1992, pp. 16–18, and passim) shows, in Britain in the mid to late 1980s, while some saw *threats* to women and children as a major cause for concern and action, others saw *exaggerated reactions to supposed threats* to women and children as a cause for concern. As in all topics social, *interpetations* of conditions as threatening, benign, or neutral form the core of the subject matter of moral panics.

A Critic of the Moral Panics Concept

The validity of the concept of the moral panic has not gone unchallenged. Waddington (1986) attacks Hall et al.'s (1978) argument that in the early 1970s, mugging represented a moral panic in Great Britain, one engineered by the ruling elite to divert attention away from the crisis in British capitalism. While much of Waddington's argument is sound – contrary to Hall et al.'s claim, the figures actually demonstrate the growing severity of street crime, rather than its diminution – its failure to acknowledge the very existence of the moral panic represents a major weakness. The moral panic, Waddington claims, "is a polemical rather than an analytic concept." It implies "that official and media concern is . . . without substance or justification . . . It is, of course, perfectly possible to panic about even the most genuine problem. People may panic in a fire, but this does not imply that the building is not burning nor that there is no threat" (p. 258). The "principal difficulty" of the moral panic is in "establishing the comparison between the scale of the problem and the scale of response to it . . . Conceptually, the notion of a 'moral panic' lacks any criteria of proportionality without which it is impossible to determine whether concern about any . . . problem is justified or not" (p. 246). Perhaps, Waddington argues, "it is time to abandon such value-laden terminology" as the moral panic (p. 258).

Clearly much of the field has chosen to ignore Waddington's attack on the moral panic concept. Whether it is referred to specifically as a moral panic (Ben-Yehuda, 1986, 1990a; Zatz, 1987; Ajzenstadt, 1989; Thompson, 1990a; Ungar, 1990; Jenkins, 1992; Jenkins and Meier-Katkin, 1992), a "rumor-panic" (Victor, 1989), simply a "panic" (Goode, 1990; Victor, 1993), a "menace" (Markson, 1990), a "craze" (Whitlock, 1979; Ben-Yehuda, 1980), or a "scare" (Richardson, Best, and Bromley, 1991; Levine and Reinarman, 1988; Reinarman and Levine, 1989; Ungar, 1992), much of the field regards the concept as viable. At the end of February, 1993, in an editorial, *The Economist* dubbed the outrage generated in Britain by the murder of a two-year-old boy by a stranger who was, moreover, a minor – a "moral panic." It is possible that our critic of the moral panic has overreacted.

Criteria of Disproportionality

Waddington's supposed problem of proportionality is readily resolved. How do we know that the attention accorded a given issue, problem, or phenomenon is disproportional to the threat it poses? Is referring to a certain issue as a "moral panic" nothing more than a "value judgment," an arbitrary claim that it does not deserve to receive as much attention as it has? While we agree with Ungar (1992, p. 497) that, with *some* conditions, "it is impossible to determine the nature of the objective threat" – and therefore, for that condition, to measure the dimension of disproportionality – this is most decidedly not true for many, possibly most, conditions. Threats that are "future-oriented" and potentially catastrophic, such as the greenhouse effect, the earth's shrinking ozone layer, and the risk of nuclear warfare, in all likelihood, *are* impossible to calculate. In contrast, threats that are more familiar, ongoing, and based on the behavior – and impact – of many individuals are, in our view, far more readily calculable.

Here are four indicators of disproportionality.

Figures Exaggerated

First, if the figures that are cited to measure the scope of the problem are grossly exaggerated, we may say that the criterion of dispro-portionality has been met. In May 1982, a member of the Israeli parliament, the Knesset, and representatives of the police released figures to the media to the effect that half of all Israeli high school children used hashish. This disclosure touched off a brief flurry of concern in the form of media attention and a demand for investigations. All available evidence indicated that the figures that were cited were fabricated; the actual figures, as indicated by systematic surveys, were in the 3–5-percent range (Ben-Yehuda, 1986, 1990a, pp. 101,

104, 106, 129, 133). Figures as discrepant as these provide a clue to the fact that we may have a moral panic on our hands.

Figures Fabricated

Second, if the concrete threat that is feared is, by all available evidence, nonexistent, we may say that the criterion of disproportionality has been met. Some fundamentalist Christians claim that satanic kidnap-murders are responsible for the lives of roughly 50,000 children in the United States each year. Careful examinations of the factual basis for this claim has turned up no evidence whatsoever to support it (Hicks, 1991; Richardson, Best, and Bromley, 1991). This enables us to argue that satanic kidnap-murders may constitute a moral panic among a segment of fundamentalist Christians.

Other Harmful Conditions

Third, if the attention that is paid to a specific condition is vastly greater than that paid to another, and the concrete threat or damage caused by the first is no greater than, or is less than, the second, the criterion of disproportionality may be said to have been met. The use of illegal drugs generates vastly more concern than the use of legal drugs, in spite of the fact that legal drugs cause far more disease and death than illegal drugs. According to the Surgeon General of the United States, in the US the use of tobacco cigarettes is responsible for well over 400,000 premature deaths each year, while alcohol use causes some 150,000 deaths; a crude extrapolation from hospital and medical examiner's data yields premature acute deaths for illegal drugs (or the illegal use of prescription drugs) in the 20,000 or so territory (Goode, 1993, p. 117). Again, discrepancies such as these should cause us to speculate that, perhaps, currently or recently, concern over illegal drug use might provide an example of a moral panic. (But for another side to the issue, see Goode, 1990.)

Changes over Time

Fourth, if the attention paid to a given condition at one point in time is vastly greater than that paid to it during a previous or later time without any corresponding increase in objective seriousness, then, once again, the criterion of disproportionality may be said to have been met. Between the middle to the late 1980s, newspaper and magazine articles on the subject of drug abuse virtually exploded, the percentage of

Americans saying that drug abuse was the nation's number one problem skyrocketed from the 2–3 percent range in the mid 1980s to 64
percent late in September 1989, and lawmakers proposed a huge spate
of bills and laws during the 1986–9 period, but far fewer before and
after. Yet during that period of time, the proportion of Americans who
used illegal drugs actually declined. (Again, see Goode, 1990.) This
tells us that the criterion of disproportionality has been met and that,
possibly, a moral panic about drugs gripped the nation in the late
1980s.

Determining Harm: The Anti-pornography Movement

Is the anti-pornography crusade a moral panic? Is the concern that
anti-pornography activists feel in excess of what it "should" be, given
pornography's objective harm or threat? This may not have a clearcut
answer. At least three questions have to be answered before this issue
can be addressed; their answers would determine whether the movement can be characterized as a moral panic. First, are the movement's
adherents primarily concerned about, and motivated by, the concrete,
objectively determinable harm they attribute to pornography? Second:
does pornography *in fact* cause the concrete harm that anti-pornography crusaders attribute to it; that is, is the concern expressed by anti-
pornography factions appropriate to or commensurate with the actual
damage it causes? And third, do anti-pornography activists characterize
the *nature* and *extent* of pornography acurately?

Reading the anti-pornography literature, especially that portion of it
produced by a certain wing of feminism, one gets the feeling that the
primary concern of its authors is that pornography is a *blasphemy
against women*, that each manifestation of pornography, each photograph, novel, film, video, each issue of *Playboy* and *Penthouse*, is *itself,
by its very nature*, an assault against womanhood. Each manifestation of
pornography announces that women are to be regarded – even if only
within the context of the pornographic material itself – primarily as
sexual objects, objectified and exploited, leered at and ogled; it is an
affirmation that, again, even if only in their pornographic depictions, all
women are whores. The very representation of women in pornography
is empirical evidence that women are exploited and oppressed – in a
sense, the image is regarded as real life, as *itself* an instance of oppressive behavior, a form of violence.

Thus, the concern of anti-pornography crusaders may be less about
what pornography *does* than what it *is*. The concern over the pornography issue by its opponents seems almost religious in its inspiration. The
obvious parallel here is reactions to blasphemy among religious funda-

mentalists. In 1989, Salman Rushdie's book, *The Satanic Verses*, was greeted by riots, effigy-burnings, and a million-dollar bounty on his head by some religious leaders of the fundamentalist Muslim world, whose faithful found the book an offense against the prophet Muhammad and against Islam generally. Not because it was likely to arouse anyone to do anything evil, they said, but because the *very existence* of certain phrases in the book was inherently offensive to Allah and his earthly representatives. In a like fashion, the impact of pornography is beside the point to many, possibly most, anti-pornography crusaders.

Suppose it were demonstrated, conclusively and definitively, that pornography does not have the consequences attributed to it by its critics? Most anti-pornography crusaders would say it doesn't matter. The issue of the impact of porn is, in reality, empirical window-dressing, a logical-sounding argument to shore up a deeply felt moral and ideological position. Pornography, the anti-porn crusader would say, *does not deserve to exist* – regardless of its impact. *Its very existence* is an offense against women, they say, and for that reason alone, it should be wiped off the face of the earth. The obliteration of pornography is an end in itself. Hence, we cannot determine whether such concern is disproportionate to the actual harm imputed – one defining element of the moral panic – since that harm is secondary. The harm in this case is the very existence of pornography; such "harm" cannot be measured or quantified and hence, the concern over it cannot be referred to as a moral panic.

Even the answer to the question of the concrete impact of porn – does exposure to pornography cause men to inflict physical harm on women? – cannot be entirely straightforward. Contemporary research suggests that men who are exposed to violent pornography tend to act in a more aggressive fashion toward women in an experimental laboratory situation than men who are not so exposed, they tend to have less empathetic feelings toward women who have been raped, and they are more likely to believe in rape myths, for instance that women are responsible for having been raped – but the same is true of men who have been exposed to depictions of violence against women which is lacking in pornographic content. In contrast, men who have been exposed to non-violent pornography, as opposed to those who have not, are not more likely to manifest these differences. (For an insightful discussion of some of the methodological and conceptual problems in the study of pornography and violence, see Jarvie, 1986, pp. 390–475.) It seems that it is the violence, not the sexual content, that causes these behaviors, feelings, and beliefs (Donnerstein, Linz, and Penrod, 1987). It is possible that, from a strictly causal perspective, then, the focus of anti-pornography feminists on pornography of all kinds, non-violent and violent alike, might seem to be misplaced. However, when we consider the fact that the opposition of groups such as Women Against Pornography to porn is not simply on its causal impact but its very nature, its very existence, such a focus might seem quite rational indeed. In short, we cannot refer to the anti-pornography crusade as a moral panic; for this movement and many of its sympathizers, the obliteration of what they regard as anti-female depictions is an end in itself. Hence, there is no concrete means of measuring the dimension of incommensurability.

Third, do anti-pornography activists characterize the phenomenon they attack accurately? Or do they typify its nature and extent in a wildly exaggerated fashion? Do they, for example, see pornography for sale on every street corner and ensconced in every household with one or more males in America? Do they see all, or most, pornography as violent? Do they see violent porn as a trend toward which all pornography is tending? Do they see kiddie porn as a major proportion of all pornography? Do they see most minor runaways as victims of kiddie porn entrepreneurs? If the answer to these questions is a consistent yes for many or most anti-pornography activists, or characteristic of its leadership, it is possible that the nature and extent of pornography has been exaggerated and the movement has elements or aspects of a moral panic.

To put the matter in a nutshell: *to the extent that* the anti-pornography movement activists' motives are primarily protectionist and rational, *to the extent that* pornography does *not* have the harmful effects attributed to it, and *to the extent that* its nature and extent are exaggerated by activists, according to the criterion of proportionality, the anti-pornography movement represents a moral panic. To the extent that these motives express the view that pornographic depictions are an evil in themselves, an affront to or an assault against women, *or* to the extent that these motives are rational and protectionist and pornography *does* have the harmful effects attributed to it, and to the extent that activists see pornography's nature and extent accurately, the anti-pornography movement is *not* a moral panic. (See Zurcher and Kirkpatrick, 1976; Zurcher et al., 1971.) In short, the designation of the activities of the anti-pornography movement as a moral panic is not a simple matter. In some ways it is not; in other ways it is.

Determining Harm: The Anti-abortion Movement

Can we say that the concern felt by the anti-abortion forces constitutes a moral panic? In this case, somewhat more definitively, we cannot. If we were to accept the pro-life definition of human life as beginning at fertilization, then it follows that every abortion represents the actual murder of a human being. Pro-lifers argue that over 28 million babies have been "exterminated" in the United States since abortion became legal in 1973. The validity of this claim rests entirely on whether fetuses should be defined as fully-fledged human beings. To the extent that they are, abortion represents one of the most pressing and serious problems of our age; to the extent that fetuses are not considered full human beings, and therefore abortion is not murder, abortion will not be seen as a serious problem to society. The determination of objective harm in this case cannot be resolved without the resolution of what is an essentially unresolvable definitional problem. Since we cannot determine the extent of the objective damage to measure subjective concern against, the criterion of disproportionality cannot be met. Hence, the protests of the anti-abortion forces do not qualify as a legitimate example of a moral panic. Clearly, the example of abortion illustrates that the measure of "objective" or "concrete" harm is not always straightforward, and may itself be constructed. To be more specific, some measures are widely agreed upon as indicating objective or concrete harm (the death of children and adults from disease), while others may be more controversial (the death of zygotes, embryos, and fetuses). When we use the term "objective" or "concrete" harm, we will always refer to harm that is widely or nearly universally agreed upon as harm.

On the other hand, when the anti-abortion movement grossly exaggerates certain aspects of abortion – for instance, that a far higher proportion of women who undergo abortions suffer physical and psychological damage than actually do – we may very well have a moral panic-like phenomenon on our hands. The line between moral panics and phenomena we have no right to refer to as panics is, as with most social phenomena, not entirely clearcut. But, just as we might have some difficulty in distinguishing between dusk and night-time but none in distinguishing between noon and midnight, marginal cases do not prevent us from recognizing more classic cases of moral panics when we have one on our hands.

Disproportionality: A Recapitulation

Thus, each of the concrete indicators mentioned above – figures on the objective seriousness of the problem are exaggerated, the existence of a materially nonexistent problem, gross differences in concern among various conditions, and radical fluctuations in concern over time without corresponding material changes in seriousness – provides a criterion for disproportionality, the fourth element in our definition of the moral panic. Contrary to Waddington, the concept has objective validity; it is not a value judgment, but a phenomenon in the material world that can be located, measured, and analyzed. If we define the concept out of existence, we will fail to notice major social processes that have had an impact on human societies, possibly, for the duration of human history. Given the ubiquity and influence of the moral panic, it demands attention.

In recent years, some radicals who, in the 1960s and 1970s, downplayed the objective threat posed by lower-class street crime, have revised their views and now argue that street crime has real victims. Jock Young, for instance (1987), has developed a perspective that is referred to as "left realism," which emphasizes ways of protecting citizens from predatory street crime and urges that more effective yet less repressive means of administering the criminal justice system be instituted. Taking the fear of crime seriously, Young argues, avoids the "idealist" fallacy that certain concerns arise out of thin air and are not grounded in human experience.

Our reading of this approach would agree that certain fears and concerns must be grounded in the conditions of social and economic life; they do not arise for no reason at all. At the same time, these concerns *may* be fueled by specific threats that are materially nonexistent or grossly exaggerated. As we'll point out a number of times, fundamentalist Christians are fearful about satanic ritual abuse in substantial numbers, the evidence for which, most experts agree, is nonexistent (Hicks, 1991; Victor, 1993). At the same time, the very real conditions of the lives of believers in the material reality of this threat – marginality, the erosion of traditional Christianity and conservative values, the growing power of secularization, economic decline – may help explain this belief. These *conditions* are real, and so is a threat *of some kind*, but not necessarily the specific threat that is believed in. Many African-Americans believe that the whites who run food and drink companies that sell in the black community are trying to poison their bodies with contaminated products (Turner, 1993). The fact that no evidence has ever turned up to support this contention is secondary – *but nonetheless relevant*. What is crucial here is the fact that whites have inflicted, and continue to inflict, harm to the bodies of Black folk, a very real and concrete fact that helps make these conspiracy beliefs and rumors seem plausible to some. The point is, yes, fear and concern *do*, for the most part, grow out of the very real conditions of social life. But no, they need *not* be commensurate with the concrete threat posed specifically by that which is feared – indeed, that threat may not even exist in the first place. At the same time, concern is almost certainly based on *some* concretely real phenomenon – even though that which is feared, specifically, may be only tangentially related.

Moral Panics: An Inherently Ideological Concept?

It should be made clear that the moral panic is not inherently an ideological concept. It is true that most analyses of moral panics have in fact been made by social scientists of a liberal, left-leaning, or radical persuasion (Jenkins, 1992, p. 145). Clearly, the concept dovetails neatly with the view that the government, the media, and the public are excessively concerned with trivial or nonexistent problems identified as being caused by "underdogs" about which a major fuss is raised, whereas those which the "top dogs" are responsible for causing do not generate such concern or attention – for instance, muggings (Hall et al., 1978) versus corporate crime.

This supposed leftish accompaniment is not, however, one of its necessary, inherent, or defining features.

For instance, some factions of feminism, whose adherents claim some affiliation with leftish politics, seem to have taken up the satanic child molestation and murder cause in the United States (Rose, 1993). In addition, some British feminists and members of the political left supported the satanism-child abuse cause, briefly, in 1990 (Jenkins, 1992, pp. 173–6). In both cases, we have examples of adherents of a supposedly liberal or radical stance supporting what seems to be a nonexistent threat and thereby becoming participants in a moral panic. Another example: experts claim that the risk of contamination from nuclear power plants is minuscule, a proposition that the overwhelming majority of the public refuses to accept (Slovic, Layman, and Flynn, 1991; but see Perrow, 1984, pp. 324–8 and Erikson, 1990). In this case, therefore, the facts of the case presumably support a pro-industry (that is, a "conservative") position, and the exaggerated or dispro-portionate fears of the public (that is, the "panic") support an anti-industry or "liberal" position. Clearly, there is no *intrinsic* leftist slant to the moral panics concept.

Cohen (1988, pp. 260–3) argues persuasively that (while there are significant differences), many of the same arguments that the 1960s and early 1970s radicals and liberals advanced to trace out the social, political, and economic origins of the moral panics and crusades they opposed (against marijuana, homosexuality, the consumption and sale of alcohol, and so on) could be used to understand the moral panics and crusades now supported by some contemporary liberals and rad-icals (for instance, against industrial pollution, smoking, and pornogra-phy). Just as the moral entrepreneurs of earlier decades would have found the analyses of moral panics theorists offensive and critical of their efforts, likewise, the liberal and radical moral entrepreneurs of today resist such an approach to their efforts, again, sensing a subversion of their cause. In each case, the analysis of the backgrounds of these campaigns seems to *delegitimate* the cause; it seems to argue that the individuals who took up the cause, and worked to criminalize the behavior in question, were motivated not by the harm inflicted by the behavior itself, but by moral, political, economic, and ideological issues.

In fact, the legitimacy of a cause is – in principle, in any case – independent of its social, economic, and political origins. Thus, while, as a general rule, analysts of moral panics have *tended to be* leftish in their political views, observers of any political stripe could use the concept to understand the mobilization and social organization of exaggerated social fears. In the abstract, the concept is politically neutral, but using it to critically examine widespread fears usually regarded as conservative in their import, or the elite manipulation of latent public fears, has characteristically been the rule since the concept's inception. While the moral panics concept has at times degenerated into "mere debunking" (Whitlock, 1979), debunking for political ends is neither one of its necessary nor its principal features; it is measureable, it can be applied to cases supporting a wide range of political views, and it has no *inherent* political slant.

Moral Panics: An Overview

Societies everywhere have at times been gripped by moral panics and yet, as Cohen says (1972, p. 11), they have received insufficient systematic attention. More research has been devoted to the moral panic in the past decade than was true of the decade following Cohen's introduction of the concept. Still, we need to know far more about them than we do. Focusing on moral panics raises a number of questions. Who is it, exactly, whose expression of concern defines the moral panic? How much concern in how many individuals constitutes a genuine case of moral panic? Why do some panics occur among certain segments among the public but not others – that is, why are some panics socially and subculturally localized, while others grip a people society-wide? How do they get started? What, exactly, is the active agent responsible for their genesis? Do they arise as a result of enterprise – that is, the conscious efforts of the few – or do they emerge on a more widespread, grassroots, populist basis? If it is the former, is there any such thing as a moral panic without popular support? If it is the latter, are specific agents necessary at all, or can moral panics erupt without specific agents, leaders, or entrepreneurs? How do the efforts of the few effect concern among the many? Is it possible for certain incipient moral panics to fail to take hold? Why do panics over a particular issue burst forth at one time but not another – that is, why are they patterned according to a specific *timing*? Are certain individuals, types of individuals, or segments of society more likely to initiate the moral panic? If certain individuals, types of individuals, or social categories attempt to launch a moral panic, is it more likely to be successful – that is, to take hold – in comparison with the outcome of the efforts of other individuals, types of individuals, or social categories? Once started, do moral panics take on a life of their own, or do they require sustained nurturance? Why do panics over certain issues grip specific groups or categories in a society but leave others indifferent? Whose values are being expressed by the panic? Whose interests does the moral panic serve? Are certain behaviors more intrinsically frightening than others – and more likely to generate moral panics? What is the role of the media in reporting and sustaining a moral panic? What is the role of the state or the government in the generation and maintenance of the moral panic? Why do moral panics die out? What is their long-term legacy or impact? What characterizes those that have a long-term impact versus those that do not?

Moral panics frequently erupt in modernizing and modern society, a fact that should cause us to question their sophisticated, tolerant, *laissez-faire* stance toward nonconformity. In fact, it is entirely likely that moral panics serve as a mechanism for simultaneously strengthening and redrawing society's moral boundaries – that line between morality and immorality, just where one leaves the territory of good and enters that of evil. When a society's moral boundaries are sharp, clear, and secure, and the central norms and values are strongly held by nearly everyone, moral panics rarely grip its members – nor do they need to. However, when the moral boundaries are fuzzy and shifting and often seem to be contested, moral panics are far more likely to seize the members of a society (Ben-Yehuda, 1985).

Moral Panics: Four Overlapping Territories

The moral panic takes place when four territories overlap: *deviance, social problems, collective behavior,* and *social movements.* The territory occupied by deviance accounts for the *moral* part of the moral panic: behavior regarded as immoral is more likely to generate public concern and fear than is more traditional, conventional behavior. The territory that is occupied by social problems accounts for the *public concern* part of the moral panic: when much of the public is aware of and concerned about a given condition, regardless of its objective status, sociologically, it must be regarded as a social problem – and certainly the panic represents an extremely heightened form of awareness and concern. The territory occupied by collective behavior accounts for the *volatility* of moral panics: the fact that, much like fads, they erupt suddenly and usually unexpectedly, and, in a like manner, fairly swiftly subside and disappear – or lose their fervid quality in the process of becoming institutionalized. The territory occupied by social movements addresses the issue of the organization and moblization of concerned segments of the population to address and change specific social conditions. Although many moral panics do not generate full-scale social movements or social movement organizations, all activate proto-, incipient, or "germinal" social movements or social movement organizations which may or may not reach complete institutionalization.

A Representative Moral Panic: LSD in the 1960s

Psychedelic drugs were taken, in the form of peyote, the psilocybin (or "magic") mushroom, and the bark of the yagé vine, mainly for religious and ceremonial purposes, by North and South American Indians long before the coming of Europeans to the western hemisphere. Although some intellectuals and bohemians in Europe and America experimented with mescaline and peyote around the turn of the nineteenth century, it was not until well into the second half of the twentieth century that hallucinogenic drug use became fairly widespread. This development was predicated on the synthesis of, and experimentation with, a specific psychoactive chemical – lysergic acid diethylamide, or LSD.

In 1938, Albert Hofmann, a Swiss chemist, synthesized LSD in a lab. At the time, he merely noted its existence and set it aside. In 1943, he accidentally inhaled an extremely minute quantity of the drug, felt dizzy, and left his lab to go home and lie down. He experienced a "stream of fantastic images of extraordinary plasticity and vividness . . . accompanied by an intense, kaleidoscopic-like play of colors." Hofmann was, in fact, experiencing the first LSD trip in human history. He suspected that his unusual experience was the result of a chemical he was working on. The following Monday, he returned to the lab and ingested 250 micrograms of the drug, a dose that, for most drugs, would have had no measureable or noticeable effect whatsoever. He was, once again, forced to discontinue his work and, accompanied by an assistant, go home and lie down. The effects included most of those he experienced the first time, as well as a feeling of timelessness, depersonalization, and a loss of control. "I was overcome with fears that I was going crazy," Hofmann said. "This drug makes normal people psychotic!" he declared. During the 1940s and 1950s, a few researchers picked up on Hofmann's insight and speculated that the hallucinogenic drug experience might be the key to insanity. In time, they found the differences outweighed the similarities, and this line of research was eventually abandoned.

The use of LSD might have remained almost totally confined to hospitals and laboratories had it not been that in 1954, a British novelist and essayist, Aldous Huxley, famous for his classic novel *Brave New World*, took mescaline and described his experiences in a slim, poetic volume entitled *The Doors of Perception*. Though he did draw the parallel with insanity, he also added a new angle to the growing literature on hallucinogenic drug use. Being normal, Huxley wrote, is learning to shut out or eliminate most of the distracting, overwhelming, disturbing, confusing stimuli that explode all around us. Psychedelic drugs, he claimed, wash away the many years of rigid socialization and programming we have been exposed to, and permit us to perceive that which we have learned to ignore. Taking psychedelic drugs like mesaline, psilocybin, and LSD, Huxley wrote, can bring about a kind of transcendence, much like religion.

Huxley's book was read by Timothy Leary, a PhD in psychology and lecturer at Harvard University. Vacationing in Mexico in 1960, he took a dose of the psilocybin mushroom and had what he described as a "visionary voyage." "I came back a changed man," he declared. With several colleagues, he administered doses of hallucinogenic drugs to hundreds of volunteers, including Harvard undergraduates, theology students, and convicts. With all of them, Leary claimed, it "changed their lives for the better." The experiments, many observers felt, were casually administered, unscientific, and aimed mainly at proselytizing; usually, a physician was not present. By the fall of 1962, Harvard's administration voiced grave concerns about the experiments, which Leary brushed off as "hysteria" that was hampering his research. In the spring of 1963, Leary was fired, an event that touched off headline news.

One indication of the excitement stirred up by the use of LSD and other psychedelic drugs was the enormous number of articles that were published in popular magazines and newspapers on the subject. It is a phenomenon confined almost entirely to the 1960s. The first article listed in *The Reader's Guide to Periodical Literature* was published in *Look* magazine and was entitled, ominously and prophetically, "Step into the World of the Insane." In 1962, a popular article appeared reporting that LSD was being used on the street. In the entire decade before February 1963, only 11 articles on LSD had been published in all of the popular magazines indexed by the *Guide* – only one per year (not counting those appearing in *Science*, which although listed in the *Reader's Guide*, is not really a popular magazine).

However, beginning with Leary's dismissal from Harvard, the stories on LSD quickly mounted. From March 1966 to February 1967, 50 popular articles were published on LSD and indexed in the *Reader's Guide*. In March 1967, a research article appeared in *Science* which purported to demonstrate that LSD damaged human chromosomes.

(Later, it was revealed that the research was flawed and its conclusions fallacious.) That angle proved to be a major theme in the 33 articles published in the subsequent year. But by 1968, LSD had declined in newsworthiness; only 13 articles appeared from 1968 to 1969, and less than half that in each subsequent year. Only one article on LSD was published in 1974 and 1975. Clearly, as news, acid had had it.

The pre-1967 magazine (and newspaper) articles on LSD conveyed the distinct impression that those who ingested the drug stood an unwholesomely strong likelihood of losing their minds – temporarily for sure, and possibly permanently as well. The effects of LSD were described as "nightmarish;" "terror and indescribable fear" were considered common, routine, typical. *Life* ran a cover story in its March 25, 1966, issue entitled "The Exploding Threat of the Mind Drug That Got out of Control." *Time* ran a feature essay on LSD emphasizing the drug's "freaking out" aspect. "Under the influence of LSD," the story declared, "non-swimmers think they can swim, and others think they can fly. One young man tried to stop a car . . . and was killed. A magazine salesman became convinced that he was the Messiah. A college dropout committed suicide by shashing his arm and bleeding to death in a field of lilies." Psychic terror, uncontrollable impulses, violence, an unconcern for one's own safety, psychotic episodes, delusions, and hallucinations formed the fare of the early articles on the use of LSD.

The newspaper articles on LSD were even more sensationalistic, lurid, and one-sided than were those published in popular magazines. Newspaper headlines screamed out stories such as "Mystery of Nude Coed's Fatal Plunge," "Strip-Teasing Hippie Goes Wild on LSD," and "Naked in a Rosebush" (Braden, 1970). A story that circulated about two teenagers under the influence of LSD who went blind staring into the sun was later revealed to have been a hoax; it was widely reported and believed because, it was felt, "anything can happen" with this terrifying and mysterious new drug.

After 1967, the chromosome breakage angle dominated the popular press. One article, which appeared in the *Saturday Evening Post*, displayed photographs of distorted babies, explaining that "if you take LSD, even once, your children may be born malformed or retarded" and that "new research finds it's causing genetic damage that poses a threat of havoc now and appalling abnormalities for generations yet unborn" (Davison, 1967). This wave of hysteria was not quite so strong or as long-lasting as the "insanity" theme, but it did convince many users – and authorities – that the drug was extremely dangerous in yet another way. The whole LSD-chromosomes episode illustrates Stanley Cohen's thesis about "sensitization" during moral panics, since the research on which that conclusion was based (Cohen, Marinello, and Back, 1967) was extremely shoddy, based on very few cases, and poorly conducted – and yet it "demonstrated" the toxic danger of this panic-inducing drug. As we now know, the whole issue proved to be a false alarm. LSD is an extremely weak gene-altering agent, exceedingly unlikely to cause chrosomal anormalities in the doses typically taken (Dishotsky et al., 1971).

In the 1960s, LSD appeared to many observers to pose a uniquely damaging potential; to some, the threat it seemed to pose was massive. In 1966, the New Jersey Narcotic Drug Study Commission declared LSD "the greatest threat facing the country today" (Brecher et al., 1972, p. 369). Two facts make this hysteria truly remarkable. First, LSD is a drug that is taken with almost unique infrequency. Of all widely used recreational drugs, it is the one taken by users most episodically and occasionally, least regularly and chronically; users typically take LSD, when they do, on a once-in-a-while basis – once or twice a year, once a month, very, very rarely every week. And second, the use of LSD was at an extremely low level in the 1960s; at the peak of the drug's publicity, no more than 1 or 2 percent of adolescents and young adults had ever taken LSD. Between the late 1960s and early 1970s, when the publicity about the drug was declining, use was rising, and fairly sharply. (For a detailed discussion of these assertions, see Goode, 1993, ch. 8.) Here, once again, we see a strong disparity between at least one measure of concern and objective threat.

And yet, this panic evaporated in what was probably record time. Today, the use of LSD and the other hallucinogens is no longer a public issue, at least, not apart from the use of drugs generally. LSD has been absorbed into the morass of drug-taking generally – less seriously regarded than heroin or crack use, but more so than mari-juana. LSD never *materialized* into the threat to society that many people claimed it was. The drastic, dramatic, cosmic, philosophical, and religious claims for the LSD experience that were made in the 1960s now seem an artifact of an antiquated age. The psychedelic movement, which never made up a majority of users, even regular users, of LSD, simply disappeared. The fear of the conventional major-ity that users would go crazy, drop out, or overturn the social order also never came to pass. LSD has become just another drug taken occasion-ally by multiple drug users for the same hedonistic, recreational reasons they take other drugs – to get high. Interestingly enough, expressions of fear over the use of LSD were recycled in the early 1990s (Seligmann et al., 1992; Orcutt and Turner, 1993, p. 201) by turning an extremely small increase in the use of this drug into a major threat. This new fear is unlikely to generate another full-scale panic, but it shows that some threats never seem to disappear for good; if they managed to stir up concern at one time, why not another? Some moral panics manifest what communications expert Jean-Noel Kapferer refers to, with respect to rumor, as "the eternal return" (1990, pp. 113ff).

A Representative Moral Panic: Satanic Ritual Abuse

Beginning roughly in 1980, a tale has been told on a national scale that qualifies as a contemporary legend, a collective delusion, a moral panic, and, when told among believers, a rumor panic as well (Victor, 1989, 1990, 1991, 1993; Jenkins and Meier-Katkin, 1992; Thompson, King, and Annetts, 1990; Richardson, Best, and Bromley, 1991). It seems that, in the United States and England, a conspiracy of satanists is kidnapping (and breeding) children in order to use them in satanic rituals, which includes sexually molesting, even torturing, mutilating, and murdering them. Most or at least a significant proportion of cases of missing children, sexual molestations, and child pornography, the legend claims, have a satanic connection (Nathan, 1990, 1991). Geraldo Rivera, a popular talk-show host, summed up – and endorsed – the tale when he opened one of his many shows on satanism with the following words: "Satanic cults! Every hour, every day, their ranks are growing. Estimates are there are one million satanists in this country. The majority of them are linked in a highly organized, very secret network. From small towns to large cities, they've attracted police and FBI attention to their satanist ritual child abuse, child pornography, and grisly satanic murder. The odds are this is happening in your town" (*Devil Worship: Exposing Satan's Underground*, NBC television documentary, October 25, 1988).

These practices are taking place on a vast scale, these observers claim. Some 50,000 to 60,000 (even up to two million, some estimates have it) children are being murdered each year in satanic rituals. This conspiracy is being covered up at the local and national level because of ignorance, fear, and complicity on the part of authorities. Police officials, teachers and day-care workers, newspaper editors, and even judges and politicians are part of the conspiracy, this legend proclaims. Evidence of satanic ritual child abuse and murder is all around us, its supporters aver. Satanists use animal sacrifices before murdering their victims; the dead, mutilated bodies of animals may be found in communities all across the country, they argue. Hundreds of thousands of children are missing each year, and hardly anyone is doing anything about it. Sexual molestations, satanic rituals, and animal sacrifices are taking place on a routine basis in day-care centers from coast to coast, and, again, officials are silent. Accounts by dozens of cult "survivors," detailing their coerced childhood participation in satanic rituals, have been given on such American talk shows and television news programs as *Geraldo*, *Oprah*, *20/20*, and *Sally Jesse Raphael*. Dozens of books demonstrating the link between satanism and child murders have been published in the 1980s and 1990s and have received widespread attention; even *Ms.* magazine, which usually expresses a liberal, enlightened, feminist perspective, published a "survivor" account endorsing the legend (Rose, 1993). Who could doubt such convincing evidence?

The ritual sacrifice of children by evil outsiders is a tale with roots extending back in history at least two thousand years. In ancient Rome, during the time of the early Christians, ironically, Christians were said to be kidnapping Roman children and murdering them in their unholy rituals (Ellis, 1983). In the Middle Ages, Jews were said to perform blood sacrifices on Christian boys (Ridley, 1967). The fact that a nearly identical story crops up independently a number of times does not necessarily or automatically mean that the story is false. However, it does force us to wonder whether it might have been similar historical and cultural circumstances that made the story plausible to some members of a society – or the fact that it tells a gripping, dramatic tale – rather than that the story represented an accurate rendering of literal, concrete events.

Evidence

It should be said at once that, as with the historical stories of the ritual sacrifice of children by evil agents, the contemporary version of the tale has not received evidentiary corroboration of any kind. No solid physical evidence, or, in fact, evidence of any of these claims has ever been confirmed to support the satanism–child sacrifice link. Circles of satanists do exist, of course, a number of extremely tiny cults with a total national membership of no more than a thousand, not counting scattered satanic "dabblers," unconnected to any organized cult. (Actually, at least in its stated policy, the Church of Satan specifically forbids its members from abusing children, drugs, and animals.) And children are sexually molested, and in substantial numbers; roughly one in six to one in seven American children have been sexually molested at least once by their eighteenth birthday (Russell, 1986, p. 10; Finkelhor, 1979, p. 53). However, these molestations very, very rarely take place in day-care centers or organized groups of any kind; most often, they are committed by relatives, neighbors, or older friends. And child pornography rings do exist, of course, but evidence of their link with satanism has never surfaced. And all of the numbers on missing children and child murders by the advocates of the satanism claim are almost literally impossible. The official yearly number of criminal homicides – the total number of all people from all sources – in the United States given by the Federal Bureau of Investigation, is roughly 25,000. According to the FBI, over the past five years, less than 500 stranger-abducted children are still reported as missing. In contrast, about 2,000 children are murdered by their parents each year.

Not a single satanist child murder claim has been borne out by the facts.

Characteristics of Believers

However, the most interesting aspect of the satanism story to researchers and students of the moral panic (as well as other social phenomena, such as collective behavior) is not its concrete falsity. The fact that it departs *so radically* from what we know to be the facts should lead us to ask why and how it arose, circulates, and is believed. The fact that, unlike many feverish concerns – which are simply *exaggerations* of the importance of certain threats – the satanic child abuse and murder stories and fears represent a case of "imaginary deviance" (Victor, 1993) should lead us to wonder about their origin. The social setting in which this panic is located – especially when contrasted with those social circles in which it has no currency at all – tell us a great deal about its appeal where it is felt. Sociologists know, for example, that rumormongering is most likely to take place under conditions of maximum anxiety and ambiguity among people who are likely to be highly gullible and uncritical. (See chapter 7.)

In which social circles are we most likely to find these conditions? There are exceptions, of course. As we saw, *Ms.* magazine, whose readers are, for the most part, secular, urban, and well educated, seems to endorse the tale (Rose, 1993). However, on the whole, believers of the satanism tale are largely fundamentalist Christians, live in rural areas or small towns, and tend to have relatively low levels of education (Victor, 1989, 1990, 1991, 1993). The story typically takes root in areas that are hardest hit by an economic recession; individuals most likely to be gripped by the satanism panic are those who have experienced a serious erosion of traditional values in recent years, especially those pertaining to religion and the family (Victor, 1989; Bromley, 1991). The characteristics and ideology of those subject to fear of the satanism tale give us a powerful clue in understanding why such a belief has currency nowadays. It is the life circumstances of certain individuals and circles of individuals that make the satanism claim "culturally plausible" (Bromley, 1991, pp. 50, 64). It should be emphasized in the most forceful terms possible that not all or even most small-town fundamentalist Christians believe the satanist child murder and abuse legend or are consumed by a panic, concern, or fear about this nonexistent phenomenon. However, each factor mentioned above – education, fundamentalism, residence, a perception of the erosion of traditional institutions and values – increases the likelihood that a given individual will do so. (For discussions of the fundamentalist Christian world view, see Flake, 1984 and Ammerman, 1987.)

Literal Reality versus Metaphor

To us, the satanism story may be taken not so much as a literal description of concrete phenomena that exist and events that are taking place in the world – which is, in fact, how it is taken by its believers – but as a *metaphor*, a tale that represents, stands for, or symbolizes an actual state of affairs. That is, "the satanism claims may be *metaphorically* true even if *empirically* false" (Bromley, 1991, p. 68; our emphasis). To individuals with a certain kind of background living in certain life circumstances, the fear appears to be based on concrete events, the story on which the fears are based appears to be true because of events that are really happening that, to them, very much *represent* events that happen in the story. People are receptive to stories to the extent that those stories resonate with their notion of the way things are. Indisputable evidence tells some relatively uneducated, blue-collar, rural and small-town fundamentalist Christians that the satanism legend is true. The myth explains a great deal about things they know to be true. In other words, certain assertions about satanic happenings will be relatively unaffected by the lack of evidence on these events (Bromley, 1991, pp. 64, 68) because a very different form of evidence will be taken as supporting those assertions. And it will be the ideology and life circumstances of such individuals that will convince them that evidence that fails to satisfy most other individuals is true.

Subversion Myths

The first and most important fact about the panic over the satanism legend is that it is a *subversion myth* (Bromley, 1987, 1991; Victor, 1991, 1993). It is a story that explains to members of certain social circles *why* things are going wrong, why their way of life is being undermined or subverted. It also explains who has introduced the practices they regard as an abomination. Subversion myths (some of which may be at least partly concretely true) *demonologize* certain individuals or categories of individuals, holding them responsible for the evil that has rained down on the heads of the righteous; these individuals have been characterized as metaphorical devil – "folk devils," in Stanley Cohen's terminology (1972). These individuals are depicted as subversives; satanists "embody quintissential evil" (Bromley, 1991, p. 58). Such individuals become scapegoats for the troubles of the members of the social circles who propagate such myths.

Institutional Crisis

The second crucial aspect of the satanism story and panic about it is that members of certain segments in American society are facing what Bromley (1991, p. 50) refers to as an *institutional crisis*. That is, events are sweeping over them that make previous desirable traditions and practices difficult, untenable, or impossible. In nearly all social change, there are winners and losers. Over the course of the twentieth century, and especially since the end of the Second World War, many traditional institutions have been eroded or undermined. Families have gotten smaller and there has been a decline in domesticity, a loss of family control, prestige, and power; government and business have become larger and more impersonal, more powerful and bureaucratized; traditional religion has lost influence and prestige, become less integral to mainstream culture, and markedly secularized. In the eyes of many traditionalists, there has been a virtual explosion of drug use, pornography, teenage sex, abortion, crime and delinquency, and non- and anti-Christian cultures. The nation is wallowing in filth, corruption, and depravity, some feel. Many traditionalists feel that they are witnessing the death throes of a once-viable, meaningful, and worthwhile way of life that stood at the center of their existence. It is the decline of that which is regarded as good and the recent, immense growth of that which is regarded as evil, that convinces many fundamentalist Christians that the satanism tale must be true and that it is a cause for serious concern for the country as a whole. It is the "institutional crisis" in some quarters that has generated the moral panic over satanic ritual child abuse and murder.

Abortion

Perhaps the most prominent among these evil practices is abortion; fundamentalist Christians are deeply concerned about the legalization (in 1973) and growing legitimacy of abortion. Although not in itself a moral panic (as we saw), the concern over abortion has helped fuel one or more moral panics. In a way, if we grant some basic fundamentalist Christian assumptions, children *are* being slaughtered in extremely large numbers in the United States each year. If we agree that the fetus is a fully-fleged human being, a child in the same way that an infant is, then it follows that abortion represents the murder of children on a very large scale. Since 1973, when abortion was fully legalized in the United States, nearly a million abortions have been performed each year, more than 20 million – nearly 30 million, by some counts – during this period. Legal abortion can be seen as the triumph of a kind of conspiracy of secular humanists – who are seen as being in league with Satan – who have managed to wield their influence over God-fearing and God-loving Christians. In this sense, children *are* being slaughtered by "the forces of Satan" – not literally, of course, but metaphorically. To the fundamentalist Christian, it is a very small step from the metaphor to the concrete reality, from believing that abortions are legally performed by physicians on women who voluntarily request the operation, to believing that children are being kidanpped or bred by an organization of satanists for the purpose of unholy ritual slaughter. In short, abortion is a "concession to the Devil *little less overt* than actual ritual sacrifice" (Jenkins and Meier-Katkin, 1992; my emphasis).

Women Working

Another trouble recent change has wrought for some traditional, relatively uneducated, blue-collar, fundamentalist Christians has been in the area of women working. In the past 40 years, the proportion of women with preschool children who are employed outside the home has increased five times, from 12 percent in 1950 to 60 percent in the 1990s. To the traditionalist, this development is a catastrophe. A woman's place is in the home, caring for her young children, teaching them traditional values. By taking a job, the woman is neglecting her most important function and exposing her children – and herself – to danger. To a fundamentalist Christian mother with old-fashioned values, being forced to work because of difficult economic circumstances represents the triumph of evil over good; of secularism over religious values; of having to give up power and autonomy and independence to an alien, uncaring, godless world. To the religious right, the trend toward an abandonment of women's traditional role as homemaker in favor of a job outside the home can only erode the strength of traditional Bible religion, and strengthen the hand of modernism and secularism – tools of corruption in the hands of Satan.

Day Care

Almost as important as the legalization of abortion is the recent explosion of children in day-care centers. The decay of the family is nowhere as evident as in the proliferation of day-care centers for preschool children. Instead of remaining at home with their mothers, children are now being cared for and raised by strangers. Half of all preschool children are being cared for during a significant period during the day by someone other than their parents. Who are these people? Where do they come from? What are they doing with our children? What are they teaching them? What are their beliefs? Can we trust them? Such fears are likely to breed insecurity, powerlessness, paranoia, a suspicion that one's loved ones are being hurt and corrupted, and a receptivity to subversion myths, susceptibility to a panic that centers around children. By emphasizing that satanic ritual abuse is widespread, traditionalists are invoking a metaphor to demonstrate that day-care centers are "an extremely dangerous place for the young" (Jenkins and Meier-Katkin, 1992).

Atrocity Tales

The satanism legend represents an example of an *atrocity tale* – a real or imagined *summary event* that represents all that is wrong with one's opponents and enemies and is intended to evoke moral outrage and generate action against the alleged perpetrators (Bromley, Shupe, and Ventimiglia, 1979, p. 43). As we shall see in chapter 8, atrocity tales are routinely disseminated by social movements whose aim is to galvanize support for their cause. Such stories describe *extreme*, rather than routine examples, aspects, or practices of target groups of behaviors. Ironically, to gather support for the *typical* conditions they oppose, social movements must invoke *atypical* ones. Stories about the satanic ritual abuse and slaughter of innocent children serve as "atrocity tales" for Christian fundamentalists. It is not enough to argue that American society has become secular, irreligious, and humanistic. Most audiences listening to such a statement are likely to respond with, "So what else is new?" The satanic legend offers a dramatic and extreme realization of the fears of religious traditionalists. It provides a concrete reason for the fundamentalists' opposition to secular humanism, documentation of the fruit of contemporary developments. It declares, "You see what happens when godless secularism is allowed to fester?" And it purports to describe in graphic terms what most of us would regard as just about the worst thing that could possibly happen: the unpunished murder of countless numbers of our children. Such an appeal, if true, cannot fail to galvanize outrage, a call to action, and, in some circles, renewed support for the fundamentalist Christian cause. The fact that no solid evidence exists to support such claims makes it difficult for most individuals who are not located in rural or small-town, blue-collar, relatively uneducated, fundamentalist Christian social circles to accept the legend and get caught up in the panic.

The Ritual Abuse Panic in Great Britain

The satanic ritual child abuse and murder panic erupted in Great Britain in the late 1980s, almost a decade later than in the United

States. By fall 1990, "ritual abuse had become a national scandal"; even *The Times* devoted 25 items to the topic in September of that year alone. But unlike the United States, the concern over ritual abuse in Britain both captured much of the general public and declined fairly swiftly; by late 1990, a backlash emerged in the press and significant segments of the public, and by some time in 1991, the panic had almost totally fizzled out, the defenders of these remarkable assertions having become pretty much completely discredited (Jenkins, 1992, pp. 151ff).

The panic emerged, roughly in 1988, as a result of a coalition of American moral entrepreneurs and a "network" or British evangelical and fundamentalist religious groups. Groups and organizations such as the Evangelical Alliance Committee and the Christian Exorcism Study Circle took up the ritual abuse cause. Occult survivors, women who claim to have been abused by satanic cults in their childhood but managed to escape with their lives, were given respectful interviews in the media (pp. 166–7). A claim, put forth by Christian representatives of two social welfare agencies, Childwatch and Reachout, to the effect that, each year in Britain, some 4,000 babies "are born into covens to be used for sacrifices and cannabilism" (p. 167), was widely circulated in the press.

Within a very brief span of time from its introduction, the satanic ritual child abuse idea had become "domesticated" and "increasingly adopted by social work and child protection groups anxious to assert the serious and pervasive nature of child abuse" (Jenkins, 1992, p. 158). Lists of symptoms or "indicators" of ritual abuse, originating from the United States – most of which are common and normal preoccuptions of small children – were photocopied and widely circulated by child welfare investigators. Efforts were made to make these "essentially medieval allegations palatable to . . . progressive left/feminist" circles (p. 175). By 1990, an "odd coalition of religious and radical groups . . . emerged," thereby creating "an atmosphere conducive to the rapid spread of ritual abuse allegations" (p. 176).

But by the end of 1990, a series of court cases involving baseless allegations on which dubious evidence had been gathered began to discredit the ritual abuse cause in Britain; "it became apparent" to much of the British public, the press, the police, and representatives of the judiciary "that the panic had little substance" (p. 181). Draconian seizures of children from their homes on flimsy evidence began to harden public opinion and the media against the idea of ritual abuse (pp. 183, 185). Social workers were depicted as "obsessed with finding evidence of satanic abuse," and "browbeating children in custody" (p. 184). Charges of ritual abuse were made in small, remote, close-knit communities where such practices would have been impossible without general knowledge of it. In one rural Scottish village, "children from four families suddenly found their lives interrupted without even the opportunity to take a few toys with them." The action was justified by the authorities on the ground that the coven posed a grave threat to the community. Evidence seized included a shepherd's crook, academic gowns, a cloak, and a book with a goat on the cover (p. 186). The charges were deemed preposterous and they, along with belief in ritual abuse generally, were dismissed and discredited.

In the late 1980s, in Britain, "a panic had been manipulated into existence out of practically nothing." But by late 1990, "the press with few exceptions launched an uncompromising attack against the ritual theorists, and the police and social workers who had accepted their views" (p. 187). By the spring of 1991, the press was involved in a "strident campaign against the social work profession in general" (p. 188). The images that emerged in the press "were of innocent families persecuted by incompetent, heartless, and ignorant social workers, who knew so little of children that they could wrench such sinister meanings out of their families" (p. 189). The press reported on "gestapo tactics," "bureaucratic rape" of communities, and "power mad" social workers snatching children from innocent parents (p. 190). Consistently, social workers "were depicted as gullible victims of propaganda by religious theorists, who employed ritual abuse to establish their social and sectarian agenda" (p. 190). By 1991, the whole notion of ritual abuse had been "thoroughly undermined;" belief in it was "almost wholly discredited" among media, policymakers, and much of the public (p. 193). While the concern over satanic ritual abuse is still felt in fundamentalist circles in Britain, it is essentially dead outside those circles.

4

DEVIANCE AND MORALITY

Morality – views of right and wrong – can be looked at from two radically different perspectives: it may be taken as relative, that is, as *subjectively problematic,* or as absolute, or *objectively given* (Rubington and Weinberg, 1987, pp. 3–5). The absolute or objectively given approach is the traditional, conventional perspective; it assumes that we all know – or should know – what good and bad, right and wrong, virtue and evil, are. The quality of evil or immorality resides in the very nature of an act itself; it is inherent, intrinsic, or *immanent* within certain forms of behavior. If an act is wrong, it is wrong now and for ever, it always was and will always be evil, it is wrong here and everywhere; it is evil *in the abstract,* an offense against nature, science, medicine, God, or the universe – depending on the appropriate rhetorical vehicle which conveyes the argument. Behavior is wrong if it violates an absolute, eternal, final law. It need not be *seen* or *judged* by external human observers to be regarded as wrong; its immorality is a simple, objective fact, even if it takes place in a society or group that condones it. The belief held by anti-abortion pro-lifers that abortion is murder is an example of this line of thinking. So is the fundamentalist Christian's belief that homosexuality is an abomination in the eyes of God, and the anti-pornographer's view that, in and of itself, pornography represents an assault against women. It matters not to these denouncers of evil that the activities or phenomena in question are seen, defined, or conceptualized in a different way in other quarters; they see them as inherently, abstractly, immanently evil – wrong everywhere and at all times, irrespective of social and cultural definitions of right and wrong.

Moreover, the objectively given approach assumes that "evil causes evil," or "the doctrine of evil consequences," that is, that consequences universally agreed to be negative and harmful inevitably flow from immoral practices; *it is inherent in the very nature of the behavior itself* that addicts die of drug overdoses, homosexuals contract AIDS (a "retribution from God" for engaging in immoral behavior), pornography causes men to brutalize women, alcoholics contract cirrhosis of the liver, illegal drug use causes moral degeneration and criminal behavior, and so on. The harmful consequences of evil actions are self-evident and verify what the absolutist already knows: that there is a *moral economy* in the universe, that punishment – of onself or others – is to be *expected* from violating the rules of morality. Wrongdoing is harmful and pathological in ways that conventionality is not; harm and pathology are *immanent* or inherent in evil actions. It is not possible to fool around with immorality; eventually, society has moral dues to pay and negative consequences to deal with.

Relativity

Taking morality as relative or *subjectively problematic* looks at matters the other way around: it attempts to understand how and why behavior is regarded as evil or deviant. The focus is on the definition or understanding that members of a society hold with respect to the acts designated as undesirable. The existence of the evil in the indwelling, objectively given, or immanent sense is not so much negated as put aside for a focus on how morality is defined and acted out. What is regarded as evil in one place or situation, or at one time, may be acceptable or even rewarded in others. Morality, to repeat an oft-used cliché, is relative. To put it another way, designating certain behaviors and individuals as deviant is problematic, not commonsensical, and it is the members of the society who decide, not the external observer.

Morality is relative geographically and culturally, historically and temporally, situationally and subculturally. Adulterers could be stoned to death in Iran, yet in Sikkim, adultery is tolerated, often encouraged, even, upon occasion, rewarded. An assassination on one side of a border or against the member of a particular group is seen as murder, a brutal act of butchery and cowardice; on the other side, or against the member of another group, the same killing may be regarded as laudible, an act of heroism, liberation, and triumph. Ancient Aztec priests cut open the chest of a human sacrifice and tore out his still-beating heart; in contemporary Mexico, the same act would be cause for arrest, prosecution, possibly commitment to a mental institution. Even within the same society at the same time, there is considerable variation from one group, category, and subculture to another in evaluations of and reactions toward certain behaviors. As we saw, among the members of Women Against Pornography, the consumption of pornographic material is an evil in itself – a blasphemy against women – that presumably causes men to engage in even more seriously evil actions; such material, they say, must be excised from the society altogether. Among the readers of *Playboy*, *Penthouse*, and *Hustler*, consuming pornography is regarded as a harmless, pleasureable activity that expresses and satisfies a simple, natural male impulse or need. To the pro-life movement, abortion is murder. To most feminists and sexual and sex-role liberals and libertarians, abortion is the removal of unwanted tissue, an expression of a woman's free choice and control over her own body.

To the adherent of the relativist or subjectively problematic approach, no quality of absolute evil lurks immanently or inherently in adultery, homicide, human sacrifice, pornography, or abortion. What is crucial is how the behavior is defined, judged, and evaluated in a particular context. What counts is these varying definitions and evaluations; it is they and they alone that determine the status of an act with respect to morality and immorality. *It can be determined that* such relativistic definitions and evaluations exist, are believed, and are acted upon; we can investigate and determine the religious practices of the ancient Aztecs, the attitudes of contemporary Iranians, the views of Women Against Pornography, how pro-lifers view abortion. On the other hand, in the abstract, *how do we know* that adultery is immoral, killing is evil, abortion is murder? *According to whose perspective?* What measureable criteria will allow us to establish these positions?

Our view is that the relativistic, subjectively problematic perspective is far more fruitful in helping us to understand morality than is the objectively given approach. We take *evaluations* of behavior as our point of departure. In doing so, we insist on two points: one, that the subjectively problematic dimension is worthy of study in its own right; and two, that it is impossible to predict the subjective dimension from the objective. Definitions of morality arise as a consequence of factors that are to some degree independent of the objective consequences of behavior. The populace is not outraged at a killing solely because it results in the loss of human life; many types of killing are condoned. Drug use, possession, and sale are not condemned and criminalized exclusively because they – supposedly – cause users to commit crime and violence, get sick, and die; homosexuals are not regarded as outcasts by the heterosexual majority simply because their behavior causes some objective damage or threat to the society; pornography does not generate hostility in segments of the public mainly because it causes behavior that nearly all of us would regard as undesirable. It is our contention that something else is at work here, and we intend to understand what that something else is. Judgments of evil or immorality cannot be reduced to or subsumed under objective harm.

Everything Is Relative: Or Is It?

Too often, a valuable insight is pushed to its logical extreme, caricatured into an absurd, meaningless formula. A focus on the subjectivity inherent in judgments of wrongdoing by different audiences implies relativity from one society, epoch, group, category, and subculture to another. To the naive observer, the subjectively problematic approach is reduced to the cliché, "Everything is relative." In fact, "everything" is *not* relative. The concept of relativity has its limits, although they are broad. *Radical* relativity seems imply that all behaviors stand an equal chance of being sanctioned. Taken literally, the "everything is relative" cliché implies that any, or almost any, behavior is deviant to some people and that no behavior is deviant to everyone. While literally true, this statement is not very useful. Relativity is limited both on the cross-societal and the intra-societal levels.

On the cross-societal level, it is clear, worldwide, that some actions are more likely to result in condemnation and punishment than others. Willfully killing a member of one's own group is highly likely to result in negative sanctioning just about everywhere; to say that *some forms of killing* are tolerated in one place and punished in another does *not* mean that *other* forms of killing are not punished in all, or almost all, cultures of the world. Incest is widely, nearly universally, condemned; robbing members of one's own group is accepted by almost no peoples on earth; betraying one's own country or society when it is at war with another is regarded as heinous, and is punished, just about everywhere. To the extent that radical relativity implies no patterns whatsoever in the moral codes from one society to another, it is fallacious.

Even within the same society, the idea of relativity has its limits. Different categories and groups in a society, each with its own views of right or wrong, are not equally powerful or numerous in the population. Consequently, someone who enacts behavior that is opposed by a small number of relatively powerless individuals stands a low likelihood of being condemned and punished, whereas someone who enacts behavior that is opposed by large numbers of relatively powerful individuals is highly likely to be condemned. Thus, the radically relativistic, "everything is relative" cliché is wrong because not all individuals who enact different sorts of behavior stand the same chance of being condemned as deviant. A priori, one can predict that, when detected, murdering an infant in its crib, say, is more likely to result in punishment than is chewing gum. The number of circumstances which would excuse the former action and seriously punish the latter are extremely limited.

Attitudes toward and reactions to potentially deviant behavior are held and expressed by differing numbers of people, as well as people with differing quanta of power. We are not interested in a mere patchwork mosaic of different beliefs and customs in a given society. Rather, we have to direct our attention to the *dominant moral codes*. Looking at different definitions of deviance as if they existed side by side without impinging on one another, as if they existed in a kind of ethical "free enterprise system," belies the *hierarchical* nature of deviance. What we want to know here is *which forms of behavior have a high likelihood of being condemned and punished.* To each form of behavior enacted by specific individuals we can attach a certain *probability* of exciting moral outrage or censure. To the degree that radical relativity implies that, within a given society, any and all actions are equally likely – or unlikely – to be condemned or punished, it is fallacious.

At the same time, we must always focus on the specific audience that is relevant to the behavior under scrutiny. It is one thing to say that certain behaviors stand a low likelihood of being condemned in a society generally; it is an altogether different matter to focus on the dynamics of censure within a given setting or context. The likelihood that members of western society generally will be censured, for example, for engaging in mixed-sex dancing is small; therefore, we can say that dancing is not a deviant act – to most westerners. On the other hand, if it is behavior within the context of extremely strict, orthodox, fundamentalist religious sects in which we are interested, their definition – that coed dancing is a degenerate, immoral practice – becomes relevant. Some forms of behavior may be deviant to very small, relatively powerless audiences, but to someone subject to their definitions of right and wrong, such definitions are central, because they determine the likelihood of censure.

Deviance

Sociologists refer to behavior that is widely condemned, which, if someone engages in it and it is observed, is likely to attract or generate hostility, condemnation, or punishment from others, *deviance* or *deviant behavior.* How widespread does this condemnation have to be? There cannot be a clearcut answer to this question; what is clear, though, is that the more widespread the condemnation, the more a given form of behavior qualifies as deviant. Deviance is not an either-or proposition; "deviantness" is a matter of degree. The important point is, to the sociologist, the characteristic of deviance is defined not by the quality of the act but by the nature of the reaction that the act engnders or is likely to engender. To most people, the terms "deviance" and, even more, "deviant," are pejorative and condemnatory; they imply that there is something wrong, sick, or pathological about the behavior and the person being referred to. In contrast, to the sociologist, these terms are simply descriptive; they imply nothing whatsoever about the behavior or the person referred to except that such behavior or person has attracted widespread public scorn. No condemnation whatsoever is implied by the use of the terms "deviance" and "deviant"; they refer to behavior that, or persons who, are widely condemned – that, and nothing more.

Audiences

The sociologist's focus on deviance as subjectively problematic implies the importance of an *audience*, that is, those individuals who directly or indirectly witness, hear about, and evaluate the behavior or the individuals in question. Audiences can include parents and other relatives, teachers, employers, a spouse, friends, acquaintances, neighbors, psychiatrists, the police, eyewitnesses, onlookers, and bystanders – anyone who can and does evaluate what one is doing and who one is. In fact, one can even be an audience to onself and one's own behavior. Again, what counts with the subjective or relativistic approach, is that audiences evaluate behavior and other individuals. To answer the question of whether a certain form of behavior is deviant, we are forced to ask a series of questions: deviant *to whom? Whose* evaluation is relevant? *Which audience's* reaction are we interested in? The issue of deviance is completely meaningless without reference to a specific, relevant audience. *To audience X*, behavior A is evil and immoral; *to audience Y*, it is not.

"Societal" versus "Situational" Deviance

The distinction between the likelihood of attracting censure in a given society as a result of committing categories of behavior and the punishment that is incurred within a specific setting, group, subculture, or category is nicely captured by the distinction between "societal" and "situational" deviance (Plummer, 1979, p. 98). "Societal" deviance is made up of widely condemned classes or categories of behavior. It would be difficult to argue that, in western society generally, robbery, homosexuality, transvestism, or alcoholism are not widely regarded as censurable, unacceptable, deplorable behavior; "societally," they must be regarded as deviant. One is far more likely to be stigmatized than praised for engaging in them. One need not agree with this judgment to recognize that it is generally true. In contrast, "situational" deviance ignores such broad, society-wide judgments and examines only concrete negative judgments of behavior and individuals in specific contexts. Not all alcoholics are condemned for their excessive drinking in all places at all times; though most are in most contexts. Widely accepted views of a given form of behavior may not be acted upon everywhere. In order to determine whether an act is "situationally" deviant, it is necessary to observe actual, concrete reactions in specific, real-life, micro-interactional settings and situations (Plummer, 1979, p. 98).

Stereotyping

By definition, according to many – in all probability, most – sociologists, deviance is a quality that implies hostility, stigma, and condemnation; it is intrinsically negative, invidious, a quality that attracts scorn. (But see the debate between Ben-Yehuda [1990b] and Goode [1991].) Whenever scorn and condemnation are called forth, strong, harsh, emotionally charged feelings often accompany them. The fact is, many conventional members of society have strongly negative feelings toward individuals who are regarded as deviants and toward the behavior that attracted that label. Deviants are seen, for the most part, as belonging to a despised category. Whenever strong emotions are activated, especially strongly negative ones, fantasy, selective perception, stereotyping, and an inventory of predictable and readily recognizable elements usually accompany them (Young, 1971a, pp. 49–79; Cohen, 1972, pp. 44–8; Goode, 1973, pp. 26–37, 1978, pp. 89–102). Stereotyping permits the conventional member of a society to feel justified in strong, even savage condemnation; if an individual is a member of a despised category, and shares a host of undesirable characteristics with them, then unambiguous hostility toward him or her should not only be expected – it is demanded. To feel any other way would be to encourage evil behavior and collude in its further enactment.

Deviant Categories Old and New

While some forms of behavior have been widely (if not universally) condemned for millennia – incest and in-group murder, rape, and robbery come to mind as obvious examples – the deviant status of many others is much more recent. In the United States, marijuana use was not condemned – in fact, it was barely even heard of – until the 1930s. LSD as a psychoactive agent did not exist until the 1940s, and its use was unknown until the 1960s; only during the latter decade did its use become a target for censure. Rock and roll music was not listened to on a widespread basis until the 1950s, and only then did the conventional adult public regard it, and its listeners, in a negative light. It was not until roughly 1980 that the supposed links between satanism, pornography, and child abuse were forged in the minds of some contemporary fundamentalist Christian observers. Prior to the turn of the nineteenth century, addicts were viewed as sick rather than wilfully deviant and criminal. Prior to the 1960s, most parents who beat their children were seen as strict disciplinarians rather than child abusers.

Does Relativism Condone Injustice?

It is possible to simplify and vulgarize the relativistic view of deviance and argue that, in adopting it, we are forced to tolerate and excuse all manner of atrocities. Relativism, this line of thinking goes, views Nazism, anti-Semitism, slavery, racism, sexism, and warfare as acceptable and normative at certain times and in certain places, and therefore, the sociologist has no right to criticize the people who practice such atrocities; the societies in which they take place have a perfect right to continue to practice them. (See, for instance, Henshel, 1990, pp. 10–14, for an ethical criticism of the relativity of social problems defining.) To our way of thinking, this is an inaccurate understanding of the concept of relativity.

Saying that values and definitions of deviance – or social problems – are relative to time and place does *not* condone oppressive practices. It says nothing about the right of a society, or certain members of a society, to continue practicing atrocities upon others. It simply makes an objectively true statement: around the world, and throughout history, peoples, cultures, societies, and groups have defined right and wrong differently. That is a fact. How *we* feel about it is a entirely different matter. The fact is, many southern landowners prior to the Civil War *did* believe that slavery was acceptable; during the 1930s and 1940s, many Germans *did* believe that Jews were responsible for most of their problems, and that they should be punished for it; during much of human history, in societies around the world, killing unwanted babies was *not* considered wrong.

The relativity of deviance does not say that we must condone, accept, or tolerate practices or beliefs such as these – only that they exist or existed, and are or were a part of the societies in which they are or were located. Their existence and practice cannot be denied; how we feel about them and what we do about them exists in an entirely different dimension. Relativity simply says, Let's see how this belief or practice works in this context; it says nothing about an outsider's views of the belief or practice. Accepting relativism poses no ethical "dilemma," as some have argued (Henshel, 1990, p. 14); it does not advocate a "hands off" policy toward practices we consider evil. It simply says that what we consider evil may be seen as good to others – that is a fact we have to face – and before we attack that evil, we have to understand how others come to view it as good, and come to practice it. Relativism simply says that our personal view of things may be irrelevant to how beliefs are actually put into practice in a given context.

Deviance and Moral Panics

By viewing deviance as subjectively problematic, we raise the possibility of the concept of the moral panic. If the condemnation of certain behavior as deviant is not an inevitability, but grows out of the characteristics of a particular society, and the social structure of a certain time and place, we admit the possibility that intense public concern can emerge to some degree independent of a condition's objective threat. Indeed, we must agree that the members of a society can become wildly hostile to a certain category of people, or a certain form of behavior, that does not endanger them in any concrete way, and may remain indifferent to others that represent a very clear and present danger to them.

More broadly, the key ingredient in the emergence of a moral panic is the creation or intensification of hostility toward and denunciation of a particular group, category, or cast of characters. The emergence or the reemergence of a deviant category characterizes the moral panic; central in this process is the targeting of new or past "folk devils." In Brazil in the 1890s, Canudos were a previously unfamiliar deviant category; they became a target of ecclesiastical, media, popular, and official condemnation and punishment because they seemed to threaten to drag the country back into what was seen as a primitive and altogether unacceptable state of affairs. In the 1950s in Boise, Idaho, homosexuals – including those who had sex with underage boys – were members of a category that already existed but, in all likelihood, few residents gave much thought to. Prior to the panic that erupted in 1969 in Orléans, France, the chances are, very few citizens would have spontaneously thought of "sexual slavery" as a category of evil, immoral behavior, a form of behavior that was worthy of their hostility and condemnation.

However, during moral panics, suddenly, witches are burned at the stake; abortion clinics are bombed; sex shops are picketed; propagandists for psychedelic drugs are denounced; homosexuals are beaten; laws criminalizing marijuana possession and sale are passed, and users are arrested; suspected or known communists are dismissed from their jobs; pamphlets explaining how to protect children from abductions by strangers are distributed to parents; the police use more repressive measures against misbehaving or delinquent adolescents. In most cases, a deviant category or stereotype exists, but is latent and only routinely activated. During the moral panic, the category is either created or, more often, relocated, dusted off, and attacked with renewed vigor. New charges may be made, old ones dredged up and reformulated. In the case of child kidnap-murders by satanists, an ancient charge (found in many societies with two or more conflicting groups, lodged, as we saw, by the ancient Romans against the early Christians) is put together with novel features. In the case of marijuana in the 1930s, charges against other forms of drug use (mainly cocaine and, to a lesser extent, opiates) were transferred to the use of a previously unknown substance. During the AIDS crisis, a new charge – in this case, empirically true – was lodged against a category of people whose members have been regarded as deviant for centuries.

Thus, while the deviant characters acting out their assigned parts may have existed prior to the emergence of a particular moral panic, the part they play in a particular one may be emphasized or partly, or wholly, reinvented. The part that individuals who are designated as deviants play in moral panics is crucial – indeed, central – but their precise role is creatively assigned, dynamically acted out, and to some degree reformulated with each episode. It must be investigated in detail with each new moral panic.

During times of crisis or panic, deviants may serve as scapegoats, secondary targets to deflect attention away from some of society's most pressing but insoluble problems (Best, 1990, pp. 180–1). Just before Prohibition, conservative, small-town, native-born, White Anglo-Saxon Protestants feared an erosion of their prestige and power; brewers and drinkers became folk devils and deviants whose defeat would restore positive values to American society (Gusfield, 1963). The sexual psychopath laws emerged during two crises in American history, the first (1937–40), when the country was struggling with the most serious economic depression in its history, and fearful of the gathering storm of war, and the second (1949–54), during the Cold War, when two super-powers faced one another across the chasm of nuclear destruction (Freedman, 1987). The period during which hostility toward satanic ritual abuse emerged (roughly, post-1980) marked a time when small-town, working-class, fundamentalist Protestants experienced joblessness, deskilling, an erosion in their standard of living, and serious challenges to their traditional way of life (Victor, 1989, 1991, 1993; Bromley, 1991). Of course, deviants have always existed, and the hostility toward certain categories is notable far more for historical continuity than decade-by-decade variation. Yet, as we saw, deviant categories are often refurbished over time; the reasons for hating them vary according to temporal circumstances. Moral panics provide one important context for the understanding of variations in the denunciation of deviants.

5

DEVIANCE, MORAL ENTREPRENEURS, AND CRIMINAL LAW

In fairly small, relatively homogeneous societies – those based on a hunting and gathering technology – the collective conscience that Emile Durkheim argued held societies together tends to be strong; there are few serious challenges to society's moral universe; and there is usually a single moral "center." Moreover, in such small societies, even when members are tempted to violate the norms, surveillance and informal social control tend to stifle that temptation; everyone knows everyone else, members care about the opinions that others hold of them, and it is difficult to do anything outside the gaze of the fellow members of one's band or village. Moreover, members of the society are dependent on others for a variety of services, favors, activities, and life-sustaining functions; angering certain parties may mean doing without, exile, or death. Violations of the norms, when they occur, tend to be handled informally, on a face-to-face, interpersonal basis by the aggrieved party or parties or their representatives. A violation, for the most part, is against a specific, aggrieved, private party – that is, a family's grain has been stolen, a man's wife has been seduced, a mother's son has been beaten. Some form of compensation is called for, and that is adjudicated on an informal, case-by-case basis.

In large, complex, pluralistic, agrarian, and, especially, industrial, societies, the collective conscience tends to be weak, at least, far from universal, society's moral universe is often challenged, and there almost always exist a number of competing moral "centers." In larger, more complex societies, informal, interpersonal social control is no longer effective to ensure that norms are followed and the social order remains unchallenged; members of the society can ignore or discount the views of others of them or their behavior; they may not care about how others view them, and they are unlikely to be dependent on their favors. Consequently, some form of *formal* social control becomes necessary to ensure that normative violations do not threaten the social order. This includes criminal law, the police, courts, methods of punishment, and, eventually, jails and prisons. In formal social control, the state has been aggrieved, not simply a private party; an abstract rule has been violated, regardless of its impact on private parties. Agents who, in principle, have no direct stake in the sanctioning process – and may not even know the parties involved – are called upon to administer abstract justice. In becoming larger and more complex, societies move from relying almost exclusively on informal social control to relying more and more on formal social control.

Thus, in this transition, the crucial question is how behavior becomes *criminalized*. By what process do crimes get defined, the criminal law created, and violators punished? Are definitions of crimes a natural outgrowth of a society's system of morality? In this process, does deviant behavior automatically become defined as criminal? Is a society's criminal code a reflection of its moral code? How do laws get passed? Why are they enforced?

The Objectively Given or Grassroots Approach

The traditional, *objectively given* approach to deviance and morality adheres to the following points with respect to the process of deviance and criminalization. First, societies define as deviant behavior which is intrinsically harmful, that is, harmful acts tend to offend the common conscience; second, this tends to be true regardless of whether the society is more complex or less; third, to the extent that behavior is harmful to a society, it will be defined as a crime; and fourth, as a consequence, the criminal law tends to represent an expression of the culture of a society, the collective conscience, widespread public sentiment.

The objectively given approach also harbors a *grassroots* approach to the emergence of law, in that notions of right and wrong somehow "percolate" up from the general population and become translated into the criminal code; the criminal law is the natural extension of the culture of a given society. No particular effort on the part of special interest groups is necessary to form, shape, or crystallize the moral views of the members of a given society into the law. What is defined as a crime is simply a natural and inevitable extension or outcome of people's views in general. The grassroots assumption sees a close connection between morality and law: the laws a society passes criminalizing certain behaviors are the expression of the views of right and wrong held by the majority; law is a "barometer of the moral and social thinking" of the society (Friedmann, 1964, p. 143). What is harmful is widely condemned; what is widely condemned is legislated against and criminalized. Another way of saying this is that, for the grassroots perspective, the creation of the criminal law is not problematic; it is not a process that needs much explaining. How laws come into being is intuitively obvious and commonsensical. To the extent that there are exceptions – laws that neither protect the society from objective harm nor are supported by the majority of the population of a society – in all likelihood, they are laws that are on the books but are not enforced, laws that have either fallen into disuse or were not intended to be enforced even when they were passed.

The Subjectively Problematic Approach: Crime as a Political Phenomenon

In contrast to the objectively given approach, with its protectionist and grassroots assumptions, the subjectively problematic view argues that definitions of crime and morality represent a distinctly *political* phenomenon (Schur, 1980, pp. 3, 25ff). Designating certain acts as criminal serves at least three functions: first, it *legitimates* a certain category's definition of right and wrong; second, it symbolizes the respectability of one category vis-à-vis another; and third, it punishes members of one category for engaging in behavior that has been proscribed by another.

Definitions of right and wrong do not drop from the skies, nor do they simply ineluctably percolate up from society's mainstream opinion; they are the result of disagreement, negotiation, conflict, and struggle. The passage of laws raises the issue of *who will criminalize whom* (Ben-Yehuda, 1990a, p. 55). Each definition attracts adherents who attempt to persuade others that their view is right and that of their opponents, wrong – and, failing persuasion, each side will impose its version of right and wrong on the other. Criminalization is the explicit use of power to impose the view of one specific symbolic-moral universe on other universes (Ben-Yehuda, 1990a, p. 65). Adherents contend with one another in attempting to establish their view as acceptable, legitimate, valid. If possible, each side attempts to crystallize its views into the legal structure – to pass laws compatible with, or prevent the passage of laws incompatible with, its own ideological, moral, and politicoeconomic system. Where groups, categories, or "symbolic-moral universes" meet, compete, negotiate, and clash, each is "vitally interested" in demonstrating its moral superiority. This entails attempting to "widen the basis of its legitimacy," which inevitably entails controlling the criminalization process. The dissemination and acceptance of a particular view of morality as crystallized in the criminal code represents the victory of one group or category over another.

Groups and categories in the population do not have equal access to the powers of persuasion or the legal process; some are, for example, more likely to influence the media, the political process, legislators, and the educational system, than others are. Views of right and wrong do not triumph by becoming widely accepted in a society simply because they are objectively true or because they best preserve the social order or generate the greatest benefit for the greatest number of people. The power to "define and construct reality" is linked to the "structure of power in a society" at a particular time; constructions of crime and the law, as with deviance generally, "are linked to the dominant control institutions" in society (Conrad and Schneider, 1980, p. 17).

The subjectively problematic perspective sees morality and immorality, crime and law-abiding behavior, not as a quality contained in certain actions, but as the outcome of a process – a process of definition on two levels: (1) defining a certain *class of actions* as criminal, and (2) defining certain specific *individuals* as criminals. Behavior and individuals are criminalized that is, *made* criminal by the definitional process, that is, *defined* as against the law.

Far from the law representing a crystallization of custom, it is in many ways the *antithesis* of community consensus, that is, the collective conscience. A legal order that sits above the community becomes necessary when the solidarity and cohesion of the community has disappeared, when the community has disintegrated into competing and conflicting factions. Prior to the emergence of the modern state, custom was sufficient to maintain order. Everyone, more or less, either believed in the righteousness of custom, or at least was motivated to please others who did believe in it. Societies were held together by common interests and common beliefs. The more complex societies became, the more divergent belief, behavior, and custom became. And the less concerned each person became about the opinions of others – the less one cared about the condemnation of others, the more one could discount the negative things others said about what one did. Where societies became internally divided, custom lost its hold on the population. What was needed was an externally imposed set of edicts administered by a body of specialists hired specifically for the purpose of law enforcement. Where primary social control – custom, interpersonal contact, gossip, ridicule, personal disapproval – began to break down, secondary social control – law, courts, the police – assumed importance. The criminal law, then, may be seen not as an outgrowth of a grassroots social and cultural consensus, but as an outcome of social and cultural dissensus, hostility between groups, a clash in ways of life, social conflict. The legal order becomes necessary when community solidarity breaks down and society is broken up into competing and conflicting factions and interests (Diamond, 1971).

Rule Creators and Moral Entrepreneurs

The subjectively problematic perspective, then, argues that rules of morality and systems of law do not merely evolve in a natural, nonconscious, "grassroots" fashion; rather, they emerge, are institutionalized, and become influential in a society as a result of enterprise – somebody doing something to make sure they take hold and are enforced. Who are these enterprising agents? Howard Becker (1963, pp. 147–63) emphasizes the role of what he calls moral entrepreneurs in defining behavior and individuals as deviant and criminal. Moral entrepreneurs are crusaders who believe that some members of the society are willfully engaged in immoral and therefore damaging behavior and are not being sufficiently punished for it. Something must be done, they believe, to discourage or eliminate such behavior. Becker delineated two types of moral entrepreneurs – rule creators and rule enforcers.

Rule creators

> are interested in [changing] the content of rules. The existing rules do not satisfy him [or her] because there is some evil which profoundly disturbs him [or her]. He [or she] believes that nothing can be right in the world until rules are made to correct it. He [or she] operates with an absolute ethic; what he [or she] sees is truly and totally evil with no qualification. Any means is justified to do away with it. The crusader is fervent and righteous, often self-righteous. (pp. 147–8)

It is not entirely appropriate, Becker states, to think of moral entrepreneurs simply as meddlers who are interested in enforcing their rules on others; all moral entrepreneurs believe that other people should be forced to do what's right, and if they do the right thing, it will be good for them and for others as well – in fact, for the society as a whole. For instance, "Prohibitionists felt that they were not simply forcing their morals on others, but attempting to provide the conditions for a better way of life" (p. 148). Moral entrepreneurs believe themselves to be humanitarians, doing good for all concerned, even though many others in the society may not realize it and may even oppose their efforts.

The creation of the rules and the laws entails designating a *specific type of behavior* as deviant and criminal, and the enforcement of the rules entails designating *specific individuals* as deviant. Once rules are created, organizations must be instituted to punish the evildoer. If rules already exist for a wide range of deviant and immoral practices, and the perpetrators have gone unpunished, a crusade must be launched to make sure the existing rules are enforced. The rule enforcer – the police officer is the paramount example – tends not to be as ideological or as self-righteous as the rule creator, involved, as he or she is, in the practical, day-to-day operation of searching out and apprehending evildoers. The police officer typically has a more detached and pragmatic view of the job of enforcing rules. He or she

> is not so much concerned with the content of any particular rule as he [or she] is with the fact that it is his [or her] job to enforce the rule. When

the rules are changed, he [or she] punishes what was once acceptable behavior just as he [or she] ceases to punish behavior that has been made legitimate by a change in the rules. The enforcer, then, may not be interested in the content of the rule as such, but only in the fact that the existence of the rule provides him with a job, a profession, a raison d'etre. (Becker, 1963, p. 156)

Rule creators and rule enforcers should not be thought of as isolated individuals acting on their own, however. It must be emphasized that they tend to create and enforce rules and laws, either directly or indirectly, *as representatives* of specific categories, factions, or groups in the society. Their efforts will be endorsed or supported by members of these categories, factions, or groups *to the extent that* they reflect their sentiments, views, or interests. Thus, however influential individual prohibitionists were at the turn of the century, their efforts could not have resulted in a national alcohol prohibition unless they articulated, as they did, the views of small-town, middle-class, native-born, southern, fundamentalist Protestants at the time (Gusfield, 1963). Likewise, the marijuana laws of the 1930s were enacted largely because of the efforts of crusaders who saw a growing threat to society because of the drug's use and the need to control that use by enacting legislation against it (Becker, 1963, pp. 135–46). These efforts did not reflect these crusaders' views alone, but also the sentiment of certain segments of the public – for instance whites living in western states who feared that Mexican-Americans were especially prone to use marijuana became especially violent under its influence, and likely to seduce white youths into use as well (Musto, 1973, pp. 219–21; Himmelstein, 1983, pp. 27–30). Thus, moral entrepreneurs do not spring, fully formed, out of a social or cultural vacuum; their efforts tend to represent, reflect, and grow out of the views and concerns of groups which they represent or to which they belong.

Moral Entrepreneurs and Moral Panics

It must be emphasized that the concept of the moral entrepreneur applies not only to the definition of behavior as deviant and the creation (and enforcement) of the criminal law, but also to the moral panic as well (and to definitions of conditions as social problems, as well shall see shortly). That is, though strengthening society's social control apparatus through legislation is certainly one way of expressing a moral panic, there are others. Moral entrepreneurs operate on a wide range of fronts. The many efforts of moral entrepreneurs relevant to the generation and maintenance of moral panics include: attempting to influence public opinion by discussing the supposed extent of the threat in the

media; forming organizations and even generating entire social movements to deal with the problems the threat presumably poses; giving
talks or conducting seminars to inform the public how to counter the
threat in question; attempting to get certain views approved in educational curricula; influencing legislators to allocate funds which would
deal with a given threat; discrediting spokespersons who advocate
alternative, opposing, or competing perspectives.

At the same time, attempting to criminalize certain behaviors is one
of the central fetures of the moral panic. Participants in almost all
panics aim to influence the content and enforcement of the law.
Cohen's Mods and Rockers stimulated proposals at both the municipal
and parliamentary levels, and the police made more vigilant use of laws
that were already in place. The American drug panic of 1986 to 1989
resulted in major pieces of congressional legislation which were passed
in 1986 and 1988. The sex scandal in Boise, Idaho, in 1955–6 resulted
in the arrest of nearly two dozen men accused of homosexual acts,
some with minors, and the imprisonment of over a dozen of them. Fear
of Canudos in Brazil in the 1890s touched off a military campaign
which obliterated the entire sect and killed thousands of adherents.
Intense concern about satanic ritual child abuse has resulted in arrests
and highly publicized trials of day-care workers from North Carolina to
California on charges that, many observers feel (Nathan, 1990, 1991),
are entirely groundless. Whenever the question, "What is to be done?"
is asked concerning behavior deemed threatening, someone puts forth
the suggestion, "There ought to be a law." If laws already exist address-
ing the threatening behavior, either stiffer penalties or a law enforcement crackdown will be called for. Legislation and law enforcement are
two of the most obvious and widely resorted-to efforts to crush a
putative threat during a moral panic. No examination of the moral
panic is complete without a consideration of legislation and law
enforcement.

Power

Let us emphasize a crucial point we made earlier about the relationship
between morality and the law: the more power a group or social
category has, the greater the likelihood it will be successful in influencing legislation which is consistent with the views, sentiments, and
interests of its members, which its members support. Small, weak,
unorganized social categories are less likely to have their views translated into the criminal law; large, powerful, well-organized groups are
far more likely to do so. For instance, street crime – robbery, rape,
murder – is more often committed by lower- and working-class individuals than by members of the middle, upper-middle, and upper

classes; typically, these crimes call for harsh penalties and long sentences. White-collar and corporate crime – embezzlement, fraud, stock market swindles – are committed by individuals located at the higher end of the socioeconomic ladder; typically, these crimes (assuming that such actions are defined as crimes in the first place) call for, and almost always result in, comparatively mild punishment – 30 days in jail, 60 days, even more often a fine and no jail or prison sentence at all (Coleman, 1993; Ermann and Lundman, 1990; Weisburd, et al., 1991). While this difference cannot be attributed solely to socioeconomic differences between offenders – most of the public condemns robbers more than white-collar criminals because they are more likely to fear being harmed by the former than the latter – such differences cannot be discounted. Jack Douglas points out that:

> Every . . . police force has a vice squad and narcotics squad, but no police force has a professional squad, a medical squad or a lawyer squad. Doctors, lawyers and other professionals . . . are allowed to police themselves, so that their criminal activities do not often become officially categorized as crimes, whereas the lower classes have their policing done for them by the police. (1971, p. 92)

It has been argued that the reason why national alcohol prohibition failed was because the groups who supported it (small-town, middle-class, native-born, southern, fundamentalist Protestants) suffered a decline in national power, while the groups who opposed it (urban, foreign-born, or native-born of foreign-born parentage, northern, secular or liberal Protestants, Catholics, and Jews) gained more power on the national scene (Gusfield, 1963). In the United States, the liquor lobby has more power than the cocaine lobby; the pro-gun lobby is stronger than the anti-gun lobby; in most of the industrial world, industrialists, who oppose pollution controls, are more influential than environmentalists, who support them. If women were to wield more power than men, it is possible that the rape laws would be stiffer and more vigorously enforced. Laws are passed at least in part because they reflect the views, ideology, sentiment, interests, and demands of the more powerful and influential groups and categories in the population; less powerful and less influential groups and categories tend to be less successful in criminalizing behavior they oppose.

We are *not* saying, with Wellford, that "crime is a form of behavior defined by the powerful to control the powerless" (1975, p. 335). This formulation is altogether too simplistic and crude. "The powerful" may not always get their way in defining the content of the criminal law; the criminal law is not an attempt to control categories of people ("the powerless"), but behavior that categories of people – or the entire population – may or may not engage in; law is a result of conflict, struggle, negotiation, and politial compromise, and not an edict, ukaze, or fatwa handed down from above. The greater influence of elites, the wealthy, and the politically well placed in the legislative and policy spheres is a relative, not an absolute assessment. We are not saying that the more powerful get their way on every issue, that the less powerful lose out in every debate, question, or struggle against the more powerful in defining what should be against the law. Who triumphs on which issues is an empirical question, and through a variety of means, groups or categories with seemingly little power may manage to prevail. Abstract, general power is not necessarily translated into the power to criminalize behavior or effect policy in each and every instance. Seemingly powerless groups or categories can, under certain circumstances, generate the power to criminalize or influence policy on certain specific issues. A study of the exercise of power can only be fully understood on a case-by-case basis.

In Israel, one outstanding example is the Haredim, or ultra-orthodox, who make up less than 5 percent of the total population. For the most part, individually, the Haredim lack financial resources – the majority are in the bottom half of the economic hierarchy in Israeli society – nearly always lack a secular education, and very rarely hold positions of power or influence in Israeli society generally. Moreover, in principle, ultra-orthodox beliefs – and in practice, most Haredim – do not even acknowledge the legitimacy of the Israeli state (arguing that the Jewish state should be instituted only when the Messiah manifests himself), and most haredi sects do not permit the teaching of Israel's official language, modern Hebrew. (Hebrew is to be used for the study of sacred texts, not in everyday language.) Yet, on numerous key issues, the Haredim have managed to influence Israeli law and policy to the point where their will prevails over the far wealthier and more powerful secular majority.

For instance, while the vast majority of Israeli Jews must serve in the armed forces (three years – and decades of reserve duty – for men, and two years for women), the ultra-orthodox do not have to serve at all (or may serve a very brief token alternative service, with no reserve duty). While other Israelis must support themselves financially when they pursue a secular education, haredi males who study the Talmud in approved yeshivas may receive stipends from the state for an indefinite period of time. When ancient Jewish gravesites are uncovered in an archaeological or construction site and this fact is discovered, the Haredim will mount protests that, in a substantial proportion of cases, have managed to call a halt to the digging. All marriages and divorces that take place in Israel must be sanctified by a religious ceremony; no religious intermarriages are allowed. In all cities except Haifa, public transportation does not run on the sabbath; likewise, in Jerusalem, nearly all stores and places of public entertainment are closed on the sabbath. Non-kosher food is extremely difficult to obtain in all of Israel. Public streets – paid for by all taxpayers – in predominantly haredi neighborhoods are closed off to vehicular traffic from sundown Friday to sundown Saturday.

All of these laws, practices, and restrictions are the result of haredi protests, demonstrations, lobbying efforts, threats, and political pressure. The Haredim exert influence out of proportion to their numbers for several reasons. First, they are highly organized and very cohesive on many issues. Second, they represent the last piece of the political puzzle in an extremely complex coalition government. Third, in certain struggles, they can count on an alliance with some orthodox (but not ultra-orthodox) organizations and sects. (And on some issues, even a substantial number of secular Jews support the ultra-orthodox position, in principle if not in practice.) And last, they hold their beliefs much more strongly than the seculars and are willing to fight much harder to translate them into policy and practice. These existing laws and policies represent a triumph of ultra-orthodoxy over secularism, in spite of the fact that secular Jews are wealthier, much more numerous, and hold far more powerful positions than the Haredim. Thus, which groups or categories win out in a legal or policy struggle cannot always be predicted from power alone. Power must be regarded as a major factor in criminalization and legal policy, but it is not the only factor.

Common Law or "Primal" Crimes

There are, of course, numerous criminal laws that both have widespread community – indeed, worldwide – support and are directed at clearly damaging actions. Many of these are referred to as "common law," or what Cohen (1988, pp. 236–8) calls "primal" or consensus crimes – actions which, in communities around a country and in nations around the world, are defined pretty much everywhere as crimes – rape, murder, and robbery being outstanding examples. These laws cannot be seen as having been created at a specific time and place by moral entrepreneurs exercising enterprise in engineering their passage. Still, as Cohen argues (pp. 236–8), a fascinating criminological project would be to investigate just how and why, and by whom, certain actions come to be criminalized, how they come to be seen as "common law" crimes.

While actions such as rape, murder, and robbery are regarded as deviant and criminal in societies everywhere, the way that such laws are applied and enforced in concrete, real-life cases, is at least somewhat variable. In some places at some times, actions that would be almost universally regarded as rape, murder, and robbery may be seen as such only if committed against one's own group. For instance, in warfare, it is common, even routine, for conquering soldiers to rape local women as a means of demoralizing the enemy (Brownmiller, 1975). Political struggles and interethnic and interracial hostility will often erupt in mass killings which are excused, indeed, even perpetrated by the ruling government or by segments of the population, as in Palestine/Israel prior to 1948, in Bosnia in the 1990s, in Cambodia in the 1970s and 1980s, and in much of Africa during most of this century. It is difficult to think of murder as a universal crime when slavery was responsible for the deaths of millions, possibly tens of millions, of Africans between the sixteenth and the nineteenth centuries, lynching was responsible for the deaths of thousands of African-Americans in the South (and some in the North as well), Nazism for the deaths of some six million Jews between 1933 and 1945. In India and China until well into the second half of the twentieth century, the crime of female infanticide has not been prosecuted to the full extent of the law. In any case, even if we agree that "common law" crimes are widely (although not universally) recognized as crimes, it is important to note that these actions are relatively few in number. The more recent, less widely enforced, and less strongly ideologically supported laws – those whose passage and enforcement are largely a product of enterprise and group interests – are far larger in number and, frankly, more sociologically interesting.

Recapitulation

Laws, then, are not seen by the subjectively problematic perspective solely as an expression of a broad consensus, or as an altruistic desire to protect a large number of the members of a society from objective, clear, and present danger. Rather, they are seen as the embodiments of the beliefs, lifestyle, and/or economic interests of certain segments of a society. In other words, they are the product of the lobbying of special interest groups. In a sense, then, the law is a means of forcing one group's beliefs and politics on the rest of the society. Many laws are passed and enforced not solely because they protect society in general, or because most of the people in a given society believe in their moral correctness; the fact that they uphold the ideological or material interests of a certain sector of society also enters into the picture. Laws serve to stop certain people from doing what others consider evil, undesirable, or unprofitable; or they make them do something others consider good, desirable, or profitable. The passage of a law represents the crystallization of one group's economic or ideological interests into the criminal code. In the usual case, "criminal law marks the victory of some groups over others" (Quinney, 1970, p. 43). The subjectively problematic school takes the passage and enforcement of laws out of the public sphere of public safety and the collective conscience and places it squarely in the arenas of ideology, politics, and economics.

6

SOCIAL PROBLEMS

What is a social problem? How should it be studied? In what ways is it similar to the moral panic? There are two basic perspectives on or approaches to social problems: the objectivist and the constructionist; clearly, they parallel the "objectively given" and the "subjectively problematic" approaches toward morality and deviance.

Objectivism

The objectivists argue that what defines a social problem is the existence of an objectively given, concretely real damaging or threatening condition. What makes a condition a problem is that it harms or endangers human life and well-being. People need not be concerned or even aware of such conditions; what is important is that they do damage to our lives in some clearcut, non-ideological fashion. Any condition that causes death or disease, which shortens life expectancy or deteriorates the quality of life on a large scale, must be defined as a social problem (Manis, 1974, 1976). Presumably, the greater the number of people so damaged or threatened, the more important the social problem. According to this view, the final arbiter of the reality of social problems is the expert, armed with empirical evidence and scientific insight, and not the untrained general public. To cite Manis, a proponent of the "objectivist" school: "Social problems are those social conditions identified by scientific inquiry and values as detrimental to human well-being" (1976, p. 25). The objectivist model is a variant of the functionalist paradigm, in that it sees social problems largely as a product of dysfunctions, social disorganization, role and value conflicts, and a violation of norms – that is, a discrepancy between what is and what ought to be (Merton and Nisbet, 1976). Likewise, the traditional Marxist position accepts the idea that social problems should be defined objectively – by the harm that is inflicted on large numbers of people as a result of such practices as exploitation, oppression, racism, sexism, and imperialism (Liazos, 1972, 1982).

Constructionism

On the other side of the debate, representing the newer, more contemporary or avant-garde approach, we find the "constructionists," "subjectivists," or "relativists," who argue that what markes a given condition a problem is the "collective definition" (Blumer, 1971) of a condition as a problem, the degree of felt public concern over a given condition or issue. The constructionists see parallels between social problems and moral panics, while the objectivists do not. To the objectivist, a social problem is defined objectively, while a "panic" implies a totally different dimension – fear and concern, and irrational fear and concern at that. To the constructionist, in contrast, objective conditions become social problems only when they are defined as or felt to be problematic – disturbing in some way, undesirable, in need of solution or remedy.

To the constructionist, social problems do not exist "objectively" in the same sense that a rock, a frog, or a tree exists; instead, they are *constructed by* the human mind, *called into being* or *constituted by* the definitional process (Spector and Kitsuse, 1973, 1977; Kitsuse and Spector, 1973; Schneider and Kitsuse, 1984; Schneider, 1985). The objective existence of a harmful condition does not, by itself or in and of itself, constitute a social problem. Merely because a disease kills the members of a society does not mean that it constitutes a social problem among these people; if they do not conceptualize or define the disease as a problem, according to the constructionist, to these people, it is not a social problem. (Of course, the consequences of that disease may produce conditions that are defined as a social problem, but that is an entirely separate matter.) Indeed, to the subjectivist, a given objective condition need not even *exist* to be defined as a problem – witness the persecution of witches in Renaissance Europe and colonial New England (Erikson, 1966; Currie, 1968; Ben-Yehuda, 1980, 1985). In the words of Fuller and Myers: "Social problems are what people think they are, and if conditions are not defined as social problems by the people involved in them, they are not problems to these people, although they may be problems to outsiders or scientists" (1941, p. 320). More contemporaneously, Spector and Kitsuse define social problems as "the activities of individuals or groups making assertions of grievances and claims with respect to some putative conditions" (1977, p. 75).

In sum, a social problem exists when: (1) a group of people recognize or regard something as wrong; (2) they are concerned about it; and

(3) they urge or take steps to correct it. Thus, a social problem exists not only when substantial numbers of individuals in a society consider something wrong; it must also be seen as a remediable condition – something should be done to correct it. If the members of a society believe that nothing can be done about a condition – say, it is regarded as their fate, an act of God, or the whim of nature – constructionists do not see it as a social problem.

But note: a condition may be objectively serious in that it kills or harms many members of a given society. To the constructionist, that still does not make it a social problem; what makes a condition (concrete or "putative") a social problem is the degree of felt concern about that condition, whether it is objectively serious or not. During much of human history, infanticide, or the killing of unwanted babies, was widely practiced and was hardly ever considered a problem; in that sense, to the constructionist, infanticide was not a social problem. Today, it is widely considered a problem, and in all nations of the world, it is a crime, punishable by law. To the objectivist, to the extent that it results in the loss of human life, killing unwanted babies has always been a social problem; to the constructionist, killing unwanted babies became a social problem only when it was recognized, and action was taken against it. (Indeed, as we saw, even the very concept of harm may be socially constructed; the right-to-lifers construct killing unwanted fetuses as a major social problem, since they define fetuses as fully-fledged human beings.) Certainly warfare is one of the most serious social problems in human history if we measure it in concrete or objective terms, that is, by the loss of human life. Yet, only very rarely have large numbers of the members of any society declared war to be a problem – the protests during the American war in Vietnam in the 1960s and early 1970s provide one rare exception. Societies almost never declare a "war on war."

Put another way, a given condition (or "putative" condition) becomes a social problem when individuals or groups engage in *claims-making* activities with reference to that condition. Claims-making represents "a demand made by one party to another that something be done about some putative condition" (Spector and Kitsuse, 1977, p. 78). So, if a rally is held by a thousand demonstrators in a square in front of the governor's mansion to protest a state tax hike, then rising taxes can be seen as a social problem to those who are assembled. If a march is held through the streets of a white neighborhood in which a Black youth was assaulted, then violence by whites against African-Americans can be taken as a social problem to these marchers. If seminars are held and talks given which claim that tens of thousands of children are being kidnapped and killed by satanists each year in the United States and that the police must crack down on these fiends, once again, such activity manifests the existence of a social problem for those who hold, give, and attend such seminars and talks. In each case, certain parties are making a claim about the injustice of a certain aspect of the society as well as a demand that steps be taken to end it. It is in such claims-making activities that the existence of social problems can be determined.

It should be emphasized that referring to such demands as "claims" neither denies or affirms their moral validity or material facticity; a "claim" may be empirically valid or not, but it is a reality that is socially structured and is in need of examination. For instance, drug abuse is both a problem objectively in that it kills a great many people and subjectively in that it is widely regarded as a problem. To say that drug abuse is a condition that is constructed into a problem does not deny that it also has objective consquences. Too often, observers seem to belittle the drug problem by emphasizing its constructed character (Goode, 1990). Of course, as to whether it is more, or less, objectively harmful than other conditions – ones that attract less concern – is an entirely separate matter.

Note that it is not necessary for individuals to formulate, utter, or use the exact phrase, "*X* is a social problem," or "*X* is a social problem in this society." The problemhood or problemness of conditions is expressed in a variety of ways – including expressed attitudes, activism, voting on issues, participation in social movements, rebellion, revolution, consuming media stories about certain issues or conditions, and so on. More concretely, to the constructionist, the subjective reality of social problems can be measured or manifested in some of the following ways. Four such manifestations include: (1) organized, collective action or campaigns on the part of some members of a society to do something about, call attention to, protest, or change (or to prevent change in) a given condition – in short, "social problems as social movements" (Mauss, 1975; Best, 1990, pp. 2–3); (2) the introduction of bills in legislatures to criminalize, outlaw, or otherwise deal with the behavior and the individuals supposedly causing the condition (Becker, 1963, pp. 135ff; Gusfield, 1963, 1967, 1981; Duster, 1970; Best, 1990, pp. 2–3); (3) the ranking of a condition or an issue in the public's hierarchy of the most serious problems facing the country (Best, 1990, pp. 2–3, 151–75; Jensen, Gerber, and Babcock, 1991; Goode, 1993, pp. 49–50) – what Manis derisively calls "the public opinion paradigm" or the vox populi approach (1976, pp. 18–20); and (4) public discussion of an issue in the media in the form of magazine and newspaper articles and editorials and television news stories, commentary, documentaries, and dramas (Becker, 1963, pp. 141–3; Goode, 1978, pp. 230–2; Himmelstein, 1983, pp. 152–4; Best, 1990, pp. 2–3; Jensen, Gerber, and Babcock, 1991).

Why do certain conditions become thought of as social problems while others do not? Why are certain conditions looked upon as problems at one point in time, and considered as neutral or benign in their impact at another?

Why was alcohol accepted as little more than a wholesome beverage (referred to by Increase Mather, a seventeenth-century theologian, as "the good creature of God") in the United States until the turn of the eighteenth century, when consumption was quite high, while by the turn of the ninteenth century, when consumption had declined considerably, sizeable segments of the American population defined alcohol as an unmixed evil, a scourge – "demon rum" itself (Lender and Martin, 1987)?

Why is the teaching of evolution a problem in one community and *banning* the teaching of evolution a problem in another? Why, in one West Virginia community in the 1970s, were certain books that were assigned by the school board considered so damaging to schoolchildren that some local residents attempted to remove them from the curriculum? Why did different members of that same community struggle to reinstate those books back into the community's school curriculum (Page and Clelland, 1978)?

How did the use of psychiatry to silence political dissidence, particularly in the Soviet Union, come to be regarded as problem to the members of the American Psychiatric Association (Spector and Kitsuse, 1977, pp. 97–129)?

How did smoking come to be seen as a major social problem in the 1970s and 1980s (Markle and Troyer, 1979; Troyer and Markle, 1983; Troyer, 1989)? What were the dynamics behind this definitional process? What sorts of steps have been proposed to reduce or eliminate it?

Why was child abuse not thought of as a serious problem before the 1960s? How and why did it get recognized as problematic? Who "discovered" it? Publicized it? What was the outcome of this definitional process (Pfohl, 1977; Nelson, 1984)?

To the constructionist, it is the *social construction* or *subjective interpretation* of conditions that defines a social problem, not the nature of the condition itself. How do conditions come to be defined or felt or seen as problematic? Why does public concern emerge over one condition but not another? Why do the members of a given society get aroused about certain issues? Why are there year-to-year or decade-by-decade fluctuations in how seriously the public regards certain social conditions? These are some of the focal questions of constructionists.

The "Discovery" of Social Problems

It is absolutely crucial for the constructionist position to understand exactly how, and by whom, social problems are "discovered." Awareness of and concern about certain conditions as a problem does not arise spontaneously from the social body; millions of people do not wake up one day and realize that a given condition is a serious problem that must be addressed. Members or representatives of certain categories, organizations, or groups are more likely to be moved to bring a condition to public awareness that others.

Who "discovers" social problems? No single generalization applies to all social problems. Still, constructionists emphasize the role of *interests, resources,* and *legitimacy* in this process (Gusfield, 1981; Best, 1990, pp. 11–13; Jenkins, 1992, p. 3). Members or representatives of organizations or groups that stand to profit from the discovery of a problem are likely to be motivated to do so; organizations or groups that can command resources – many members, access to the media or to influential political figures, financial resources, and so on – are likely to be more successful in defining a condition as a social problem; and spokespersons who are considered credible, reliable, and respectable, likewise, are more likely to be taken seriously as the definers of a new problem.

Some conditions are discovered as problems by a single crusader who, initially, had little or no access to organizational resources. Such a crusader, for example, may write a book that touches a responsive chord and places a condition squarely in the public consciousness – witness Rachel Carson's discovery of pollution in her influential bestseller *Silent Spring.* Sometimes a single crusader who has been personally harmed by a condition, or by someone's behavior, launches a social movement and manages to define a social problem for much of the public. A good example is drunk driving. In 1980, the 13-year-old daughter of Candy Lightner, a divorced homemaker, was struck and killed by a drunk driver. The man's absurdly light sentence (21 months in jail and a community halfway house) moved Lightner to start an organization to ensure that her daughter's death had some meaning. By the early 1990s, Lightner's organization, MADD (Mothers Against Drunk Driving) had managed to define drunk driving as a major social problem, was instrumental in raising the drinking age to 21 in all states, and influenced stricter legislation against drunk driving (likewise, in all 50 states) (Reinarman, 1988). Today, MADD boasts a membership of a million, a full-time staff of 40 workers, and an annual budget of over $13 million.

In being "discovered" by more or less isolated outraged individuals rather than organizational representatives of a group or cause, environmental pollution and drunk driving represent exceptions to the rule. Most social problems are brought to public awareness by representatives of institutions or organizations whose interests are advanced in some way by the discovery.

In the summer of 1987, several motorists were shot by other motorists on the freeways in and around Los Angeles. Articles were published on the freeway shootings in the *Los Angeles Times*, and the national media, convinced that a problem of potential national scope was in the making, publicized the episodes, bringing it to the public's attention. Rashes of roadway shootings had taken place previously (and at least one occurred subsequently as well) – in Los Angeles in 1977, Houston in 1982, and Detroit in 1989 – but the 1987 Los Angeles outbreak, unlike the others, became defined as a social problem by the media. And here, the discoverers of the problem were the representatives of the media. The *Los Angeles Times* is an authoritative, prestigeous source, the outbreak took place during the summer, normally a slow news period, and the story was dramatic, if noncontroversial (Best, 1991). The story managed to generate a certain media excitement, but the projected trend did not develop, and within two or three months, the problemhood of freeway shooting simply evaporated.

In other cases, the discovery is made by professionals who act as an interest group in promoting a certain condition as a social problem. Child abuse existed for millennia, but it was not regarded as a major social problem until the 1960s. Within a scant four years, it became universally regarded as a problem, legislation was passed in all states criminalizing the abuse of children by their parents or caretakers, and physicians and social workers were henceforth alerted to the possibility of abuse in their clients. The abuse of children by parents and other caretakers was not prompted by an increase in abuse itself. What forces brought about the "discovery" of child abuse as a major social problem?

The condition was recognized not by family or general practitioners or hospital physicians, but by pediatric radiologists. One analysis (Pfohl, 1977) suggests that family practitioners did not bring the condition to public awareness because of the strength of the norm of confidentiality between physicians and their clients, because of the fear of liability in violating the norm of disclosure, because the parent, not the child, is regarded as the real patient, and because of the unwillingness of physicians to get drawn into the judicial process. On the other hand, these restraints did not apply to pediatric radiologists. They do not interact directly with the family, do not have parents as clients, are not legally liable for violating the confidentiality of the doctor–patient relationship. Moreover, as the discoverers of an important medical condition, pediatric radiologists were able to establish legitimacy over a major domain and advance the position of what was then a comparatively marginal medical speciality (Pfohl, 1977).

In short, in the discovery of any condition and its advocacy as a social problem, we must be alert to the matter of whose interests are being advanced in the process. Asking who profits does not mean that, if such motivation can be found, the problem that is being attacked is therefore inconsequential and trivial. Pediatric radiologists were simultaneously advancing a worthy cause by diagnosing child-battering *and* their own interests in bringing child abuse to the fore. Locating special interests does *not* disqualify a claim – it only locates its source and dynamics. Moreover, some causes *are* advanced by more or less disinterested parties – witness Rachel Carson's discovery of environmental pollution and Candy Lightner's efforts to control drunk driving. At the same time, we fail to understand the problem-definition process if we fail to consider who "discovered" a given harmful condition and why. Organizational self-interests are *often* at work in this crucial process.

Strict Constructionism

The social constructionists split into two camps – the "hard" or *strict* constructionists and the "moderate" or what Best (1989a) calls the *contextual* constructionists. Both are concerned with the social construction of social problems. Where they differ is in the relevance of the objective dimension. The moderate constructionists do not hold that social problems are *defined* by the objective severity of social conditions, but they do argue that they can be determined, that the subjective definition of conditions is to a large measure *independent of the objective seriousness* of those conditions. In contrast, the strict constructionist argues that it is impossible to determine the relationship between objective damage and subjective concern because *there is no such thing as objectivity in the first place.* Even scientists are involved in making claims about the social problems status of certain conditions (Aronson, 1984). All claims to objective reality are equally subjective, equally motivated by the impulse to define conditions as social problems. Scientists, armed with empirical data concerning the objective seriousness of a given condition, have no special or privileged position to define the nature of concrete reality.

To the moderate or contextual constructionists (for a representative sampling of the view of this camp, see the selections in Best, 1989a), one of the most intriguing features of social problems is the fact that extremely harmful conditions are not defined or regarded as social problems, while, objectively speaking, relatively benign conditions are. The answer as to why people become concerned about certain conditions cannot be found – at least not entirely – in the realm of objective damage. Something else is at work, and the moderate constructionists intend to unearth just what it is. In the 1980s, the absurd rumor that the Proctor & Gamble logo, the face of the man in the moon on a field of 13 stars, was proof of the corporation's support of satanism; this rumor generated some 6,000 calls a month to the company, which finally had to drop the logo from its packages (Anonymous, 1985). Why was crime against the elderly thought to be a major concern at a time when the elderly were, and still are, the *least* criminally victimized segment of the population (Yin, 1980; Fishman, 1978, 1980, pp. 4ff)? Why is the public far more aroused over illegal psychoactive drug use than the use of the legal substances, tobacco and alcohol (Reinarman and Levine, 1989; Goode, 1993, pp. 46–7, and passim)? The problematic nature of these questions can only be appreciated if we have some concretely determinable standard by which to measure public concern against. It is the discrepancy between such concern and the concrete threat posed by or damage caused by a given condition that forces us to raise such questions. If we insist that we have no right to determine the nature of the threat posed by certain conditions, such questions are not problematic – indeed, they are not even possible – in the first place.

In contrast, the strict constructionist does not recognize the existence of the objective dimension at all; *all* dimensions are equally subjective. When scientists determine and publicize the objective seriousness of a given condition, they are simply engaged in a "claims-making activity" (Aronson, 1984), essentially no different in any important respect from someone standing on a street corner handing out leaflets denouncing the use of flouride in the water, claiming that UFO abductions are the major problem of our time, or that Blacks are inferior to whites, dangerous, and should be rounded up and placed in concentration camps. Objectivity does not exist; there is no possibility of stepping outside the definitional process, according to the strict constructionist. We are all involved in defining social problems; we are all making claims about the seriousness, or lack of seriousness, of certain conditions, and there is no scientific way of resolving these conflicting claims, because objectivity is a myth. All claims are constructed, including the scientist's. Or so say the strict constructionists.

The factual correctness of a given statement – if such could be determined – of a given position is irrelevant; what counts is where that statement stands in relation to the social problem-defining process. Strict constructionists cannot determine or even inquire about the relationship – whether causal or independent – between the objective and the constructed dimensions because for them the objective dimension simply does not exist. It does not matter – indeed, sociologically, it cannot even be determined – that: in Renaissance Europe, women did, or did not, consort with the devil; charges of satanic kidnappings, ritualistic torture, and murder are, or are not, true; legal, or illegal, drugs kill more people; listening to rock and roll music in the 1950s did, or did not, cause or encourage moral decay and juvenile delinquency; and so on. What counts – and that alone – is how such charges come to be constructed, believed, and acted upon. The effort by contextual constructionists to privilege a scientific version of reality over a popular or public one represents a fallacy, a bias, an inappropriate mixing of levels of analysis, a case of "ontological gerrymandering" (Woolgar and Powluch, 1985). It is an improper sociological enterprise, they argue.

More important to our concern in this book, to the strict constructionist, *the objective basis for moral panics does not exist*. Indeed, it *cannot* exist, because the objective dimension cannot be determined and hence, the criterion of disproportionality cannot be applied. Consequently, if we are interested in moral panics, we *cannot* approach it from the perspective of strict constructionism. We can study concern (although exactly how this can be done if we do not accept the reality of the material world and our ability to determine that reality is not clear), but we cannot, for any given condition, compare levels of concern against levels of concrete threat. Thus, to the strict constructionist, the moral panic does not exist; therefore, this book is about a nonexistent topic. Clearly, the authors of this book do not, and cannot, accept the validity of strict constructionism.

Contextual Constructionism: Concern versus Harm

Our position conforms closely to contextual constructionism rather than to objectivism or to strict constructionism. A number of crucial assumptions flow from this position.

Contextual constructionism does not imply that a study of the objective seriousness of certain conditions is, in and of itself, fallacious or uninteresting. On the other hand, for us, the objective dimension does not *define* the social problem, nor does it strictly *determine* subjective concern. We do not see the objective and the subjective dimensions as contradictory so much as independent. But for us, definitions of and concern about conditions are far more sociologically relevant, while the objective threat that conditions present stems from a wide variety of sources – medical, ecological, economic, geological, pharmacological, and so on. If we were to focus on the conditions themselves and the threat they pose as our primary concern, we would be wandering in a theoretical wilderness, an unfocused, uncentered hodge-podge. While we do not deny the existence of the objective dimension, we do not believe that the objective seriousness of a given condition, not that alone, determines the public's reaction to it. Social movement activity, legislation, a prominent ranking on the public's list of society's most serious problems, and media attention, and all generated by a variety of factors, each of which needs to be investigated.

In a nutshell, public concern need not reflect objective seriousness (although media attention to the objective seriousness of a given condition may be a *factor* in influencing some of the public to be more concerned about it). Why should we assume that the public has an accurate notion of how serious certain conditions are? Few people have even a rough idea of the size or extent of many of the harmful – or not-so-harmful – conditions that exist in a given society. Which causes more deaths – accident or disease? In one survey, they were judged to be equally frequent, in spite of the fact that disease takes about 15 times as many lives as accidents (Slovic, Fischoff, and Lichtenstein, 1980b). Events that are dramatic and easy to recall are judged to be more common, other things being equal, than those that are less dramatic and difficult to remember; this is referred to as the "availability" heuristic (Tversky and Kahneman, 1982; Taylor, 1982). The media play a role in this process; more dramatic events are more newsworthy, more likely to be recalled by viewers and readers, and therefore more likely to be thought of by the public as frequent. Though disease takes a hundred times as many lives as homicide, newspapers contain three times as many articles on death from homicide as death from disease (Slovic, Fischoff, and Lichtenstein, 1980b). The extent of fear of crime in a community is less strongly correlated with the actual crime rate than with the amount of news about crime – and the nature of that news – in the media. How can the public possibly assess the relative objective seriousness of various conditions if their capacity to estimate that seriousness is fatally flawed by biases and systematic judgmental errors (Kahneman, Slovic, and Tversky, 1982)?

Public concern and action about a certain issue rise and fall in part for political, ideological, and moral reasons. There is, in other words, a "politics of social problems." As we saw, the public may be stirred up as a result of the efforts of a "moral entrepreneur" or moral crusader – an individual who feels that "something ought to be done" about a supposed wrongdoing, and takes steps to make sure that certain rules are enforced (Becker, 1963, pp. 147–63). At times, issues emerge as social problems because a social class, an industry, a professional group, or specific segment of the public will profit – or lose – as a result of certain changes in the society. Clearly, the American tobacco industry's – increasingly failing – attempt to define restrictions on public smoking as violations of the public's constitutional rights (invoking the Bill of Rights in this attempt) falls into this category. Politicians may make speeches about a particular issue and generate concern in the public that a problem exists where none was previously suspected. Events may take place in the lives of celebrities that publicize a condition and galvanize public sentiment toward seeing it as a serious problem; clearly, the death of Rock Hudson from AIDS in 1985 is a dramatic example. An especially horrifying murder may electrify the public and convince millions that a social problem of a certain type exists that needs to be rectified. While one or another of these various factors has been emphasized by different observers, they all play a role in generating subjective perceived crises at different times and in different places.

In short, in looking at social problems, our focus will be on public concern and only secondarily on the objective nature of conditions themselves. We believe that the relation between objective conditions and subjective concern is problematic: that is, there is no automatic, one-to-one correspondence between the two dimensions, and how they are in fact related is something that has to be investigated in specific cases, and is likely to be systematically connected to a variety of crucial factors and variables.

However, the contextual constructionist position holds to a second point as well. It most emphatically necessitates regarding the objective dimension as being capable of verification. Independent of the interests of those who make claims in a given controversy, we *can* determine, in a more or less objective and definitive fashion, that cigarettes cause cancer, that more people die of legal drug use than illegal, that automobile accidents claim more victims than mountain-climbing, that AIDS is not transmitted by hugging or kissing an infected party, that hundreds of thousands of women are raped in the United States each year, that most of the children who are kidnapped in the country are abducted by their parents, that urban residents are more likely to be the victim of a violent crime than small-town, suburban, or rural dwellers. To argue, as some have (Kitsuse and Schneider, 1989; Aronson, 1984), that such statements cannot be validated empirically (or that sociologists – as sociologists – have no right to play a part in this validation process), that making such statements is qualitatively no different from claiming their opposite, and places one squarely in the social problems-defining fray, reduces the study of social problems to an examination of a series of claims by contending parties, their social origins, and the struggle over their validation. To adherents of the strict constructionist view, there is no way of empirically verifying or refuting any such claims.

For instance, can we seriously argue that the claim that extraterrestrials have abducted and now inhabit the earthly bodies of thousands of humans worldwide, and that this represents the most serious problem of our age, cannot be disconfirmed? That such a claim is on an equal footing with – and is no less a special claim from a social problems definer than – saying that little if any evidence supports the claim of extraterrestrial abductions? Is the claim by white supremacist groups that Jews represent a conspiracy to corrupt and destroy the Christian nation of the United States really no less valid than the fact that not a shred of evidence exists which demonstrates the conclusion that Jews are involved in no such conspiracy? The strict constructionist position is, in our view, inhibiting, chilling, and paralyzing. It makes a critical perspective toward contemporary society impossible.

In addition, it is impossible to ignore the question of the objective *size* and *scope* of a given problem, an issue which the strict constructionist believes to be indeterminate. As we saw, claims-makers attempt to maximize the size and scope of the problem to legitimate their claims; presumably, the larger the problem, the more attention it deserves, they will argue. As Best shows, "big numbers are better than little numbers" (1989a, p. 32, 1990, p. 61). For the most part, the public, lawmakers, the mass media, and the other problem validators agree that size is a measure of seriousness. However – and this is where the strict constructionist runs into difficulty – when exaggerated size estimates are made by claims-makers, and they are not validated by the available evidence, this will seriously hurt a movement.

The problem is, size is one of those elements in an argument which has widespread acceptance; nearly everyone in a given debate pays some homage to it as a relevant factor. And, likewise, certain types of evidence have widespread, nearly universal, acceptance as legitimate. Consequently, when experts who gather such evidence declare that the size of the problem is drastically smaller than movement advocates claim, this invalidates their claim and damages the movement. This is not a simple matter of "who says what," as the strict constructionist seems to be saying, but of making use of certain materials at hand. Size estimates may be an important rhetorical device in an argument, but there must be some rough correspondence in the material world with one's claims, otherwise, one's cause is worse off than if one had made no such estimates. Of course, if no credible, externally validated evidence exists in the first place, and no potential challenges to one's size estimates are possible, almost any potentially believeable estimates can be offered. On the other hand, as we saw, the missing-child movement was seriously damaged when its original, exaggerated claims as to the size and scope of the problem were successfully challenged; the exposure of the "numbers gap" returned to haunt the movement (Best, 1990, pp. 48–50). Fears of "Halloween sadism" assaults against children (putting razor blades in trick-or-treat apples, for instance) never materialized into a social movement, in part because evidence supporting claims as to the serious size and scope of the problem simply never existed (Best, 1990, p. 147). On the other hand, one of the strengths of the ritual child abuse movement is that the phenomenon simply does not exist; hence, no evidence can be gathered to challenge its claims – until *specific* supposed offenders are accused, of course.

In addition, the strict constructionist argument runs into difficulty when we consider the fact that it accepts the validity of *certain kinds* of empirical evidence but rejects other kinds. More specifically, it is acceptable to the strict constructionist to make claims about the *social construction* of claims, but not about their validity. But *how do we know* that such struggles or contradictory claims exist and what their social locations are? The strict constructionist says that sociologists have the right to study the empirical nature of the *construction* of claims, but we cannot know the empirical nature of the *validity* of such claims. In so doing, strict constructionists privilege access to one domain of inquiry but close off another. We can determine the existence and dynamics of claims in the same way that we know that certain claims are more valid than others – we look, we listen, we investigate, we apply evidence, logic, and our reasoning powers to our understanding of social phenomena. Why we are allowed to study one class of sociological phenomena but not another is contradictory. (See Best, 1993.) To most sociologists, the strict constructionist approach simply makes no sense whatsoever. (For a recent defense of the strict constructionist position, see Ibarra and Kitsuse, 1993.)

Multiple Definitions of Problems

It is absolutely necessary to emphasize that, as with deviance, there is enormous variation in definitions of social problems. If social problems are what the members of a society think are social problems, it follows that what is considered a problem varies from one individual to another, and from one segment of society to another. There are "multiple definitions of social problems by various interested groups" (Becker, 1966, p. 10). It is not merely the existence and the extent of a problem that are socially constructed, but the nature of the problem as well. Conditions are seen and presented as problems in particular ways and not in others. One or another aspect of the condition will be focused on as the problem. For instance, is the use of marijuana a problem of hedonistic indulgence, temporary psychosis, chemical dependence, the prelude to even harder drugs, or the dampening of motivation (Best, 1991, p. 327)? The answer is likely to vary from one party, audience, or group to another.

Likewise, Gusfield (1981) argues persuasively that the *problemhood* of drunk driving is not inherently locatable to a single aspect of the phenomenon. *What is the problem* in drunk driving? Is it the fact that specific improperly socialized individuals drink too much and have accidents while driving? Is it a matter of law enforcement? Is it a traffic problem? Do we need more sobriety checkpoints on the road? Or is it caused by lax enforcement of the laws governing serving liquor in public bars and restaurants, forcing us to seek a very different solution? Or, instead, is the problem one of permitting the manufacture and sale of unsafe cars – not having strongly enforced state laws governing seat belts or safety bags? Or is it a matter of unsafe or improperly maintained roadways? Or perhaps the problem is an inadequate public transportation system – too many cars and not enough busses, subways, and trains? After all, fewer cars, fewer drunk drivers, fewer traffic accidents and fatalities. Exactly what problem is buried in the drunk driving issue or phenomenon is a matter of definition or construction. It is not, as the objectivists would have it, a matter that indwells in the issue itself, a property that imposes itself on the consciousnesses of all reasonably well-informed observers.

So crucial is the multiple definition of social problems that certain conditions can be interpreted as problems in almost precisely the opposite fashion. Industrialists think that the government meddles too much in the affairs of industry and that environmentalists exaggerate the extent to which industry pollutes the water and contaminates the air. Environmentalists think that the government should regulate industry more than it does and a stop should be put to the unregulated pollution that industry is allowed to engage in. Many white males believe that Blacks and women are given preference in hiring, and that this is a major problem facing the society today; a substantial proportion of Blacks and women argue that discrimination against them is, and historically has been, one of the most important problems in American society. To the pro-choice advocate, the abortion problem is that abortion is difficult to obtain and unavailable in many areas; to the right-to-lifer, the abortion problem is that abortion is legal and available in the first place. Few conditions will be viewed in precisely same ways by the overwhelming majority of the population.

Was slavery a social problem in the United States prior to the Civil War? Slavery was certainly a problem to African-American slaves. Many resisted it in numerous ways, large numbers escaped from plantations, some even engaged in armed rebellion against it. If valid public opinion polls had been conducted on the attitudes of slaves toward slavery, can anyone doubt that the vast majority would have seen slavery as undesirable, onerous, exploitative, and oppressive, an institution that should be destroyed? The fact that thousands of ex-slaves fought on the Union side in the Civil War to defeat the South and put an end to slavery is a certain indication that it most decidedly was a problem to them. In addition, a not inconsiderable number of northern whites joined abolition movements to end slavery – again, a measure of the social problemhood of the institution for them. Thus, to much of the African-American population in the slave-holding South and to some northern whites, slavery was a problem prior to and during the Civil War (Geschwender, 1990, p. vii).

On the other hand, to landowning southerners, slavery was not a problem. Indeed, the election of a northerner, Abraham Lincoln, to the presidency in 1860 *was* a problem to many of them, because that event spelled the first step toward the elimination of slavery in the United States. The action taken by the Confederacy as a result – cession – indicated the problemhood of Lincoln's election, at the very least, to political figures in the South and, in all probability, the mass of the white population generally. Once again, the same condition, slavery, was defined as a problem by some Americans, and its inevitable end was seen as a problem to others. (But once again, saying that slavery had a constructed or socially viewed and acted-upon aspect does not deny that it *was* a concrete, real-world institution that exploited, harmed, maimed, and killed uncountable numbers of human beings. One of the authors attended a conference at which an African-American writer objected to looking at slavery as a constructed phenomenon, arguing that that denied the objective harm that it inflicted. In fact, the constructionist perspective does *not* deny objective harm, but only insists that objective harm neither defines problemhood, nor determines social concern.) The vastly different conceptions of problemhood held by different members of a society underscores the constructed character of social problems.

In fact, as a general rule, what is referred to as a social problem is simply a condition or an area *into which is read* one or another interpretation of what the problem is (Becker, 1966, p. 7). To the educator, the problem of education may be getting more money out of legislators; to the legislator, the problem may lie in educating more students better on a shrinking budget; to the teenager, the problem of education may be in making sure that academic work does not interfere too much with an active social life; to parents, the problem of education may be as basic as ensuring the physical safety of their children while they attend school. Each party may designate "education" as an important problem, but each may have a somewhat different interpretation as to exactly what the problem is within that broad area. To many AIDS sufferers and to homosexuals generally, the AIDS problem is getting the government to devote a larger budget to curing and treating the disease; many heterosexuals may see the problem as avoiding contamination. However reasonable or unreasonable the designation of problemhood may appear to one or another party, all social problems are broad areas of concern which may be interpreted differentially according to the audience. At the same time, consensus is a matter of degree, and some social problems attract more consensus than others. During the moral panic, an unusually high degree of consensus about the problem and its solution tends to grip the members of a society or segments of that society.

Social Problems and Moral Panics

Clearly, social problems and moral panics overlap. From the constructionist perspective, both are generated by a specific definition of the situation; both are measured or manifested by attitudinal and behavioral concern about conditions that are widely regarded as undesirable; with both, steps are taken to eliminate those conditions; both entail "claims-making" about a condition and its solution; and with both, the concern need not encompass all or most members or all or most segments of a given society. However, while there is a heavy overlap between moral panics and social problems, there are at least three basic differences between them.

First, there is no necessary *folk devil* in the social problem, while it *is* an essential component of the moral panic. While some social problems are based on the harmful behavior of certain individuals who may be designated as deviant (criminals, rapists, murderers, drug addicts, pornographers, child molesters, and so on), many social problems do not contain the deviance or "folk devil" component – for instance, aging, the threat to the ozone layer and the resultant greenhouse effect, and the worldwide population problem. For many of our humanly created conditions, no specific deviant individuals or groups have materialized as being responsible; with social problems, we cannot always heap scorn and condemnation on a particular "folk devil's" head.

A second difference between the social problem and the moral panic is, as we saw, the *discrepancy* between the degree of concern over a given issue or condition and the magnitude of the supposed threat it poses. The term "panic" implies that the concern is disproportionate in relation to its concrete threat, or in comparison with a similar, or objectively even greater, threat. People are not said to "panic" over a real and present danger; they are said to panic when their reaction is excessive or unwarranted. However the social problem is defined, there is no necessary disjunction between a conditions's "objective" threat and the fear or concern it generates; in contrast, this is an essential and defining element in the moral panic.

Third, the concept of the moral panic also implies that huge *fluctuations* take place in the degree of concern over a given issue over time, from one year or decade to another. For a subantial stretch of time, little or no – or a routine, stable level of – concern is expressed; then, the condition is "discovered" (or rediscovered) and a moral panic breaks out; concern is feverish for a time; and, finally, for another stretch of time, the concern subsides, and the issue lies dormant. In contrast, there is no necessary fluctuation in the seriousness of a social problem (although there often is empirically); such fluctuations in social problem magnitude are not one of its defining elements. In principle, a social problem could remain at the same level of seriousness – however that is defined – decade after decade.

7

COLLECTIVE BEHAVIOR

Stanley Cohen not only launched the term "moral panic," he was also the first to notice its collective behavior-like quality (1972, pp. 11–12, 144ff). Collective behavior is defined as behavior that is relatively spontaneous, volatile, evanescent, emergent, extra-institutional, and short-lived; it emerges or operates in situations in which there are no, or few adequate, clearcut definitions as to what to do from mainstream culture. Collective behavior operates outside the stable, patterned structures of society; it reflects the "maverick" side of human nature. Compared with conventional, everyday life, collective behavior is less inhibited and more spontaneous, more changeable and less structured, shorter-lived and less stable (Goode, 1992, pp. 17–21).

From day to day, week to week, year to year, and even decade to decade, we can make certain predictions about the behavior of the members of a given society. We know – within broad limits – that a certain proportion of the population will vote in a given election, purchase specific products, show up for work, attend religious services, go to sleep at night and wake up in the morning, attend class, and obey traffic laws. It is possible to refer to this type of behavior as "conventional" or "everyday" behavior. On the other hand, certain behavior is more labile from day to day, week to week, or year to year. The stock market is a great deal more volatile – the price of a given stock, the overall industrial average, the total number of stocks traded – than are, say, supermarket purchases; this is especially the case during feverish "boom" and "bust" trading periods (Kindleberger, 1987; Galbraith, 1990). The purchase of certain novelty products or fad items is considerably more unstable, and fluctuates far more from year to year, than is the purchase of refrigerators, washing-machines, or vacuum cleaners. The movement of a story through the rumor mill is far more unpredictable than the description of a historical event in scholarly books and articles. Although social movements tend to be far more stable than collective behavior, still, support for most social movements is a somewhat chancy affair, and rises and falls more quickly, than it does for mainstream political parties. The unpredictability and disorderliness of charismatic authority in contrast to bureaucratic authority has been a staple of sociological analysis since the pioneering work of Max Weber early in the twentieth century (Goode, 1992).

The forms of collective behavior Cohen mentioned as having direct relevance to moral panics were mass hysteria (p. 11), mass delusion (pp. 11, 148), disasters (pp. 11, 144ff), including the convergence process during disasters (p. 159), riots (p. 11), including race riots (p. 155), crowds (p. 11), especially the milling process that takes place during crowd assemblies (p. 154), mass vilification (pp. 11–12), rumors (pp. 155–6), and legends (p. 156). Let's look at the most basic collective behavior processes and their relation to the moral panic.

Rumor

Rumor is both a process and a product, an accelerator of collective behavior and a form of collective behavior itself, both a mechanism that pervades collective behavior and an example of collective behavior. Rumor is popularly taken to be stories that are by definition false; actually, experts define rumor not by its falsity – nor its content at all – but by its lack of substantiation. By definition, rumors are told without reliable factual documentation; at some later point in time, they could turn out to be verified, or be shown to be false – what counts is that they are unverified. Rumors are hearsay; they are told, believed, and passed on not because of the weight of the evidence presented, but because of the expectations by tellers that they are true in the first place (Rosnow and Fine, 1976).

Four factors facilitate the rumormongering process: topical importance or "outcome-relevant involvement"; uncertainty or ambiguity; personal anxiety; and credulity. When these four factors are high, many rumors are likely to fly about; when they are low, rumors are unlikely to be circulated (Rosnow, 1988, 1991).

As a general rule, a story about a situation that is felt to be inconsequential in its implications is not a source of speculation (Rosnow, 1988, p. 23). Rumors about events that are felt by listeners to be unimportant, to have little or no relevance for their lives, are far less likely to be passed on and are more likely to be dead-ended if told than rumors about events that are felt to have important consequences, both good and bad. People in the United States simply do not spread rumors about the price of camels in Afghanistan because the subject does not have any importance for them (Allport and Postman, 1946–7, p. 502). Other things being equal, the more subjective importance a given topic has for an audience, the greater the likelihood that rumors will be told about it; the less important that subject is regarded, the lower the likelihood is. Rumor tends to fly thick and fast under certain conditions, when topical importance is maximized: wartime, disasters, the stock market, politics, mass-produced products, race and racial tension, the doings of friends and other intimates, an especially sensationalistic crime, the doings of celebrities. Remember, we are talking about subjective importance. In the grand scheme of things, that is to say, objectively, what celebrities are doing makes no difference whatsoever to the lives of most people – it has no impact on their lives – but it is deemed or felt to be subjectively important to the public, and hence, it is of importance to them.

For the most part, rumor contexts are those that are problematic, that is, about which not enough is known, or which present a puzzle or a problem; thus, the second "rumorgenic" (Rosnow and Fine, 1976, pp. 22ff) factor is uncertainty or ambiguity, a state of mind "produced by doubt, such as when events are unstable, capricious, or problematical" (Rosnow, 1988, p. 20). Rumor thrives on doubt.

The third factor that feeds the rumor process is a state of anxiety or apprehensiveness, an emotional, negative state "produced by apprehension about an impending, potentially negative outcome" (Rosnow, 1988, p. 20). Anxiety is both a personal and a structural variable – that is, some individuals are more prone to anxiety than others, and some conditions are more likely to generate anxiety in nearly everyone than others. Another way of saying this is that "rumor flies on fear" (Goleman, 1991). Individuals who are fearful are more likely to believe and pass on rumors than individuals who are not (Kimmel and Keefer, 1991). And situations that maximize fear are those in which rumors are more likely to be told and believed.

And lastly, there is the factor of credulity, that is, a willingness to believe, to suspend disbelief, to hold one's critical faculties about the validity of a story in abeyance. Rumors must *seem* to be true; if they are clearly false to a listener, then they tend to be dead-ended rather than passed on. A critical set (Buckner, 1965) is the enemy of rumor – a tendency to be questioning and skeptical about the truth of a rumor, or stories one hears in general – while credulity is a friend of rumor. As a general rule, the more knowledgeable one is, both about the subject of the rumor and generally, the lower the likelihood that one will pass on a rumor one hears.

Moral panics represent periods during which all of these four factors are maximized. Shibutani argues that rumor is "improvised news"; it is a substitute for news, it replaces news when established or institutionalized channels of communication have broken down, or are silent or unreliable concerning events of importance. For Shibutani, rumor is an effort at collective problem solving; it allows people to cope with the uncertainty of life (Shibutani, 1966; Rosnow and Fine, 1976, pp. 12,

30). Where the unsatisfied demand for news is moderate, and degree of interest or excitement about a given subject, likewise is moderate, people generally engage in some form of critical deliberation; they check assertions and verify the reliability of their sources. However, when unsatisfied demand for news is great, and the subjective excitement and interest in a given subject likewise is great, rumor is more spontaneous and extemporaneous. Here, rumors are more likely to be taken at face value from almost any source. Shibutani claimed that such conditions are very rare.

Shibutani's theory has been criticized for overemphasizing the *cognitive* and *rational* factors in rumor (Goode, 1992, pp. 284–6). Certainly information-seeking is only one of an array of motives for rumor-mongering. Moreover, under certain conditions, the last thing people who tell rumors want is verified information; the "reality testing" that Shibutani posits as central to rumor transmission (pp. 148–55) may not characterize the actions of many rumor tellers and listeners. Much of the time, rumor is a distinctly "irrational" process, that is, it often represents the need to verify deeply held beliefs and values far more than concrete facts. Often, rumor affirms in-group membership, virtue, and victimization, and out-group exploitation and wickedness. Although Shibutani's theory was developed well before the moral panics concept came into being, it is clear that one of the conditions that is likely to inhibit critical deliberation is the moral panic. By their very nature, during moral panics, many people regard the putative threat of personal importance to them, they are uncertain about its impact on them, the subject makes them apprehensive and fearful, they hunger for more news than is available, and they tend to suspend or lower their level of disbelief.

Fundamentalist Christians are both more likely to believe that satanists are sexually abusing and killing tens of thousands of children in the United States yearly, and they are more likely to tell rumors to that effect, than is true of agnostics, atheists, and religious skeptics; this is especially likely to be the case with less educated, rural, more traditional couples who are distressed by the secular trend of contemporary society, among whom the wife works, who have children in a day-care center, and who feel guilty about the arrangement. When tradition has broken down or is no longer possible, and the sources of information that are customarily sought (the government, the media, big business) are seen as the very forces that are causing the problem, alternative sources will be sought out and legitimated (Richardson, Best, and Bromley, 1991).

Individuals living in communities that are strongly racially divided and conflicted are more likely than those living in more racially harmonious communities to see threat in the actions of another racial category and to believe and pass on atrocity stories concerning what

evil things a representative of that other racial category did to one of
their own members. During periods when conflict flares up and the
press is seen as an unreliable source of information – by many whites
and conservatives as being too sympathetic to rebellious African-
Americans, and by many Blacks and liberals as too sympathetic to the
government, the police, and established interests – rumors are likely to
fly thick and fast (Rosenthal, 1971; Knopf, 1975).

Stories about what drug dealers are doing are more likely to be
countenanced on the basis of less evidence in neighborhoods whose
residents feel threatened by drug abuse than in those in which drug
abuse is felt to be a more distant or less common phenomenon. The
fact that the press, the government and, again, big business are often
seen by some members of such communities as deeply implicated in
contributing to the problem makes statements which issue from their
representatives suspect, and rumormongering more likely.

Rumor is one of the basic processes that both fuels and is fueled by
the moral panic. A moral panic sets the stage and provides a context for
rumormongering; when rumors take place, they provide the justification for fears, exaggeration, and a sense of threat. Rumor is a vital
element in the moral panic. It is one of the reasons why the moral panic
must be regarded as a form of collective behavior.

Contemporary or Urban Legends

There is a particular type of rumor that is so important it deserves
special mention: the "urban" or *contemporary legend*. Like rumor, contemporary legends have an unauthorized, unofficial, subterranean
quality. They arise more or less spontaneously, they are told with great
frequency and intensity for a time, after which they subside; some are
reborn in a somewhat different guise at another time in another place.
Like rumor, urban legends are dynamic, evanescent phenomena. Contemporary legends are stories that are told as true, and are widely
believed, but lack factual verification – which means that they qualify as
rumors. On the surface, they seem to be about specific people and
events; in reality, they have an abstract, general, or cartoonlike quality.
In the run-of-the-mill rumor, what counts is the details of the subject
of the story – the fact that the story is about specific events or a
particular person. In contrast, the tales told in contemporary legends
are stereotypical; they have a standard, dramatic form, they adhere to
a fairly fixed formula; they contain a fairly simple plot and readily
recognizable characters. They represents a "folk soap opera" in minia-
ture and thus have a widespread and almost timeless appeal. Unlike
classic fairy tales or ancient myths, which are fantastic tales about
magical events or superhuman characters in a far-off, nonexistent land,

modern legends are mundane, seemingly plausible events which took place in the recent past, usually in the local area, to perfectly ordinary people (Brunvand, 1981, 1984, 1986, 1989).

Urban legends circulate for much the same reasons that rumors are told, believed, and passed on; the factors that encourage them include topical interest, ambiguity, anxiety, and credulity. However, since the urban legend (unlike gossip) tends not to be about concrete people whom the listener is likely to know or know about or events with which he or she is personally familar, there have to be some additional factors which propel it into circulation. A few include: they tell a strong, interesting, dramatic story; they tell a story with a meaningful moral or message; they reflect contemporary fears; they contain a grain of truth with respect to what is currently believed; they supply supportive detail or local color; they supply or point to a credible source (Brunvand, 1981, pp. 10–12; Dickson and Goulden, 1983, pp. 128–35; Mullen, 1972).

Many urban legends contain an element of threat; they tend to be about events that were, or nearly were, harmful to the subject of the story. They often infuse the everyday, mundane world with shock, apprehension, wonderment, and fear; they exploit the fear that many people have that danger is lurking around every corner. These stories make that fear a seeming reality. As we saw, anxiety or fear is a major component of rumors; it is one of the forces that propels them. As a general rule, the more frightened listeners are when they hear a rumor (and, it can be assumed, the same applies to legends, a form of rumor), the greater the likelihood they will repeat it. One of the motives for repeating a scary story you've heard is to discover facts from the listener than contradict it. Very often, however, the story is believed and one's fears escalate (Kimmel and Keefer, 1991; Goleman, 1991; Rosnow, 1991).

Moral panics are the perfect breeding ground for urban or contemporary legends. They arise in spheres of life about which threat is perceived and insecurity is rife. As we saw, urban legends are rumors, but they are more than rumors, in that they pretend to be about actual, real-life individuals while, in reality, they have an abstract, cartoonlike, substitutable quality. A given contemporary legend could be about anyone – or anything – with the appropriate characteristics. For instance, in the early 1980s, a legend circulated that Proctor & Gamble, a large, international household products corporation, contributed 10 percent of its profits to the Church of Satan. Something quite specific made P&G the target of the urban legend – its logo, the face of the man in the moon on a field of 13 stars, was capable of being interpreted by means of what was thought to be satanic imagery – but , in principle, the rumor could have been told about any large corporation. To many small-town fundamentalist Christians, such corporations were both a symbol and a cause of bewildering social change and the decline of a traditional way of life.

One special type of urban legend that most successfully propels and expresses the moral panic is the "atrocity tale" (Bromley, Shupe, and Ventimiglia, 1979) or "horror story." In a moral panic, horror or atrocity stories "help identify the threat" (Thompson, King, and Annetts, 1990, p. 3). The ideology of specific social categories, sub-groups, or social movements provides a framework that makes certain horrifying (but empirically unlikely) events seem possible, plausible, or even likely; tales about such events are believable because, in certain circles, they give life to fears and threats that have been articulated on a more abstract or general level. Legends narrating atrocity tales express and validate what tellers and listeners believe and want to hear in the first place. A good example of an atrocity tale in the form of a contemporary legend is the story that was circulated in the late 1970s and early 1980s among certain feminist circles of the existence of "snuff" films, movies in which women or girls were actually raped, mutilated, and killed on camera for the entertainment of male viewers. Although no solid documentation exists that any such films are authentic, the fact is, their existence and circulation was believable among feminist separatists who were willing to believe that man's deepest desire is to brutalize and kill women – or, failing that, to watch other men brutalize and kill women (Dworkin, 1981, 1982). Stories of "snuff" films provided the documentation for that belief (Thompson, King, and Annetts, 1990).

Best (1990, pp. 131–50) takes the existence of urban legends as one indication of fear and concern about a given perceived threat. Certain conditions generate social movements; the response to others is less organized, less institutionally based, more "subterranean." Certain themes can be regarded as "unconstructed social problems" when they become the subject of legends and folklore (pp. 144–8). The fact that legends are told, believed, and widely disseminated measures or indicates the degree or extent of the seriousness with which the problem is taken. As we saw, the number of actual incidents involving serious harm to children as a result of "Halloween sadism" was quite small, indeed, practically nonexistent. This means that there was a diminished likelihood that a social movement would have emerged to deal with it in a concrete, practical way. At the same time, the fear that such a claim tapped was sufficiently strong and widespread to launch a score or more legends conveying the message that children were acutely vulnerable to such a threat. This argument applies even more strongly to moral panics, which generate intense fear for a period of time, but do not necessarily grow into fully-fleged social movements. Indeed, the fact that a number of contemporary legends are circulated about a given perceived threat provides an important clue that we may have a moral panic on our hands.

Mass Hysteria and Collective Delusion

A great deal has been written about hysterical contagion, epidemic hysteria, mass panic, or *mass hysteria*. (Sirois, 1974, summarizes the literature as of two decades ago.) Note that at least one observer (Bartholomew, 1990) has objected to the term, "mass hysteria," holding it to be pejorative and inappropriately pathology-oriented. He prefers the term "collective exaggerated emotions." According to Miller (1985, pp. 98ff), there are three qualities necessary to define mass hysteria: a mistaken belief concerning the threat from a certain agent, heightened emotion, particularly fear, and mobilization, especially flight, on the part of a substantial proportion of the population supposedly threatened by the agent.

If we are quite strict and literal about applying these three criteria, mass hysteria is so rare as to be virtually nonexistent. The classic cases of the mass hysteria literature – including reactions to the radio broadcast of *The War of the Worlds* in 1938 – virtually never entailed mass mobilization. While a substantial proportion of the population has sometimes felt threatened by a nonexistent agent and, upon occasion, even felt fearful as a consequence, it is practically never the case that such a belief or emotion has triggered irrational, mass, headlong flight. If the mobilization that mass hysteria triggers is restricted to flight, then the phenomenon is extremely rare, practically nonexistent.

On the other hand, mass mistaken beliefs or *collective delusion*, the belief component of mass hysteria, are quite common. As we saw, the moral panic is predicated on an exaggerated fear, "taking alarm without due cause" (Rose, 1982, p. 29), or, at least, taking more alarm at a supposed threat than is warranted by a sober assessment of the evidence. Panic arises both from "a nervousness about catastrophic possibilities" and "an inability or reluctance to check" the facts (p. 29). Taking only the belief component of the mass hysteria, then, by definition, all cases of moral panics are based on an aspect of mass hysteria. One of the essential defining aspects of the moral panic is an exaggerated fear; in this sense, the moral panic is a kind of mass hysteria. In the early 1980s, certain segments of the American public feared that tens of thousands of children were being kidnapped by strangers, when the real number was no more than a few hundred. Beginning in the early 1980s, many fundamentalist Christians came to believe that satanists were torturing and killing children in the tens of thousands each year, when very little, if any, evidence had been unearthed to support the contention that any such practices ever occur. Americans fear a greater threat from illegal drug use than from the use of legal drugs, when the latter kills more than 20 times the number of the former. If we understand mass hysteria to be based on a grossly exaggerated sense of threat, then the frequent outbreak of moral panics disproves the contention that at least one element of mass hysteria is practically nonexistent.

But moral panics are made up of far more than a mass collective delusion. Note that the criterion of irrational mass, headlong flight is sometimes used to define mass hysteria (Miller, 1985, 98ff). While, it is true that such irrational or self-destructive headlong flight in the face of a nonexistent threat is practically unknown in human history – or, at least, in the sociological literature – there are other forms of mobilization which are extremely common: rallies, protests, marches, speeches, petitions to politicians, organizing a social movement, giving and attending talks, speeches, seminars, and publishing articles and books about the putative threat. If the mobilization in response to an exaggerated sense of threat can include a wide range of activities to avoid or deal with the supposed threat, then the phenomenon of mass hysteria is quite common indeed. Some components of mass hysteria, then, form building-blocks of the moral panic.

Persecutions and Renewals

Many moral panics qualify as persecutions or renewals (Rose, 1982, pp. 137–82, 183–242). Persecutions have been defined as "severe repressive actions" taken against "some category of persons" as a result of "an almost obsessive public fear of the dangers emanating from" representatives of that category (p. 137). The members of the targeted category are not in fact engaged in the evil deeds, or do not represent the threat ascribed to them. A feeling of insecurity on the part of much of, or segments of, the public leads to "some degree of fantasy or exaggeration of danger" (p. 146); "a category of people become defined as a likely causal agent in producing current social misfortunes" (p. 148). As a consequence, the representatives of these agents are targeted as the enemy, scapegoated, and dehumanized. Examples of persecutions include anti-Semitic pogroms, the Stalinist purges that took place in the Soviet Union in the 1930s, the witch-hunts of Renaissance Europe, and the anti-communist campaigns initiated by Senator Joseph McCarthy in the 1950s. In persecutions, evildoers are seen as taking part in a conspiracy; relatively "simple conspiatorial explanations" leave "no doubt about good and evil" (Levin, 1971, pp. 94, 95).

As a result of these beliefs and ascriptions, mobilization – collective action – is taken against those "defined as enemies of the people"

(Rose, 1982, p. 151). For sustained, widespread persecutions, some government approval or sponsorship is likely to be present. At the same time, such episodes also require "the support of a substantial part of the general public" (154). "The degree of popular support for a given persecution is an important background factor" in the success of a given episode of persecution, as is the "dispositions of the popular press" (p. 154). In addition, it must be recognized that persecutions are generally not "simply a reflection of sudden outbursts of general public rage. To succeed, therefore, they often require access to support from various organized groups" (p. 155). Consequently, persecutions are as much a product of social movements as collective behavior.

Renewals are defined as episodes of awakened enthusiasm "for commitments that had lapsed into relative indifference" (Rose, 1982, p. 185). Millenarian movements represent one of the most "enthusiastic" of religious renewals; they are episodes in which participants "anticipate a sudden radical transformation of the world" (pp. 186–7). The most often studied of millenarian movements are "nativistic" or "revitalization" movements among colonial peoples. Millenarian movements necessitate not only a disaster that destroys or threatens the viability of a traditional culture, but also a charismatic leader to prophesy the coming utopia (p. 195). A less extreme version of renewals than millenarian movements is represented by the revival, in which a coming utopia-like condition of the society is anticipated through the widespread awakening of a dormant spiritual state. Such revivals are said to have gripped much of the American public through much of the nation's history. Some historians believe that four such revivals (or "Awakenings") took place between the 1740s and the 1960s (Rose, 1982, pp. 185–6).

Disasters

There are some strong parallels between disasters and moral panics, as Stanley Cohen (1972, pp. 22–9, 144–8) pointed out. In many natural disasters, there is a period of advance warning during which the threat of imminent danger is perceived and communicated within the community. Tornados can usually be predicted with some degree of precision, although no one knows for sure just how damaging one will be. Volcanos often give off signs of future eruptions; such advance warning may have saved hundreds of lives in 1980, when geologists predicted that Mount St Helens, located in Washington State, was about to erupt. There is, then, in some natural disasters, a "warning phase" and a "threat," a period when the community fears that it will be hit, although, again, it does not necessarily know the precise nature or scope of the oncoming events. In the warning phase (Cohen, 1972, pp. 22, 144–8), the community is sensitized to cues of trouble. In the moral panic, sensitization sometimes exacerbates the seriousness of the problem. For instance in the Mods and Rockers disturbances in England in the 1960s, increased police presence and readiness ("we will crack down on them immediately") often brought on an escalation in violence; a slight scuffle easily turned into a full-scale mêlée (pp. 146–7).

In both the disaster and the moral panic, there is the "impact" phase, during which the threatening agent strikes the community, and its residents must take an "immediate and unorganized" response to the damage that follows (p. 23). And in both, there is an inventory of the damage, a "rescue" of the survivors, a "remedy" proposed, and a period of "recovery." In the disaster literature, during the past generation or so, there has been a stress on the formal organizations that have been set up to cope with future disasters, which maximizes preparedness and minimizes surprises; in this way, the original reaction to a novel disaster, one for which a community is not prepared, will be organized, effective, and community-wide rather than "immediate and unorganized." Likewise, in a moral panic, authorities in a community organize against the threat so that not only do the threatening agents know the community is ready for their onslaught, but the members of the community know that steps are being taken against the threat as well. In time, relations between the threatening agent and the community become institutionalized and routinized.

Another parallel between natural disasters and the moral panic is that there is something of a community *overreaction* to the threat. Researchers have identified the phenomenon of *convergence* in many, possibly most, disasters. In a widely publicized disaster, people and supplies typically *converge* on the stricken area, often to the point where coordination and distribution becomes itself another disaster; in addition, all too often, curious onlookers also converge on the scene, impeding rescue operations (Goode, 1992, pp. 210–11). In a moral panic, likewise, as we have already seen, the community – or a segment of it – overreacts to a given condition, issue, phenomenon. And in both, public attention on the event or issue is usually fueled by media focus; often, when that media focus fades, public attention fades as well.

Disasters and moral panics even share a number of dilemmas and conflicts in common. How to counter the claims of individuals and agencies who argue that the threat is not as substantial as most believe, That the solution to the threat or problem proposed by some is at odds with the one proposed by others? How to make use of the services of organizations that traditionally do not deal with this particular threat? The schools, the churches, businesses? How should the media be regarded – as allies in the struggle, a resource for communicating the correct position, as impartial observers, or as an enemy? How to enlist the government's help and avoid its interference? What is the proper role of the police? In a given crisis, who sould be designated as an expert, a spokesperson for a given position, be given the authority to make crucial decisions? Which agencies or organizations should be funded and given the authority to coordinate the operation of dealing with the crisis? Should organizations that are already in place deal with the problem, or should new ones be created? When the crisis has passed, which organizations should stay in place and continue to be funded? Which ones should be dismantled? These are precisely the sorts of questions that have to be addressed in a disaster, and ones that individuals involved in the moral panic also have to resolve. And in both situations, the ways that they are answered are to some degree unknowable in advance, which is one of the reasons why the field of collective behavior is so fascinating.

Of course, moral panics are not *exactly* like disasters. In some ways, the differences are stronger than the similarities. With disasters, the agent is generally far more clearcut and identifiable – a hurricane, a volcano, a tidal wave, an earthquake – and universally agreed to be damaging and undesirable; just *how* the agent damaged the society is fairly unambiguous – it generates a substantial level of consensus. With moral panics, by contrast, there is usually less agreement as to just *who* the agent is and what damage, of any, it inflicts. In the natural disaster, there is are fairly clearcut phases – the threat, the impact, the post-disaster or recovery phases. With moral panics, these phases are not so clearcut. And with disasters, there may be disagreement as to whether the society responded in a fashion commensurate with the threat, but that is not a *necessary* component of the disaster; with the moral panic, by definition, the response is out of proportion to the threat of the issue, behavior, or condition being responded to. And in natural (as opposed to technological) disasters, there is no "folk devil," no deviant, no human agent responsible for the suffering they inflicted. (At least not until the post-disaster, recovery, or clean-up phase; for accusations of inappropriate behavior in the recovery phase, see Goode, 1992, pp. 227–33.) Actually, the parallels between moral panics and *technological* disasters – especially those involving contamination by toxic substances – are much stronger than those with natural disasters, as we explain in chapter 9. In technological disasters, there is often no period when the threat has subsided, and there may be a "folk devil" or human agent responsible for the suffering the disaster inflicted; there is, in short, a *moral* dimension to the technological disaster not found in most natural disasters.

8

SOCIAL MOVEMENTS

The generation of "action groups" – "germinal social movements" – is one accompaniment of the moral panic (Cohen, 1972, p. 120). In fact, social movement organizations or movement-like groups represent one means by which the moral panic is expressed. Many, indeed, most, of these "germinal" social movements die on the vine; a few years after they break out, no lasting legacy, inheritance, or trace of the furor that had once been mobilized remains. The two action groups discussed by Cohen that sprang up in the wake of the concern over the Mods and Rockers never became full-scale social movement organizations, and did not survive past the late 1960s. Some other moral panics generate social movements and social movement organizations that manage to survive beyond the period of excitement into the more temperate period that inevitably follows. For instance, in spite of the fact that illicit drug use stirs up considerably less excitement today than it did in the late 1980s, scores of activist organizations that were put together at that time still remain in existence.

Social movements are defined as organized efforts by a substantial number of people to change, or to resist change, in some major aspect of society. Social movements, by their very nature, express *dissatisfaction* with the way things are or with the way, some fear, others want to make them. Thus, they require three conditions to come into being. First, some real, potential, or even imagined *condition* to which some people may object; second, a *subjective feeling* on the part of some that this condition is undesirable and should be changed; and third, an organized means for making this dissatisfaction collective, that is, a social movement *organization*. The participants of social movements feel that their own values, needs, goals, or beliefs are being threatened by certain conditions or people, and they wish to "set things right" (Goode, 1992, pp. 407–8).

The principal aim of social movements is to *establish the legitimacy of a specific claim about a social condition*. Social movement activists believe that a given condition does not receive enough attention and is not regarded as a sufficiently serious social problem in a society; no, or insufficient, steps are being taken, they believe, to remedy the supposed problem. Members of the various animal rights groups believe that animals have the same rights as humans, and should be protected from pain and exploitation. To that end, they protest animal experimentation, the use of animals for fur, and factory-like farms that cause cows, calves, sheep, pigs, and chickens needless suffering. In the Middle East, members of Hamas, a fundamentalist Muslim organization, believe that Israel should be driven out of existence and that orthodox, Iran-like Islamic states be established throughout the region, indeed, eventually, throughout the entire world. Toward that end, some of their members assassinate Israeli Jews, especially soldiers, and Arabs whom they believe cooperate with Israel. On the other side of the ledger, several Jewish Israeli terrorist groups (for instance, Terror Against Terror and The Fist of Defense) believe that Israel must absorb and incorporate occupied lands once inhabited by the ancient Jews, including Judea, Samaria, and Gaza, and that these lands be "Arab-free." To that end, they have placed bombs on Arab busses, attempted to assassinate mayors of some Arab towns, murdered Arabs, raided at least one Islamic university, and conspired to blow up mosques on the holy site of Temple Mount (Cromer, 1988).

Interest Groups: Insiders versus Outsiders

Although all social movements and social movement organizations are interest groups in that they seek to advance the cause or interests of a specific social group or category, or a cause that a specific group or category deems important, not all interest groups are social movements. This distinction is especially crucial for the study of moral panics and other collective behavior phenomena.

Some interest groups may be referred to as *established lobbies* or *established pressure groups* (Useem and Zald, 1982; Best, 1990, pp. 13–16). They are "insiders" in the political process. They have direct access to policy-makers, legislators, and politicians. They employ a paid professional staff who represent their interests, or the interests of their clients. Their representatives can call a senator, a governor, or the head of a federal or state agency, arrange a meeting or conference, explain their aims, and possibly have some influence on the political process. In addition, they have continual access to the media; a major statement issued by the head of a large, established pressure group or lobby is usually broadcast in the press and often on television news. Examples of established lobbies or pressure groups include the National Rifle Association, the American Medical Association, and the Sierra Club. In effect, established pressure groups are an integrated component of the mainstream political process, the "Fourth Estate," nearly as central as the executive, legislative, and judicial branches of government.

Social movements are somewhat different from established pressure groups. They are, of course, pressure groups, but of a distinct sort. Their activists are "outsiders" in the mainstream political process. They do not have direct access to policy-makers, nor do their statements receive automatic attention in the media. In effect, they have to "try harder." In the absence of being integrated into political and media institutional networks, social movements and movement organizations, for the most part, have only four methods of attracting members, acquiring resources, and achieving some of their goals: violence, protests and demonstrations, gaining access to the media, and direct appeals to the public.

For most social movements, violence is an extremely risky method of achieving movement goals; only a small proportion of activists are willing to engage in it; it usually backfires, and it entails a high likelihood of arrest and imprisonment. Protests are unconventional, unorthodox, and occasionally illegal mass actions against undesirable targets, institutions, organizations, establishments, or symbols. They sometimes achieve movement goals, but at least as often, they alienate the very factions movement activists wish to appeal to. Gaining access to the media usually represents an attempt to appeal to the public directly and thus generate attention for a cause, define a problem or issue in a certain way, recruit new members, and generate funds. This may entail, again, holding a protest or a demonstration, or even initiating a riot, getting arrested, holding a press conference, making a statement challenging the position of a politician or some other mainstream figure, appearing on a talk show or granting an interview for a feature story (Best, 1990, p. 14). Public campaigns – direct appeals to the public – usually take place through the media, but they may also be launched through a mass mailing of movement literature.

Social Movements: Claims and Arguments

All social movements begin with a *premise*; more specifically, they begin with the claim that something is wrong that can and should be remedied. Thus, the claims that movements make fall into two parts: "What's wrong?" and "What is to be done?" As we saw, the conditions that social movements address – "What's wrong?" – may exist and be as serious as they say, may exist but not be as serious as they say, or may not even exist at all. It doesn't matter: in order to attract recruits and donations, motivate activists, gain media attention, and move lawmakers to enact favorable legislation, social movement leaders and publicists must formulate an argument and marshall evidence supporting their position. Claims-making is one of a variety of methods or tools social movements have to help them achieve their goals. It is part of the struggle for the hearts and minds – and consequently, the time and the pocketbooks – of the public, legislators, and the media (Goode, 1992, p. 434).

In other words, social movements are engaged in "the politics of reality" (Goode, 1969), that is using evidence (or supposed evidence) as a means of defining for others how things are and how they ought to be. Convincing others that one's definition of reality is correct – that the condition really is serious and in need of solution – represents a kind of victory for a movement, one milestone along the way to achieving its goals. Definitions of reality are fought over and debated in public forums. Much of the struggle and the give-and-take between social movement representatives and their constituents, their opponents, the public, the media, and legislators entails the attempt to legitimate a certain view of the reality of the condition being addressed. Indeed, even getting others to pay attention to certain previously ignored conditions represents a major victory for a social movement. Another way of saying this is that movements attempt to define their cause as "politically correct" and opposition to their program – or even simple inaction – as politically incorrect, almost unthinkable. Anti-abortion groups refer to abortion as "killing babies," a form of murder; what crime could possibly be worse than murdering babies? Who could possibly be in favor of such monstrous behavior? The animal rights people refer to favoring humans over animals as "speciesism," a sin no less wrong than racism and sexism. Clearly, much social movement activity represents a struggle over what certain actions should be called, how they are to be defined or referred to (Goode, 1992, p. 435).

Arguments put forth by social movements very rarely weigh the pros and cons of both sides in a reasoned, scholarly fashion and come out with the conclusion, "On the one hand . . . but on the other . . ." They nearly always "make a case," much as a trial lawyer does in arguing for or against a defendant in court. Typically, the evidence is presented in a one-sided fashion. Evidence suggesting that the other side might have a point is presented – if it is – as a foil, a device to demolish its claims. Movements are more likely to formulate an argument in black-or-white, either–or terms than in shades of gray. The wrong they struggle against must be seen as an atrocity, not simply a condition that is bad in some respects and not so bad in others. This technique of argumentation is not unique to social movement participants, of course; the opponents of a position taken by a given social movement, likewise, tend to engage in one-sided arguments. Just as the environmental movement is likely to exaggerate the extent of an oil spill, in a like fashion, industry spokespersons are very likely to minimize it. Much of the process of claims-making in social movements is taken up not only with validating the view of one's own group but also discrediting those of one's opponents (Goode, 1992, p. 435).

Extremely rarely the case – although it sometimes happens – are conditions a movement focuses on worse than its activists' claim. With most conditions, nearly all the time, movement participants must make them out to be worse than they are; they tend to focus on the worst aspects of the condition *as if they were typical*. In this sense, the justifications that social movements construct to support their position are similar to gossip, rumor, legends, and paranormal beliefs – that is, they "tell one hell of a good story." In order to grab the observer by the throat, get his or her attention, and insist, *"This condition is important, it is bad, and something must be done about it!,"* it is almost always necessary to lie or at least exaggerate a little. It would be difficult to contest the point that, while some participants in some social movements describe the conditions they wish to change accurately, *taken as a whole*, social movement participants and activists tend to exaggerate their extent and seriousness. To be plain about it, exaggeration is a great deal more effective as a movement strategy than the complex task of literal, point-for-point truth-telling. Movement claims-making makes demands on people's limited time and attention; there are many issues to deal with, and movements must convince potentially interested parties that this particular issue needs dealing with (Goode, 1992, pp. 435–6). This is likely to be especially the case with recycled problems or conditions, which must insinuate themselves into an already-crowded social problems agenda.

For instance, in their attack against pornography, anti-pornography groups focus almost exclusively on violent pornography and pretend not to know, or explicitly deny, that the overwhelming majority of it is non-violent – or they arbitrarily define all non-violent pornography as violent – and ignore or dismiss evidence that suggests that non-violent pornography does not cause or influence men to become violent toward women. To say that a tiny percentage of all pornography depicts violence against women is to elicit a "ho-hum" response from an audience; to say that pornography depicts women being "bound, gagged, sliced up, tortured" (Dworkin, 1982, p. 255) is to stir up a sense of outrage. To say that the evidence suggests that, over the short run, witnessing violent films with sexually explicit content is correlated with men inflicting simulated pain in a laboratory setting, but watching non-violent films probably is not, does not cause many women to run out and enlist in the anti-pornography crusade. In contrast, chanting "Pornography is the theory, rape is the practice" – the slogan of Women Against Pornography – is far more likely to generate that movement-joining fervor (Goode, 1992, p. 436).

Anti-abortionist groups claim that abortion is not simply harmful to the fetus, it is also extremely dangerous to the women who aborts a fetus; after an abortion, women supposedly suffer a serious "syndrome" of "physical or emotional trauma" (Garb, 1989). In contrast to this claim, the evidence is clearcut: a woman is more than 10 times as likely to die in childbirth than as a result of undergoing an abortion, according to statistics gathered by the National Center for Health Statistics. Anti-abortion forces never mention the increased risk of childbirth when discussing the issue of the impact of abortion on a woman's health. They do mention that there is a medical risk when undergoing an abortion; they do not mention that that medical risk is greater for childbirth than abortion. (Of course, in a parallel fashion, the pro-choice forces underplay the fact that abortion always results in death to the fetus – which is, after all, a potential human being.) Bringing in all the facts, in all their complexity, makes strong advocacy of a given cause more difficult (Goode, 1992, p. 436).

Exaggerated and one-sided claims stimulate more outrage, attract more attention, and generate more resources for the cause than assertions that are nearer the literal truth. To an activist, carefully weighing the evidence is tantamount to saying that the condition isn't really terribly serious and isn't much in need of remedy. It is seen as a *betrayal* of the cause. Activists may challenge those who insist on factual correctness by claiming that they are petty, nit-picking, missing the main point – as if facts are little more than a distraction from their goal. Indeed, in terms of movement activity, this is often the case (Goode, 1992, p. 437). Unfortunately for some movements, exaggerated claims can often backfire, generate a reaction that is harmful to movement goals if they prove to be wildly off the mark. This is precisely what happened to the "missing children" movement which at one time claimed that there were some 50,000 child victims of stranger abductions, when more disinterested estimates based on available evidence yielded no more than 300 children who were kidnapped by strangers for more than 24 hours, or who were kidnapped and then harmed by them (Griego and Kilzer, 1985; Gentry, 1988; Best, 1990; Forst and Blomquist, 1991). The exposure of this fabricated, exaggerated, and wildly inaccurate claim dealt a damaging blow to the "missing child" movement (Best, 1990, pp. 49–50; see also Jenkins, 1992, pp. 142–4).*

---

* The most recent study, based on several systematic data sources (a national household survey, a survey of police records, and an analysis of FBI data) estimated that in the United States, in 1988, between 200 and 300 "stereotypical" kidnappings took place, that is, those in which a stranger perpetrator took a child overnight, or a distance of 50 miles or more, or killed or ransomed the child, or demonstrated a desire to keep the child. Some 3,200 to 4,600 children were kidnapped by strangers according to the legal definition of a kidnapping, but these acts lacked all elements of the stereotypical kidnapping – that is, children were "moved, detained, or lured over shorter distances or time periods, usually in the course of other crimes like sexual assault" (Finkelhor, Hotaling, and Sedlak, 1992, p. 238).

As we said above, not only do social movement representatives attempt to establish the validity of certain claims about the seriousness of a given condition, they also engage in *discrediting their opponents*, or individuals or agencies they see or define as their opponents. To many movement activists, it seems obvious and self-evident that their cause is important and just; they simply cannot see why anyone would disagree with their position. There must be an explanation for why others put obstacles in their path. Two readily come to mind: those who do so are either stupid or evil. In an argument with them, this basic fact must be pointed out; bystanders must be made to realize that this is the case. Thus, anti-AIDS activists publicly charge that AIDS workers or commentators are liars and guilty of "murdering" AIDS patients. In a smilar vein, the animal rights lobby accuses fur trappers, ranchers, garment manufacturers, the employees of stores that sell fur garments, and purchasers of furs of being "murderers." Likewise, anti-abortionist or pro-life advocates claim that abortionists, women who undergo abortions, and pro-choice advocates are, once again, guilty of "murder." Of course, murder is simpy the most extreme charge that movement activists can hurl at their opponents; practically all movements charge opponents with a wide range of crimes and outrages in an effort to discredit them, their character, their arguments, their behavior, and their position. One of the most important claims-making activities that social movement participants engage in is *vilification* (Vanderford, 1989; Goode, 1992, p. 438).

Social Movements and Moral Panics

In sum, the social movement – or at least, the incipient or "germinal" social movement or action group – is one manifestation of the moral panic, one means by which the panic is expressed. A threat is perceived; members of the community discuss that threat and organize to deal with it. They make demands on their local, state, and national political representatives; they appeal to the public, usually through the media, to recognize the threat and join in the struggle against it; they confront the threat directly through pickets, demonstrations, boycotts, even acts of violence. Proctor & Gamble, in the 1980s thought by some small-town fundamentalist Christians to contribute 10 percent of their profits to the Church of Satan, received 6,000 calls a month protesting this offensive practice; in the early 1980s, the photographs of missing children appeared on milk cartons all over the country; in the late 1980s, new penalties were proposed for drug offenses by hundreds of politicians from coast to coast. Speeches are made, lectures are given, members of Congress receive letters, calls, and telegrams, government subcommittee meetings and hearings are held, books and articles are published, stores are picketed, products are boycotted, bills and laws are proposed – these and countless other activities are generated and coordinated largely by social movements and other action groups rather than by isolated individuals. It is impossible to understand the moral panic without understanding the role of social movements and movement-like organizations.

It is entirely possible that "germinal" social movements and social movement organizations thrown up in the wake of moral panics represent a somewhat different type of movement than those that arise during less heated periods. It is possible, for instance, that their claims are less likely to be checked by credible evidence, that the vilification of "folk devils" is sharper and less restrained, that matters of technical expediency and material resources are less likely to be considered by activists in attempting to achieve their goals, and so on. In short, it is entirely likely that such movements deserve special and sustained attention.

9

THREE THEORIES OF
MORAL PANICS

Why moral panics? Why do the public, the media, the police, politicians, and/or social action groups in a particular society at a particular time evidence intense concern over a condition, phenomenon, issue, or behavior that, a sober assessment of the evidence reveals, does not merit such level of concern? Two dimensions distinguish the theories that have been advanced to explain moral panics. The first is the *morality versus interests* dimension, and the second is the *elitism versus grassroots* dimension. The first dimension addresses the question of *motive*: do concern and activism coalesce around a given issue because of worldview, ideology, and morality – that is, deeply and genuinely felt attitudes and sentiments – or because actors stand to gain something of value – jobs, power, resources, respectability, wealth, recognition, ownership of a domain of expertise – if others are concerned about that issue? (Can these two motives be separated so cleanly and neatly? Of course not. At the same time, in any given action, one or the other motive is more likely to predominate.)

And second, are *many* actors responsible for the creation and maintenance of the panic, or *few*? Does the panic start from the bottom and progress up, or does it work from the top down, that is, from above? Or does a panic, perhaps, begin in the middle of society's status hierarchy, neither from the elite at the top nor from the undifferentiated general public, but from representatives or leaders of specific middle-level organizations, agencies, groups, institutions, associations, and so on? (Can these levels of power be separated quite so cleanly and neatly? Of course not. At the same time different segments of a society have more versus less power, and individuals and groups can be arranged roughly according to these categories.)

These three "levels" of society – the elite, the middle level, and the general public or grassroots – cannot be defined with a great deal of precision. Rothman (1993, p. 82) argues that position in the elite is based on "occupational position and/or accumulated wealth"; membership is defined by "ownership and/or control of major productive resources." Elites can be institutional or economic elites, that is, elites with powerful positions and elites with great wealth. (Some individuals can have membership in both categories, of course.) According to Dye (1986), in the United States, national institutional elites include: the top executives of the largest corporations, banks, insurance companies, and investment firms which control half of the nation's total corporate assets; occupations of the most powerful government and military positions; executives in the largest media organizations, presidents and ruling executives of the largest and most prestigeous private universities and foundations (Rothman, 1993, pp. 82–3). Overlapping but somewhat separate from the institutional elites are the economic elites – individuals and families who possess "vast economic resources in the form of money, property, and stocks and bonds" (p. 83). The "middle" level of power includes decision-makers in less influential institutional realms: local media, local police, professional organizations, local and even state-wide educational associations, local political parties, small-to-medium-sized businesses, social movements and movement organizations, less-than-mainstream lobby groups, and so on. Members of the middle level of power, of course, also lack significant financial resources. And the general public or grassroots level includes the rest of us, that is, everyone who possesses no significant resources and does not hold decision-making authority even in moderately influential institutional realms.

What happens when we combine these two dimensions, that is, motives based on morality versus status or economic interests and levels of status, power, and influence? Theoretically, we have six possible theories, as table 9.1 shows us.

Of course, table 9.1 is a *theoretical* delineation of the possible theories of moral panics. Not all of the possibilities are empirically likely – nor have they all attracted proponents. Cell 1, where elites generate a moral panic out of deep feelings of ideology and morality – independent of their material or status interests – we suspect, may be regarded as a null or empty cell, essentially empirically nonexistent. To our knowledge, it has attracted no proponents; this may be because, in western society, profoundly influenced as we are by Marxist thinking, it is difficult for

Table 9.1 Theories of moral panics: motives and origin

	Morality/Ideology	Material/Status Interests
	Motives	
Level		
Elite	1	2
Middle	3	4
Public	5	6

us to imagine elite ideology divorced from elite interests. For all practical purposes, when western intellectuals think of elite ideology, it is part and parcel of efforts to justify elite self-interests. It is possible, however, that examples of cell 1 do exist. For instance, in Iran after the revolution of 1979, elites (and the masses) waged a war against western values and behavior for moral, ideological, and religious reasons; in many ways, this war hurt Iran's (and Iran's elite's) material interests. Anti-communist McCarthyite witch-hunts which took place in the 1950s in the United States, which attracted some elite support, may have been more ideological in its focus than material. In our view, cell 1 should not be dismissed out of hand.

Cell 2, of course, is the classic Marxist approach; it would argue that elites "engineer" moral panics so that they will gain some material or status advantage therefrom. According to this model, elites fabricate a panic over a nonexistent or trivial threat – and one about which they themselves feel little concern – in order to gain something of value or divert attention away from issues that, if addressed, would threaten their own private interests. We will look at the "elite-engineered" model or theory of moral panics momentarily.

Advocates of arguments falling into cell 3 argue that occupants of the middle-status levels of the society – the police, professional organizations, the media, and so on – act independent of elites to either express or maximize their own morality or ideology; proponents of arguments falling into cell 4 argue that occupants of the same status levels primarily seek material or status advantage. As we shall see shortly, while these two cells can be separated in principle, in real life it is a bit more difficult to distinguish them. The interest-group model sees material and/or status interests as crucial, but argues that moral panics originate neither from the top nor the bottom, but somewhere in society's middle rungs – professional associations, the police, the media, religious groups, educational organizations: middle-level associations, organizations, groups, and institutions of every description. The interest-group model does not see society as being controlled from the top down; interest groups often have interests that contradict those of elites, and the former often, perhaps even usually, initiate crusades, panics, and campaigns in the face of elite opposition or indifference. In the interest group model, ideological and moral motives tend be downplayed or ignored because they are taken for granted, while material and status interests will be focused on as crucial because they may not be quite so obvious or commonsensical.

Cell 5, usually referred to as the "grassroots" model, argues that moral panics are generated from the "bottom up," and, concomitantly, that morality and ideology are dominant motives for activists and concerned citizens. To the grassroots theorist, moral panics are more or less spontaneous eruptions of fear and concern on the part of a large number of people about a given threat or putative threat. To our knowledge, cell 6, the argument that the mass of the public generates moral panics primarily out of material or status considerations, does not have any advocates.

These models may not be quite so mutually exclusive or contradictory as appears at first glance. One model may explain a given moral panic best, while another may be more adequate in explaining a different one. Or two different theories may explain different aspects of the same panic. For instance, Ben-Yehuda (1980, 1985, 1986, 1990a, and chapter 10 and 11 in this book) argues that the content or target of the Israeli drug panic of 1982 is best addressed by the dimension of morality, while the timing of the panic is addressed by the dimension of interests. The morality and interests dimensions can be used in conjunction to gain a fuller understanding of moral panics. It is altogether possible that, in the same panic, different actors, participants, or segments in the drama are moved by different motives – that is, morality as opposed to material or status interests. The different points along the elitism–grassroots dimension, likewise, may be more appropriate for some panics than others, more appropriate for some aspects of moral panics than others. It seems difficult to avoid an eclectic approach in the study of moral panics.

The Grassroots Model

The grassroots model argues that panics originate with the general public; the concern about a particular threat is a widespread, genuinely felt – if perhaps mistaken – concern. The expressions of concern in other sectors – in the media, among politicians, political action groups, and law enforcement – are an *expression* or *manifestation* of more widespread concern. The actions of no special group or sector is necessary to bring about the widespread concern over a given issue; this concern arises more or less spontaneously, although it sometimes requires being assisted, guided, triggered, or catalyzed. Thus, if politicians or the media seem to originate or "stir up" concern about a given issue, in reality, there must have been a general latent fear or concern about that issue to begin with. Of course, the general public is inevitably influenced by media coverage of a given condition – both in terms of extent and angle or slant – but, the grassroots advocate would argue, two issues can be presented in the same way by the media, and one will touch a nerve, and feed a panic, while the other will be met by audience indifference. Politicians and the media cannot fabricate concern where none existed initially. (In some more extreme, now no longer held, elitist formulations, public opinion, as most of the field recognizes it, did not exist apart from views elites successfully socialized the masses to accept. If the masses initiate a given action independent of the elite, they may act out of "false consciousness" and on behalf of elite interests. In short, the masses "don't know what's best for them.") In the overt expression of the moral panic, a kind of diffuse anxiety or strain simply explodes at the appropriate time; the panic is simply the outward manifestation of what already existed in less overt form. Politicians give speeches and propose laws they already know will appeal to their constituencies, whose views they have already sounded out; the media broadcast and print stories their representatives know the watching or viewing public is likely to find interesting – and, about certain topics, troubling. Action groups are launched and are successful to the extent that their constituency – that is, much of the general public – is distressed about a given issue that demands correcting. What is central to the grassroots theorist – what explains the outbreak or existence of the moral panic – is deeply felt attitudes and beliefs on the part of a broad sector of the society that a given phenomenon is a real and present threat to their values, their safety, or even their very existence.

For instance, it is difficult to imagine what elite, movement, or organizational interests were involved in the brief panic that broke out in Orléans, France, over the alleged "sex slave" abductions that were rumored about in 1969. The rumor was not initiated by local upper- or middle-level groups, was not endorsed by any local influentials, and it was not in their interests to have anyone believe it. It was entirely a spontaneous, word-of-mouth, grassroots phenomenon (Morin, 1971). The Salem witchcraft trials of the 1600s in Massachussetts have been cited as an example of a broadly based panic generated by widespread, grassroots sentiment, fear, and concern over the threat of witches. In cases such as accusations of witchcraft, the "deviant individual violates rules of conduct which the community holds in high respect; when these people come together to express their outrage over the offense and to bear witness against the offender, they develop a tighter bond of solidarity than existed earlier" (Erikson, 1966, p. 4). What earthly interests could the executives and millionaire shareholders of Proctor & Gamble – or leaders of any conceivable interest group – have had in propagating the rumor that P&G contributed 10 percent of its profits to the Church of Satan? The fact is, this rumor supported a worldview held among a certain segment of small-town fundamentalist Christians and was launched and maintained on a grassroots, populist basis.

One of the most clearcut examples of the power of populism in fueling a grassroots panic is the contemporary rumor among African-Americans – almost certainly false – that executives of major corporations are poisoning the black population by distributing heroin and crack cocaine in their communities. As Turner points out (1993), these and other conspiracy fears have a solid and valid historical basis: in the past and even currently, whites *have* harmed blacks by means of a wide variety of actions, institutions, schemes, and conspiracies. Belief in this *particular* conspiracy – absurd on the face of it – is actually contrary to the interests of the white power structure and thus is unlikely to have been elite-engineered; it emanated from the street, a genuinely grass-roots phenomenon.

Federal Drug Legislation, 1986 and 1988

In 1986 and 1988, the United States Congress passed omnibus drug legislation; the first of these represented the first effort by Congress to enact a major anti-drug law in two decades. A variety of explanations have been offered to explain why, at this particular time, federal legis-lators felt compelled to enact broader and stiffer laws against drug possession and sale. (For some representative views, see Goode, 1993, pp. 51–3.) Stolz (1990) puts forth a grassroots dynamic for the concern expressed by the 1986 and 1988 anti-drug legislation. She argues that the evidence suggests that the late 1980s anti-drug congressional policy-making may have been "a response to concerns of the general public, not just those of interest groups [or elites]." Congress reacted "as an institution to public concerns, not just as individuals responding to a threat to their own reelection" (p. 21). The 1986 and 1988 drug legislation was addressed to three "symbolic components of criminal law – reassurance, moral education, and model for the states"; it expressed "the need to reassure the public that the nation's drug problem was under control, to communicate an anti-drug message to the law abiding, and to provide model laws and programs for the states." It was these factors, and not machinations of interests groups or elites seeking to further their own material or status interests, that brought about the initiation and enactment of the 1986 and 1988 anti-drug legislation (Stolz, 1990, p. 2).

Crime

In the moral panic, the public's fears may be mistaken or exaggerated, but they are real, they do not have to be "engineered" or "orches-trated" by powerful agencies, institutions, bodies, or classes such as the media, the legislature, or the power structure. For instance, during times of stress and crisis, the public translates its anxiety into an irrational fear of being victimized by street crime, and this, in turn, leads the public to accept, even demand, punitive approaches to the crime problem (Scheingold, 1984, 1991). The actions of legislators in proposing and enacting legislation is a more or less straightforward response to public demands and fears. A "Lock 'em up and throw away the key" solution to the crime problem, the grassroots perspective would argue, emanates from the public, not from the media, law-makers, or the members of the political and economic elite. Punitive policies reflect the public's desire for scapegoats who are seen as responsible for society's problems, against whom anger, resentment, and anxiety can be directed. During times of stress, such policies "express a collective yearning" for retribution (Scheingold, 1991, p. 6).

Populism

Panics often entail populist sentiment. The threat that generates concern may be seen as emanating from powerful, high-status strata; their very power and status imparts a certain ominous quality to their capacity to harm common, honest, hardworking folk. Conspiracies hatched at the upper reaches of society comprise some of the richest seedbeds of our hostile and fearful rumors. Indeed – or so the elite conspiracy goes – elites are so powerful that they are able to manipulate and control the very content of the rumors themselves (Goode, 1992, p. 294). On many issues, the rank-and-file members of western society mistrust the rich and the powerful, and harbor suspicions that they are likely to engage in evil actions that threaten the rest of us so that they may line their own pockets. A contemporary or urban legend widely narrated and believed in poor minority communities in the late 1980s and early 1990s has it that American corporations are distributing narcotics in the ghettos to destroy African-Americans. This tale works only because its villains are rich and powerful (and white). The plot of a popular film released during the summer of 1993, *Hard Target*, had the hero, kick-boxing champion Jean-Claude Van Damme, track down and eliminate a ring of wealthy thrillseekers who pay to hunt and kill poor, homeless men for sport. Audiences find the movie entertaining specifically because of their hostile feelings toward the rich; the plot would not be as effective if the killers were poor or working class.

In the British moral panics over threatened women and children that broke out in the 1970s and 1980s, both liberals and conservatives felt it was possible that "the crimes of the upper classes would be concealed by a cover-up by an ubiquitous 'old-boy network'" (Jenkins, 1992, p. 77). The revelations during those same decades that a number of individuals with elite backgrounds and positions and Oxford–Cambridge educations were Soviet spies – and homosexuals – generated substantial hostile populist sentiment. These scandals "helped condition public attitudes to the image of upper-class perverts whose activities were concealed by their colleagues. This was a powerful weapon in populist rhetoric against the entrenched ruling elite. Politicians were repeatedly involved in scandals involving homosexuality, pedophilia, or frequenting . . . male prostitutes" (p. 78). "High society" scandals are popular in part because they tell the comon man and woman that the high and mighty aren't quite so "high" or "mighty," that even they have feet of clay. Moreover, such scandals show the public that, in spite of all the cover-ups of the unsavory doings of the respectable, occasionally, justice and retribution triumph. Populist sentment is crystallized in the words of one police officer, who, during a particular British scandal involving underage male prostitutes, said: "people always want their paedophiles to be judges or politicians" (p. 78).

Nuclear Energy and Other Dreadful Threats

A good example of the grassroots perspective toward moral panics (and other expressions of widespread concern) may be found in the extremely hostile and widespread attitudes – and actions – of much of the American public toward nuclear power. Since the Three Mile Island accident in 1979 (the news of which touched off the voluntary evacuation of hundreds of thousands of local residents, and yet, in which, in fact, no one outside the plant was injured), and especially the Chernobyl catastrophe of 1986 (which has already caused thousands, and may eventually cause as many as hundreds of thousands, of premature deaths), the building of new nuclear facilities in the United States has been brought to a complete standstill, and opposition to the dumping of nuclear waste has stymied the building of facilities for this purpose.

The cause of the nuclear standstill, grassroots theorists argue, is the fear on the part of the American public of the danger of nuclear energy. It cannot stem from the efforts of special interests or elites – principally, the nuclear power industry and the United States government – to stir up opposition to nuclear energy. Quite to the contrary, it is to the advantage of powerful special interests and elites to provide all manner of assistance in promoting the nuclear power industry. American energy needs cannot be met by domestic production, and "dependence on foreign oil" has become something of a negative watchword in encouraging alternate energy sources. But not nuclear energy; any politician who supported the interests of the nuclear industry against the wishes of his or her constituency would face an uphill battle in getting reelected. Clearly, this concern is grassroots – not interest group or elite – generated.

According to some experts, this fear is groundless and irrational, and, in this sense, is a manifestation of a moral panic. (Concern over nuclear energy is *not* a moral panic in most of the ways we have defined it – for instance, there is no "folk devil" and no sudden increase in concern. Only for the single dimension of disproprotionality between the harm or objective threat posed by nuclear power, as agreed upon by experts, versus those of other, less subjectively troubling conditions, does nuclear energy qualify.) Three decision research experts argue that feasible solutions to disposing of nuclear waste have met "overwhelming political opposition." The reason: "Public perception of the risks of a nuclear waste repository as immense and unacceptable stands in stark contrast to the prevailing view of the technical community, which believes that nuclear wastes can be stored safely in deep, underground islation." Powerful imagery – dread, revulsion and anger – "that is so strong and so impervious to influence from the pronouncements of technical experts must have potent origins" (Slovic, Layman, and Flynn, 1991, pp. 7, 11). Why this exaggerated concern, this groundless, seemingly irrational fear, this panic?

Perrow (1984, pp. 324–28) and Erikson (1990) locate this panic – this huge and almost unique discrepancy between what the experts say and how the public feels – to a factor they refer to as *dread*. It turn out that experts and the public calculate risk of harm in a drastically different fashion. Experts make use of what Perrow refers to as "absolute rationality"; the public uses "social rationality" (p. 325). The experts' calculation is made in a straightforward, rationalistic way: what is the statistical likelihood that certain harmful outcomes will occur, and how harmful are these outcomes? For instance, what are the odds of dying while traveling from New York City to Chicago by car? By plane? Although the statistical chance of dying in an automobile accident on the trip are considerably greater than the odds of experiencing death in an airline accident, far more people fear the latter than the former. The expert would find the public's fear misguided and irrational; after all, a death is a death, and if more deaths are produced by driving, on a mile-for-mile, passenger-for-passenger basis, then the fear of flying – a safer mode of transportation – more simply makes no sense. But if factors other than and in addition to the statistical likelihood of harmful outcomes enter the picture, we understand why certain threats are feared more than others. The public fears threats to the extent that they are seen as involuntary, uncontrollable, unknown, unfamiliar, catastrophic, certain to be fatal, and delayed in their manifestation. Accidents as a result of flying in – contrast to those in a car – though less likely to occur, are seen as involuntary and uncontrollable (the pilot, not the passenger, flies the plane, and, moreover, severe weather conditions can limit even the pilot's control), unknown and less familiar, catastrophic (many more people are likely to die), and are much more likely to be fatal when they do occur. Only in terms of latent, long-term, or delayed manifestations of harm are these two modes of transportation similar. It is not solely the chance of dying in an accident that generates fear of flying; it is the nature and mode of death that influences this dread.

Nuclear power stands at the extreme end of all of these undesirable dimensions of fear. Its risks are seen as "involuntary, delayed, unknown, uncontrollable, unfamiliar, catastrophic, dreaded and fatal" (Perrow, 1984, p. 325). Thus, aspects of risk not judged to be crucial in the experts' evaluations loom extremely large in the public's assessment. Radiation and other technological toxics "contaminate rather than merely damage; they pollute, befoul and taint rather than just create wreckage; they penetrate human tissue indirectly rather than wound the surface by assaults of a more straightforward kind" (Erikson, 1990, p. 120). Nuclear accidents "elicit an uncanny fear in us." People find radiation and other toxic substances significantly more threatening than most natural hazards and nontoxic technological hazards; they *dread* toxic substances far more intensely (p. 120). Instead of assessing danger by calculating odds the way experts do, perhaps we should, Erikson argues, "understand radioactive and other toxic substances as naturally loathsome, inherently insidious – horrors . . . that draw on something deeper in the human mind." Toxic emergencies "really are different" from more routine accidents, such as car crashes; "their capacity to induce a lasting sense of dread is a unique – and legitimate – property" (p. 121).

Why do toxic emergencies create so much alarm? Erikson asks. They are "unbounded," he answers; "they have no frame" (p. 121). Classic disasters, such as tornados or hurricanes, have a beginning, a middle, and end. An alarm is sounded, destruction follows, and, finally, the destruction ends, and then the "all clear" signal is sounded. "Toxic disasters, however, violate all the rules of plot"; they "never end. Invisible contaminants remain a part of the surroundings – absorbed into the grain of the landscape, the tissues of the body, and, worst of all, into the genetic material of the survivors." That "all clear" signal is never sounded (p. 121). Radiation and other toxic poisons "are without form. You cannot apprehend them through the unaided senses; you cannot taste, touch smell, or see them. That makes them ghostlike and terrifying . . . They slink in without warning . . . and begin their deadly work from within – the very embodiment, it would seem, of stealth and treachery" (p. 122).

Fear of radiation is not engineered by elites or a product of the activism of members of interest groups. It is not "some exotic form of hysteria that will subside once the media stops fanning the flames and calm returns to public discourse" (Erikson, 1990, p. 125). It stems from deep, primordial feelings that are relatively impervious to manipulations and machinations from above. It is a genuine grassroots phenomenon.

In 1993, in an unpublished internal police report based on a nationally representative survey of hundreds of Israeli citizens, the number one police problem in Israel was seen to be – not terrorism, not crime, not car accidents, not the threat of war, but – *drug abuse*. The body count from drug abuse is low; the body count from at least a dozen other sources is higher. Why drug abuse?

It is possible that the concept of dread helps explain some aspects of moral panics that focus on drug abuse. Dread does not explain the *timing* of drug panics, of course, but it does address why so many panics center on the use of illicit psychoactive substances. The control that drugs seem to have over the user is often seen as diabolical and insidious, one that creeps into the user's mind and body and "takes over"; the drug is attributed with a kind of "black magic" power that dominates and overwhelms the user. The fact that this stereotype is inaccurate – most drug users control their consumption of psychoactive substances, and only a minority become dependent to the point of completely lacking control – is not the point. What counts here is the image, the sterotype, the most visible user, the user that is "available" to the mind of the general public – that is, the out-of-control addict. To the non-using majority, dependence on drugs most decidedly appears to be involuntary, uncontrollable, unknown, unfamiliar, catastrophic, often fatal, and delayed in its manifestation (Perrow, 1984, pp. 324–8). While not nearly so dreaded as nuclear contamination, drug abuse is believed to exert a power that, at the very least, manifests certain parallels with other insidious, dreadful forces that embody "stealth and treachery," that invade, contaminate, pollute, corrupt, taint, befoul, "penetrate human tissue," and "never end," never quite seem to go away. It would be facile of us to dismiss these fears, grounded as they are in some very real, primal emotions. Certainly fear of and concern about LSD in the 1960s – however misplaced or uninformed it seems today, given what we now know about the drug's effects – was based, in part, on the dread of a foreign substance entering our bodies and "taking over" our minds and, moreover, causing a silent genetic catastrophe among uncountable descendants. Certainly the media had an independent interest in advancing the LSD panic – it was a riveting and terrifying story which sold magazines, newspapers and air time – but it was the public who *found* the study riveting and terrifying in the first place.

Not all – or even most – intense public fears or concerns follow the same pattern. What seems highly likely is that moral panics are not explicable by means of a single model. Perhaps we need to specify the nature of the panic before we agree on a theory to explain it. What seems clear is that we cannot dismiss the grassroots model out of hand. *Some* intense and seemingly exaggerated fears do arise more or less spontaneously; the flames of others are fanned with outside assistance; and with still others, the manifestations of the panic lie largely outside the sphere of public reactions.

The Elite-engineered Model

The theory that moral panics are elite-engineered argues that an elite group deliberately and consciously undertakes a campaign to generate and sustain concern, fear, and panic on the part of the public over an issue that they recognize not to be terribly harmful to the society as a whole. Typically, this campaign is intended to divert attention away from the real problems in the society, whose solution would threaten or undermine the interests of the elite. Clearly, such a theory is based on the view that elites have immense power over the other members of the society – they dominate the media, determine the content of legislation and the direction of law enforcement, and control much of the resources on which action groups and social movements depend. For example, Chambliss and Mankoff (1976, pp. 15–16) critique Erikson's grassroots analysis of the Salem witch trials, aguing that crime and the repression of crime play an important role in "enabling the ruling stratum to maintain its privileged position." According to Gerassi (1966), the witch-hunt against homosexuals in Boise, Idaho, in 1955 and 1956 was specifically launched by members of the conservative local elite on behalf of elite interests – to discredit a moderate, reformist municipal administration; on the other hand, the scandal did enjoy widespread support from the man and woman on the street. Certainly President Ronald Reagan's "drug war" speeches in 1986 prepared the way for the late 1980s American drug panic, including strong public support for his actions. (On the other hand, Richard Nixon delivered similar speeches in the early 1970s, without the same response from the public.) Clearly, the campaign against Canudos in Brazil between 1893 and 1897 was initiated at the highest levels of power and influence – major landowners, the hierarchy of the Catholic church, powerful politicians, the army; once again, however, much of the Brazilian public (largely the urban, middle-class, well-educated segments) supported the campaign.

Hall et al. (1978) have advanced what is probably the most well-known analysis illustrating the elite-engineered theory of moral panics. They argue that mugging in the early 1970s in Great Britain qualifies as a moral panic. Fear and concern over street crime increased at a time when its actual incidence was not rising. Reactions by the courts to mugging offenses, by the media to muggings, and by the public to the news of muggings, "was all out of proportion to any level of actual threat" posed by these muggings (p. 29). Why did British society react to mugging in the extreme way it did? they ask. Why the public outrage, the extremely harsh sentences in the courts, the mobilization of the police against real and supposedly potential muggers, the law-and-order solutions offered by experts and commentators, the harsh glare of the media? Why the moral panic over mugging? What is the panic *really* about? "What forces stand to benefit from it? What role has the state played in its construction? What real fears and anxieties is it mobilising?" (p. viii). The reaction was, in large part, "not to the actual threat," but "a reaction by the control agencies and the media to the *perceived* or *symbolic* threat to society – what the 'mugging' label *represented*" (p. 29).

We have already encountered the critique offered by Waddington (1987), who demonstrates that the criterion of disproportionality does not apply to mugging or, more generally, street crime. Contrary to what Hall et al. claim, Waddington says, the data show that street crime actually *did* increase between the 1960s and the early 1970s. Whether Wadington or Hall et al. are right about the increase in street crime during this period is not the issue here; it is the nature of Hall et al.'s, argument that is crucial, not its validity.

In the moral panic, the "wrong things" are raised into "sensational focus, hiding and mystifying the deeper causes" (Hall et al., 1978, p. vii); moral panics, Hall et al. argue, are about matters *other than* the seeming focus. The themes of the panic "function as a mechanism for the construction" of a definition of things that serve the interests of the powerful (p. viii). In the case of the early 1970s panic over street crime, it served to legitimate a law-and-order criminal enforcement program and to divert attention away from the growing economic recession, which was causing a "crisis" in British capitalism. Britain was facing a "crisis in profitability"; profits were falling, Britain's share in the world exports of manufactured goods dropped, her level of investment and rate of economic investment remained low, and inflation shot up to unacceptable levels (p. 263). During such crises, Hall et al. argue, the capitalist state is forced to shed its facade of neutrality and independence from special interests (p. 217) and assume "total social authority . . . over the subordinate classes" in such a way that "it shapes the whole direction of social life in its image" (p. 216). Domination not only seems to be "universal" and "legitimate," but exploitation must seem to disappear from view (p. 216). Such is an "exceptional moment" in capitalist society, the coming of "iron times," where "an authoritarian consensus" is called for (p. 217). When capitalism is in crisis, extraordinary times are called for; during such times, a moral panic may be hoked up to divert attention from that crisis. In Britain in the 1970s, mugging was just the issue to generate a moral panic and come to the rescue of an ailing capitalist system.

At several points, Hall et al. (1978, pp. 57, 59, 136, 176, 322 and others) insist that they are not presenting a "conspiratorial" interpretation of these events. Rather than being part of a conspiracy, Hall et al. argue, the ruling elite *orchestrates hegemony*, that is, manages to convince the rest of the society – the press, the general public, the courts, law enforcement – that the real enemy is not the crisis in British capitalism but the criminal and the lax way he has been dealt with in the past.

How is this sleight of hand accomplished? The media are one of the major means by which a moral panic is transmitted and sustained. How do the media come to serve the interests of the capitalist class during a moral panic? Without being in the pay of the powerful, Hall et al. write, "the media come, in fact . . . to *reproduce the definitions of the powerful*" (p. 57); they "faithfully and impartially . . . reproduce symbolically the existing structure of power in society's institutional order" (p. 58). How do the media do this? News media accept prevailing definitions of who is in authority, who is an authority – they reflect Becker's "hierarchy of credibility" (1967); the primary definers of reality are precisely the rich and the powerful, or those in their employ. The media over-access individuals " in powerful and privileged positions" (p. 58). The elite frames an issue; all other interpretations of reality must take their cue from, and argue against, elite formulations. By accepting a neutral and value-free stance, ironically, the media come to reproduce dominant definitions – those that serve the interests of the capitalist class. The media take their cue from the elite: Mugging is newsworthy, it is a crime on which media attention should be focused, it is a crime that hurts all sectors of British society, it is becoming increasingly common, it has reached epidemic and crisis proportions, and the solution is a "law-and-order society," in which the police must crack down on the perpetrators. In this – indirect – way, the news media serve the interests of the British capitalist class. They contribute, in their way, to the "control culture" so desperately needed by the elite during this period of crisis.

Even public opinion does not exist as an entity separate from and independent of dominant, elite interests. What most scholars and researchers refer to as public opinion is a creature that has been shaped by multiple elite interest-defining layers and processes. When a new issue is discussed among intimate networks of friends and acquaintances, opinion is informal, disorganized, shaped by "common-sense views and received wisdom" (p. 135). However, opinion does not remain on this informal, disorganized level for very long. If the issue is deemed important enough, "the media appropriate it" (p. 135). At which point: "Local communication channels are swiftly and selectively integrated into more public channels"; public opinion has been crystalized, "raised to a more formal and public level by the networks of the mass media . . . The more . . . an issue passes into the public domain, via the media, the more it is structured by . . . dominant ideologies" (p. 136). Public opinion, far from being spontaneous or an expression of popular views, is "structured in dominance" (p. 136).

The law, too – and its enforcers and interpreters, legislatures, the police and the courts – serves the interests of the capitalist class. The state, among other things, a legislative body, "performs its work on behalf of the capitalist system" (p. 208). The law "preserves public order"; "it frequently secures, in moments of open class confrontation, just that stability and cohesion without which the steady reproduction of capital and the unfolding of capitalist relations would be a far more hazardous and unpredictable affair" (p. 208). "The law remains one of the central coercive institutions of the capitalist state" (p. 177). But notice: the law, the police, the courts, did not conjure mugging and street crime up out of thin air. "'Mugging' was not produced, 'full blown' from the head of the control culture; it is not simply a ruling-class conspiracy" (p. 182). Rather, the focus of attention on mugging in Britain in the 1970s – all out of proportion to its concrete threat – the level of sensitization to, and mobilization against, street crime, "the scale of the measures taken to prevent and contain it" (p. 184), are what have to be explained. And, as with the media, the explaination lies in the long-range and immediate needs of the capitalist class. Over the long run, "the law will be an instrument of class domination" (p. 196). Within the immediate context of British capitalism in the early 1970s, the law, the police, and the courts reflect the interests of the capitalist class. The law-and-order campaign, using mugging as a pretext and generating societal moral panic, "had the overwhelming single consequence of legitimating the recourse to the law, to constraint and statutory power, as the *main*, indeed the only, effective means left of defending hegemony . . . It toned up and groomed the society for the extensive exercise of the repressive side of state power" (p. 278).

In short, the moral panic over mugging in Britain circa 1970–3 was *engineered* or *orchestrated* by the elite, by the capitalist class – with the more or less unwitting complicity of its allies, the media, the legislature, the police, and the courts. It did not originate with the masses – indeed, it is contrary to the interests of the masses – nor with specific middle-level interest-group representatives. And the moral panic is not about morality or ideology as such – that is, morality is not primarily what the panic is "about." Rather, it is a means by which the powerful protect their interests, primarily their economic interests. Hall et al.'s analysis of the moral panic over mugging is a classic example of the *elite-engineered* theory.

Interest-group Theory

By far, the most common approach to moral panics has been from an interest-group perspective. As we saw, Howard Becker showed us that rule creators and moral entrepreneurs launch crusades – which occasionally turn into panics – to make sure that certain rules take hold and are enforced (1963, pp. 147–63). Not all or even most of the interest-group analyses have been antagonistic to the grassroots morality argument. Indeed, once attention is focused on a particular issue *by* interest groups, broad segments of the public – the grassroots – may become seized by its urgency. Most interest-group analyses, however, *have* contradicted the elite-engineered approach, arguing that the exercise of power in the creation and maintenance of moral panics is more likely to emanate from the middle rungs of the power and status hierarchy than at the elite stratum. In the interest-group perspective, as we saw, professional associations, police departments, the media, religious groups, educational organizations, may have an *independent* stake in bringing an issue to the fore – focusing media attention on it or transforming the slant of news stories covering it, alerting legislators, demanding stricter law enforcement, instituting new educational curricula, and so on. This interest may contradict or be entirely irrelevant to elite interests. By saying that interest groups have an independent role in generating and sustaining moral panics, we are saying that they are, themselves, active movers and shakers – that elites do not necessarily dictate the content, direction, or timing of panics.

The central question asked by the interest-group approach is: *cui bono?* That is, for whose benefit? Who profits? Who wins out if a given issue is recognized as threatening to the society? To whose advantage is a widespread panic about a given behavior? Who stands to gain?

Material and ideological/moral gains have traditionally been separated; presumably, they represent two entirely separate motivations. Interest-group politics are usually thought of as cynical, self-serving, devoid of sincere belief. In real life, such a separation is not always easy to make. Interest-group activists may sincerely *believe* that their efforts will advance a noble cause – one in which they sincerely believe. (And one, it might be said, which will also help advance their status, power, and material resources.) Advancing a moral and ideological cause *almost inevitably* entails advancing the status (and often also the material interests) of the group who believes in it, and advancing the status and material interests of a group *may* simultaneously advance its morality and ideology.

In the United States in 1986, politicians helped stir up a panic over drug abuse, in part to get rerelected (Jensen, Gerber, and Babcock, 1991) – but many of them took their cue from their constituency, as we saw, and most sincerely *believed* that drug abuse was one of the nation's most serious problems (Stolz, 1990). The police in Phoenix, Arizona, in the late 1970s and early 1980s stirred up a moral panic over Chicano youth gangs to "acquire federal funding of a specialized unit" (Zatz, 1987, p. 129), but most police officers working in urban areas sincerely believe that crime in the minority community, especially among youth, is one of their top priorities. Prohibition has been analyzed as a struggle of a status group to regain lost prestige and respect (Gusfield, 1963), but no one questions their sincere wish to rid the country of the evils of drink.

Jenkins shows that the satanic ritual abuse panic that flared up in Britain in the late 1980s "offered ideological confirmation of the limitations of liberal theology. Since the 1960s, the dominant factions in British churches has emphasized social and political activism with a left/liberal slant . . . For Evangelicals and Charismatics, this was a lethal distraction from the crucial issues of personal holiness and spiritual warfare. During the 1980s, the point was reasserted by a new focus on black magic cults, ancestral demons, and ritual abusers" (Jenkins, 1992, p. 204). Not surprisingly, fundamentalist, evangelical, and charismatic Christian organizations have been at the forefront of the British (and American) satanic ritual abuse panic from its very inception. In this case, religious conservatives are arguing a certain definition of reality – that satanism is alive and well in contemporary society and doing his evil deeds – which advances *both* their material and ideological interests.

In Britain in the 1980s, social workers stood to gain from the panic both in terms of status and as a result of an increase in public funds for social welfare services. "A child abuse crisis . . . led to preceptions of a major problem requiring the urgent allocation of new resources: A larger and more specialized child protection establishment would mean more investigation and detection, and thus more concern. This spiral effect goes far toward explaining the overall growth [of the number of social workers in Britain] during the decade [of the 1980s]" (Jenkins, 1992, p. 201). Public opinion polls have shown social work to be at or near the bottom among all professions in prestige. "The only way to reaffirm the value of the profession was to show that social workers were dealing with truly menacing problems, which they were uniquely qualified to investigate and combat. Exposing a vast and unsuspected prevalence of child abuse thus fulfilled both ideological and professional needs, and fully justified the need for specialized social service agencies" (p. 202).

We are arguing that the theoretical separation between interests and morality is difficult to make in practice. Perhaps, rather than picturing these two motives as contradictory, it is better to see both as operative, but, in a given moral panic, one as more influential than the other. Of course, both cynicism and moralism come in degrees, and interest-group activists need not *necessarily* display this mix of motives. Some activists may be more or less *entirely* self-serving. Enough cynics cloak their self-interested motives in pious proclamations for us to be suspicious about the purity of their actions. At the same time, we need not be automatically suspicious about the motives of actors who, while advancing an ideological or moral cause, also advance their own group's material or status interests. After all, the two are very often found in the same package.

Conclusions

Can we draw any conclusions about the origins of moral panics aside from the trite, unsatisfying, and almost tautologically true platitude that different theories apply best to different moral panics? Almost certainly some latent fear or stress must pre-exist in the general public – or segments of the public – for a widespread panic to occur. Concern over a nonexistent or relatively trivial threat cannot be fabricated out of whole cloth by a cynical elite or by self-serving representatives of one or another interest group. Unlike the criminal law, which need not necessarily express the ideology or views of major segments of the public (see chapter 5), moral panics necessitate the concerns of segments of the society. It is almost inconceivable that they could be foisted off on the public, that the public becomes intensely concerned about a supposed threat that, in the absence of these machinations, they would otherwise ignore. The grassroots approach, therefore, can be thought of as calling attention to a *dimension* or *factor* – rather than offering a competing or independent explanation – that plays a central role in the moral panic.

At the same time, the grassroots model must inevitably be supplemented with another explanation; it cannot be regarded as complete. While widespread stress or latent public fears almost necessarily pre-exist moral panics, they do not explain how and why they *find expression* at a particular time. These fears must be articulated; they must be focused, brought to public attention, given a specific outlet. And this almost always entails some form of organization and leadership. Although large numbers of people may spontaneously feel fear or dread about a given agent or threat, this fear is sharpened, broadened, articulated, and publicily expressed by organized, movement-like activity launched by middle-level interest groups.

During a moral panic letters are written to the editors of local newspapers *not* with unfocused, idiocyncratic messages, but in large numbers, with consistent themes. Editors become convinced that their newspapers and magazines should publish articles about a given fearful subject not *simply* because many readers have expressed concern about it. Protests are held, *not* as a result of a spontaneous uprising of independent souls, but because these souls are mobilized through social movement organizations. Lectures, seminars, and talks are given – and attended – in large numbers not *solely* because, independently and separately, the grassroots is concerned about a given threat which is the subject of these talks. School boards are pressured – and filled because of a given issue not *simply* because large numbers of individuals feel a certain way about the curriculum. Public opinion polls reflect dominant fears and concerns not *solely* because each household has, on its own, decided that certain issues are scary and threatening. These various modes of expression coalesce around a particular theme or threatening agent at a particular time in part because activists who feel strongly about the nature of that threat are working to bring it to widespread attention and are activating a variety of avenues to do so. Thus, while the grassroots model cannot be dismissed out of hand, it does not *explain* moral panics. Rather, it points to a crucial *factor* in the dynamics of moral panics, in the absence of which they would not occur. All activists have to consider the "what if we threw a party and nobody came?" problem: all the organized activity in the world cannot create concern where none exists. At the same time, concern needs an appropriate outlet to express itself in a moral panic, and for that, interest-group formation and activity are central.

In the dimension stretching from morality and material and/or status interests, likewise, we do not picture mutually exclusive explanations. Morality provides a context; it provides an issue around which a panic coalesces, the content of the panic. It loads the gun, so to speak. Interests help explain the timing of moral panics: they act as a kind of triggering device. As we shall see in chapters 11 and 12, fear of drugs is both a widespread, grassroots phenomenon and is widely seen as a moral issue – but why Israel in 1982, why the United States in the late 1980s? As we'll see, some factions stood to gain by exploiting the issue at that time. (The sudden burst of fear of LSD in the 1960s may have been a creature of the drug's novelty, the nature of its apparent threat, and the fabulous media circus afforded by its previously nonexistent widespread use. And, of course, American society's experience with past drug panics.) As we shall see in chapter 10, witches were genuinely feared by the mass of the population in Renaissance Europe; to them, the threat of witches was very real, a genuinely moral issue. But why did the persecution of witches explode with such ferocity in the 1400s? Again, the specific interests of the Dominican order and the inquisitional machinery, already in place, help us understand the timing of the witch craze.

Once again, our argument goes beyond the claim that different models are helpful in explaining different moral panics. It is that the grassroots provide fuel or raw material for a moral panic, organizational activists provide focus, intensity, and direction; and it is that issues of morality provide the *content* of moral panics and interests provide the *timing*. While the elite-engineered model does not seem to work for most moral panics, the grassroots model enables us to see *what fears and concerns are made use of*, and the interest-group model enables us to see how this raw material is intensified and mobilized. *By itself*, the grassroots model is naive; by itself, the interest-group model is cynical and empty. Together, the two illuminate moral panics; interest groups coopt and make use of grassroots morality and ideology. No moral panic is complete without an examination of all societal levels, from elites to the grassroots, and the full spectrum from ideology and morality at one pole to crass status and material interests at the other.

Selecting Cases

All intellectual work reflects the interests of authors. This book is no exception. What follows in chapters 10, 11, and 12 are three cases studies, each reflecting the interests and research of one of the authors. Each case, we believe, is also *strategic* in that it reveals crucial concepts and dynamics relevant to moral panics; moreover, the differences among these cases highlights somewhat different concepts and dynamics. We attempt to avoid the ethnocentrism that is all too common in American sociology by selecting cases from three different soceities – Western Europe, Israel, and the United States. One case (the Renaissance witch craze) took place three to five hundred years ago; the other two occurred in the recent past. One case (the Israeli drug panic of 1982) was extremely short-lived; a second (the American drug panic of the 1980s) is a phase of a panic that has lasted, off and on, for a bit more than a century; the third (the Renaissance witch craze) endured, again, episodically, for nearly 300 years. The Israeli drug panic was reflected in the actions of politicians and the media, but public opinion has to be determined indirectly; in the American drug panic of the 1980s, all manner of manifestations – media attention, public opinion polls, statements and actions of political figures, and so on – is available. And with the Renaissance witch craze, attitudes of the masses must be inferred, and no mass communications (aside from its closest equivalent, witchcraft "handbooks," such as the *Malleus Maleficarum*) existed. With respect to our criterion of disproportionality, two are clearcut cases of more concern than harm (consorting with the devil was an invented form of deviance; and in 1982, Israeli drug use was exaggerated by a factor of 10), while with the third – drug use in the United States in the 1980s – the harm of illegal drug abuse has been exaggerated by its critics, but also, to a degree, underplayed by critics of existing drug laws. All in all, these three cases represent a diverse array of moral panics; their analysis highlights key concepts and processes for moral panics generally.

10

THE RENAISSANCE
WITCH CRAZE

One classical illustration of a moral panic is what has become known as the European witch craze. This craze, in its most virulent form, can be dated roughly from the early decades of the fifteenth century until 1650. During this period, a new form of crime came into being: conspiring with Satan against God and being involved in most shameful and dangerous demonological deeds. During this period, on Continental Europe between 200,000 to 500,000 witches (according to conservative estimates) were executed, as many as 85 percent of whom were women.

The European witch craze raises a number of intriguing sociological questions. Viewed from a macrosociological point of view, and focused on the issue of moral panics, the most pertinent research questions are clustered along three axes. First is the problem of *timing*: Why did the witch craze moral panic begin in the fifteenth century? Why did it become a popular and widespread craze between the fifteenth and seventeenth centuries? Why did the craze end in the late seventeenth century? Second is the question of *content*: why the suddenly increased attention to witchcraft, black magic, and the like? How to explain the emergence of a whole religious ideology concerning the witches, conceived as an antithesis to true Christianity? Why did this ideology culminate in persecutions of witches? Third is the question of the *target* of the witch-hunts: why were women singled out as its main victims?

We suggest that the vested interests of such control organs of the Catholic church as the Dominicans and the inquisition, the collapse of the authoritative framework of religion and of the feudal social order explain questions related to the first axis. The dissolution of the medieval cognitive map of the world, which also gave rise to utopian expectations, magical beliefs, and bold scientific explorations relate to questions centered around the second axis. Changes in the economy, demography, and the family, especially changes in the role of women – some of which were of catastrophic proportions – explain the nature of the target of the craze. The spatial distribution of the witch-hunt and its termination are explained as a result of the presence or absence of all or part of these conditions in different areas of Europe during the period in question, and their disappearance everywhere at the end of the period.

The explanations given to the riddle of the European witch craze are closely linked with the various specific changes in societal boundaries (in different realms) which took place between the fourteenth and the seventeenth centuries. Thus we suggest that medieval society was crumbling during the period between the fifteenth and the seventeenth centuries, as new social, political, economic, scientific, and religious forms came into being. The boundaries of the old medieval order were changing in a very significant way, along more than one dimension. These changes brought about the emergence of new, innovative institutional arrangements in the economy, family, science, politics, religion, and other social spheres. As a result of these changes, new positive societal reactions to the change became possible since old traditions, customs, and limitations were broken (for example in the areas of art and science). However, a negative reaction also grew in the form of a ferocious witch-hunt aimed at redrawing the old societal boundaries to where they had originally been.

It is well worth mentioning here that Europeans, at the time of the witch craze, *did* in fact believe in the reality of witchcraft, demonology, and witches in the very depth of their minds. Newton, Bacon, Boyle, John Locke, Hobbes – some of the greatest minds of the seventeenth century – all firmly believed in the reality of witchcraft (Hughes, 1952; Michelet, 1965; Baroja, 1965; Parrinder, 1958). As Russell (1977, p. 79) put it, "Tens of thousands of [witchcraft] trials continued throughout Europe generation after generation, while Leonardo painted, Palestrina composed and Shakespeare wrote."

Witchcraft, Witch-hunts, and the Witch Craze

Witchcraft and witches have existed throughout history (Williams, 1959; Lea, 1901, 1957; Baroja, 1965; Hughes, 1952). Until the time of the European witch craze, the basic conceptualization of witchcraft was largely technical: witchcraft could be used for bad or good purposes. In Weber's terminology, we had "magicians" looking for "ad hoc" answers (Weber, 1964). Two important points are worthy of our attention regarding this conceptualization. First, the witch/sorcerer/magician had a special, powerful position vis-à-vis the deities. His/her technological knowledge of such means as spells, charms, potions, and the like enabled him/her to force various deities into action they would not have otherwise done. If you like, the witch had a kind of key to activate deities. Thus, magicians became experts in this technological knowledge and magic became associated with *control*.

The second important point is that there was a division between black and white magic. The former was completely condemned and feared, while the latter was blessed and welcome.

O'Dea defines religion functionally as "the manipulation of non-empirical or supra-empirical means for non-empirical, or supra-empirical ends." In contrast, he defines magic as "the manipulation of non-empirical or supra-empirical means for empirical ends" (O'Dea, 1966, p. 7). Such an approach recalls the work of Weber (1964), for whom witchcraft is a kind of technology. For Weber, the magician's main function is to cope with relatively ad hoc interests and tensions. Magical powers can be enforced to serve human needs through the magician's correct use of formulas.

This, we believe, was the essential characteristic of European witchcraft practices until the witch-hunts of the fourteenth to the seventeenth centuries: its "technological" nature, the fact that it served ad hoc purposes and was used to achieve very specific goals (love potions, specific spells, love magic, and the like). At that time there was no developed, systematic conceptualization of a world opposed to our own and at war with it. The witch had a very special position vis-à-vis the gods (or deities): she could, with the correct "technological" use of spells, potions, and the like, compel them into specific actions.

In the European witch-hunts of the fifteenth to the seventeenth centuries, however, witchcraft was transformed from a technology used to solve ad hoc and specific problems into a completely evil entity which created – not solved – problems. The distinction between "good" and "bad" magic also vanished. Toward the fifteenth century a crystallized conception of magic and witchcraft as something purely and only evil became dominant. With the publication of the *Malleus Maleficarum* ("The Witch's Hammer") in the 1480s, demonological theories reached a peak in which they constituted an independent quasi-religion, and not just a technology. To carry the point a bit further, it became an anti-religion. Another important underlying trait – the pluralistic supernatural conceptualization of the world – also disappeared. (Where it remained – that is, in Russia – the witch craze was very weak and insignificant.) During this period the witch lost her former, special position vis-à-vis the deities, and her powerful ability to *force* (or control) the deities to comply with her wishes; this view was replaced by one which saw her totally subordinated to the devil. In short, the witch became Satan's tool.

These changes in the conceptualization of witchcraft were of crucial importance. Because witchcraft was regarded as a routine, day-to-day (almost personal) technology until the fourteenth century, witches were consequently classified as good and bad, depending on the objective of their magic. After the fourteenth century, witchcraft became a coherent, systematic theory; this analytical break enabled the inquisitors, and other individuals, to legitimately persecute hundreds of thousands of witches.

The Ceremony

The history of European sorcery and witchcraft extends well into Graeco-Roman times. Witchcraft, however, as the crystallization of an elaborated belief system, was a fairly new phenomenon, unknown as such before the fifteenth to the seventeenth centuries. The crystallization of the core ideology of the witch craze served as the solid anvil upon which the moral panic developed. What was this ideology?

> European witchcraft [between 1450 and 1750] was conceived of as a virulent and dangerous blend of sorcery and heresy. Sorcery is . . . anything that aims at negative supernatural effects through formulas and rituals . . . The other element, heresy . . . is the pact with the devil, the witches' Sabbath in the form of a black or inverted Mass. (Monter, 1969, p. 8)

The main feature of the European witch craze was the "witches' Sabbath," the climax of which was a huge orgy between the devil and witches. Lea (1901, vol. 3, pp. 401–8) reports that in the Teutonic tradition, there was a belief that witches were cannibals and that once a year on May 1 or on Saint Walpurgis's night (probably a local god transformed to a saint) there was a nocturnal gathering of witches. At this gathering, the witches ate and sang. Lea suggests that the Dominicans inflated this theme. The idea of the witches' Sabbath and the notion that witches rode broomsticks or beasts at night to travel to the forest for the Sabbath or other black Masses was partly created and partly crystallized by Dominican inquisitors in the late 1400s.

The Sabbath was conceptualized as a ritual performed by the devil and his helpers together with the witches. In that ceremony, homage was paid to the devil, the public profession of the pact was administered and new witches were recruited and signed with the devil's mark. Furthermore, the Sabbath ceremonies included a banquet, dancing, and sexual intercourse.

It is said that the devil generally chose a place for the Sabbath where four roads met or, if that was not convenient, a spot in the vicinity of a lake. Upon that spot nothing would ever grow afterwards, as the hot feet of the demons and witches scorched the soil of the earth so badly that it could no longer be fertile. Witches rode to this gathering place – on broomsticks (in France and England), on the devil himself, in the shape of a he-goat, in Italy, Spain, and Germany. The back of this goat, miraculously, had the capacity to become longer or shorter according to the number of witches he was desirous of accommodating. When all the witches had arrived (those who did not attend were severely punished by demons), the infernal ceremonies of the Sabbath began. Satan, having assumed his favorite shape of a very large he-goat, with a face in front and another in his haunches, took his seat upon a throne; all present kissed the face-behind. This infamous kiss (the *osculum infame* or *osculum obscoenum*) was well documented in the demonological literature, and was featured by most authorities. Robbins (1959, p. 420) quotes from a contemporary eminent lawyer, Jean Bodin: "There is no greater disgrace, dishonor, or villainy than that which these witches endure when they have to adore Satan in the guise of a stinking goat, and to kiss him in that place which modesty forbids writing or mentioning." This done, a master of ceremonies was appointed, and Satan together made a personal examination of the witches to see whether all were stamped with the secret mark. Those who lacked the mark were immediately stamped. This done, they all began furiously dancing and singing. Then they all stopped, denied their salvation, kissed the devil's back, spat upon the Bible, and swore obedience to the devil in all things. Then once again they began their dancing and singing (Mackay 1932, p. 470). When the dancing witches were looking around, they were surprised to observe nearly all of their friends and neighbors, whom they had not previously suspected to be witches. With them, there were scores of demons, their paramours, to whom they had bound themselves by the infernal pact. And, reigning above the feast, dominating them all, was the imperious master, the god of their worship – the devil himself. Although usually he appeared as a he-goat, he might also take the form of a big, black, bearded man, or a great toad. They danced to the point of exhaustion while the strange sound of macabre music made with curious instruments – horses' skulls, oak logs, human bones, and so on – continued.

Then, again, everyone kissed the devil, and having settled down, they would usually sit and recount the evil deeds they committed since their last meeting. Those who had not been malicious enough were severely punished by Satan himself (Mackay, 1932, p. 471; Trevor-Roper, 1967, pp. 94–5). After that, thousands of toads sprang out of the earth, ready to obey Satan's commands and, standing on their hind legs, danced while the devil played the bagpipes, the trumpet, or some other instrument. This dance supposedly amused the witches very much. The toads could speak, and entreated the witches to reward them with the flesh of unbaptized babies for their exertions – a command which the witches obeyed. After that, they settled down to a feast. In Germany they are sliced turnips, parodies of the host; in Savoy, roasted or boiled children; in Spain, exhumed corpses, preferably of their kin; in England, more sensibly, roast beef and beer. But, alas, these nice distinctions made little difference: the food, all agreed, was always cold and quite tasteless. Having finished eating, and at the word of command from the goat, witches and devils threw themselves into promiscuous sexual orgies. Again, these orgies were not as pleasurable as one might have thought. Robbins mentions that sexual intercourse was indiscriminate (incest, bestiality, unnatural sexual positions and acts, and the like) and, according to demonologists, most witches found it quite painful. Robbins (1959, p. 423) quotes De Lancre's account of the testimony of 16-year-old Jeanette d'Abadie: "she said she feared intercourse with the devil because his member was scaly and caused extreme pain: furthermore, his semen was extremely cold." After the feast, the dance began again, but not so intensively as before. The toads were called again, and everybody amused themselves by mocking the sacrament of baptism. The toads were sprinkled with some sort of filthy water, and while the devil made the sign of a cross all the witches (and the toads, of course) cursed it. When the cock's crow was heard (the description here is echoed in Saint-Saen's *Dance Macabre*), they all disappeared, and the Sabbath was over. (The above description is taken from several sources, but relies particularly on Mackay, 1932, pp. 469–71 and, to a lesser extent, on Robbins, 1959, pp. 414–24.)

Witchcraft as a Counter-religion

What were the main characteristics of the European witch craze ideology/demonology as it crystallized between the fifteenth and to the seventeenth centuries? The most important is the fact that this period witnessed the invention and crystallization of a demonical theory, unprecedented in quality and magnitude in earlier centuries. The totally negative description of the witch, as well as the entirely new perception of witchcraft and demonology, dramatically changed the previous dominant perception of witchcraft as technology. The kind of witches that the European demonologists of the fifteenth to the seventeenth centuries were referring to were qualitatively different from their predecessors: witchcraft was losing its neutral technological character in favor of an elaborated and complicated image of an anti-religion. This new ideology served as the cognitive base for the moral panic; as well as providing what Bromley, Shupe, and Ventimiglia (1979) called "atrocity tales," that is: "An event which is viewed as a flagrant violation of a fundamental cultural value. Accordingly, an *atrocity tale* is a presentation of that event (real or imaginary) in such a way as to (a) evoke moral outrage by specifying and detailing the value violations, (b) authorize, implicitly or explicitly, punitive actions, and (c) mobilize control efforts against the alleged perpetrators" (p. 43). This ideological transformation in the perception of the witch, however, did not take place before the fifteenth century, when it was crystallized, authorized, and accepted. This is a very important observation since these centuries witnessed the *transformation* of the concepts of witchcraft and magic from the technical realm into the ideological and emotional realms.

What was the nature of this new conception of witchcraft? We pointed to the central role the Sabbath in this definition. However, there were three additional and crucial ingredients in this conception. First, in the new conception of witchcraft, the witch lost her special position vis-à-vis the deities and, instead of controlling them, the witch became controlled by them. The witch was conceptualized in demonological theories as Satan's puppet, as someone from whom no good could come. Second, there can be little doubt that, in demonological theories, witches were identified with women. The *Malleus Maleficarum* (Sprenger and Kramer, [1487–9], 1968, pp. 41–8), perhaps the most important book on witchcraft published at the time, specifically mentions that "witchcraft is chiefly found in women" because they are more credulous and have poor memories, and because "witchcraft comes from carnal lust, which is in women insatiable." In about 1435 Nider mentioned that "there were more women than men witches because women have a slippery tongue and tell other women what they have learned" (Robbins, 1959, p. 41). Third, the theory of witchcraft represented a reversal of Christian theology. In this context, O'Dea's (1966) and Weber's (1964) definitions of magic and witchcraft as control technologies seem not to be valid when applied to the demonology of this period. The witch myth in the late 1400s was, in fact, a kind of religion, a semi- or quasi-religion. It was a coherent, unified, rationalized system of beliefs, assumptions, rituals, sacred texts, and the like. The Dominicans, who more than any other contemporary group developed and helped popularize the conception of demonology and witchcraft, based their beliefs on a dualistic assumption which viewed the world as a battlefield in which a struggle between the godly sons of light and the satanic sons of darkness was being played out. Their fear was that Satan might win this battle and turn the world into hell. From this point of view, the myth of witches can be regarded as the exact qualitative opposite of the conception of God. The stories and myths about witches were the exact opposite of what was supposed to be the true faith, that is, Christianity. This conception was strongly reinforced by the confessions of the witches.

In opposition to the central dogma of the church, which states that something (neither alien nor opposed, but utter spirit) entered into the womb of a virgin woman causing the birth of Jesus, we have stories about the perverted sexual practices of the devil and witches. Thus, in contradistinction to the idea of the holy birth of Jesus, the Dominicans tell us of a perverse and barren sexual intercourse between the devil and the witch. We are further told that the devil, appearing either in an attractive, super-sexual female form ("succubus") or in super-sexual male form ("incubus"), would come before a human male or female, respectively, in order to seduce them. However, because the "incubus" did not possess his own sperm, the human female had to steal it from her unsuspecting husband in order to copulate with the devil. There were also many reports that the succubus was in fact a revived corpse, who became a corpse again once her identity was discovered (see, for example, Robbins, 1959). Thus set against the idea of the birth of Jesus from a holy union between a Noman and the Holy Spirit, demonologists portrayed the perverted, painful, and degrading sexual intercourse between the devil and the witch.

The explicit sexual overtones of the witch-craze myth cannot – and should not – be ignored. Demonologits went to great lengths to associate witchcraft with perverted sexual practices and with the seductive behavior of the devil's legions. Emphasis was particularly laid on the "insatiable" sexual appetite of women: the "incubi," for example, outnumbered the "succubi" by at least ten to one (Robbins, 1959, p. 490).

Contrary to the day when Christians met to pray – Sunday morning – the devil and his legions preferred the night – between Friday and Saturday. Christians met in a holy church; the devil and his legions met in unusual and frightening places. In the church, people kissed the Crucifix; at the Sabbath, they kissed the he-goat's posterior. The symbols and objects used at the ceremony in the church (wine, wafers, water) were mocked at the Sabbath. Jesus was the pure good, the devil, pure evil. In contrast to the holy baptism, the devil had his own form of "baptism" – a mark imprinted on the witch, while filthy water was sprinkled throughout the ceremony, usually by stinking toads. Jesus was associated with light, the devil with fear, darkness, and stench. Music was also apparently played during the satanic ceremonies; however, as opposed to the music played in church, this music was macabre and played on strange instruments – skulls, logs, bones. While in church people tasted the holy symbols (wafers and wine), at the Sabbath they feasted on unbaptized, roasted babies' flesh. These unbaptized infants, who were aborted, strangled, or stolen from graves by witches were destined to be the main course of the Sabbath feast. Semen was collected from unsuspecting husbands for use during the orgies. The host was saved from Mass and brought to the feast to be desecrated (Mackay, 1932; Trevor-Roper, 1967). In short, the Sabbath represented a mirror-image of the true faith (see also Clark, 1980).

The Historical Development of the European Witch Craze

Monter (1969, p. 59) notes: "Until the beginning of the 13th century . . . Church and State fought against maleficia in the older, simple form. After 1230, the scholastic community investigated the possibility of a connection between human and demons . . . by 1430 this process was completed and the concept of a sect of sorceress and witches gained ground."

The timing of the witch craze is not an easy task. Most researchers (for example Monter, 1969; Kieckhefer, 1976; Russell, 1972; Robbins, 1959; Cohn, 1975; Trevor-Roper, 1967) suggest that the witch craze began in the fifteenth century, gained momentum in the sixteenth, and ended in the seventeenth century, through a few trials took place as late as the early eighteenth century.

After the disintegration of the Roman Empire and the rise into dominance of Christianity, the church made many serious efforts to convert European barbaric, pagan tribes to Christianity. Upon arrival, many Christian missionaries found that these barbarians already possessed quite a large spectrum of local deities. In the most sensible and politically astute manner, missionaries sought to convert these people by canonizing local idols so that the natives could continue to worship them as Christian saints. In this manner, not only were local deities transformed into saints but also, the old temples were converted into churches so that Mass could be celebrated in familiar places of worship (Michelet, 1965; Eckenstein, 1896, pp. 6–32, 484). The magical practices – whatever they were – were tolerated because it was felt that they would simply fall into disuse and be forgotten as the pagans would become truly Christians (Lea, 1901, vol. 3, pp. 485–96). Thus, in the years between the fall of the Roman Empire and the beginning of the Renaissance, the church remained tolerant of sorcery and witchcraft. Action was taken against sorcerers (if at all) only if the sorcery had resulted in a murder or the destruction of property (Lea, 1901, vol. 3, p. 408). In some cases, sovereigns not only punished sorcerers for wrongs they committed, but rewarded others for using the craft to benefit their neighbors, much in the same manner as in Graeco-Roman times (Nelson, 1971). This view receives more support from Michelet (1965, pp. 86–7) who states that sorcerers continued to be feared and employed at all levels of medieval society, especially among peasants.

During the period, the church remained tolerant of sorcery, the casting of spells, astrology, and the like. Even though the churchman would have – no doubt – preferred to see them abandoned, they did not persecute those practicing these arts. Official church policy regarding the actual practice (and belief) of witchcraft in particular held that the belief in witchcraft was itself an illusion. This statement appears most clearly in the famous *Canon Episcopi* (Kors and Peters, 1972, pp. 28–31; Lea, 1957, vol. 1, pp. 178–80, 494; Robbins, 1959, p. 74; Harrison, 1973, pp. 119–20), whose statement on witchcraft was adopted by later canonists as official policy. It states (Kors and Peters, 1972, pp. 29–31):

> some wicked women, perverted by the devil, seduced by illusions and phantasms of demons, believe and profess themselves, in the hours of night, to ride upon certain beasts with Diana, the goddess of pagans, and an innumerable multitude of women, and in the silence of the dead of night to traverse great spaces of earth, and to obey her commands as of their mistress, and to be summoned to her service on certain nights. But I wish it were they alone who perished in their faithlessness and did not draw many with them into the destruction of infidelity. For an innumerable multitude, deceived by this false opinion, believe this to be true, and so believing, wonder from the right faith and are invalued in the error of the pagans . . . Wherefore the priests throughout their churches should preach with all insistence . . . that they know this to be false and, that such phantasms are imposed and sent by the malignant spirit . . . who deludes them in dreams . . . Who is there who is not led out of himself in dreams, seeing such in sleeping which he never sees [when] waking? . . . And who is so stupid and foolish as to think that all these things, which are only done in spirit happen in the body? It is therefore to be proclaimed publicly to all that whoever believes such things . . . has lost his faith.

For more than six centuries this policy, namely that witchcraft is an illusion, served to discourage those in the church who might have wanted to destroy the belief in witchcraft by sheer force. The *Canon Episcopi* served as a brake on any sought-for change in the conception of witchcraft as an illusion. No wonder that when in 1458 Jacquier Nicholas wrote his important book on witchcraft he first had to tackle the *Canon Episcopi*. As long as the *Canon Episcopi* was held as official church policy, no mass-scale witch craze could take place. (Midelfort [1972, pp. 16–19] does not feel that the significance attributed to the *Canon episcopi* is justified. However, in view of the nature of the document, and especially all the other sources on the history of witchcraft, we are inclined not to accept his argument.) Beginning in the fifteenth century (Robbins, 1959, pp. 143–7; and 1978), various writers started attacking, both directly and indirectly, the policy endorsed by the *Canon Episcopi*. First, attacks were made on the authenticity and validity of the text itself (Robbins, 1978, pp. 21–2). Second, it was claimed that contemporary witches were different from the ones to which the *Canon Episcopi* alluded. In 1450, Jean Vineti, an inquisitor at Carcassonne, identified witchcraft with heresy. In 1458 Nicholas

Jacquier, an inquisitor in France and Bohemia identified witchcraft as a *new* form of heresy, radically different from the type of witchcraft mentioned in the *Canon Episcopi*. In 1460 Visconti Girolamo, an inquisitor and provincial of Lombardy, stated that defending witchcraft in itself is heresy and in 1484–6 Sprenger and Kramer published the notorious *Malleus Maleficarum* in which a theory of witchcraft was developed which crystallized into a rigid and stereotypical form for 300 years (Robbins, 1959, p. 146). The crystallization of the witchcraft ideology from approximately 1450 on culminated in the wtich craze itself, which lasted in Europe up to approximately 1650.

It is important to note the historical progress of the moral panic involving the witch-hunts. It began somewhat early with

> the most spectacular witch . . . Joan of Arc, was tried and condemned in France in 1431; three years before, Europe's first mass panic, or witch-craze, occurred in the bilingual Swiss Alpine land of Valais, when over 100 people were tried by secular judges for murder by sorcery, for stealing milk from cows and ruining crops by hailstorms, for worshipping the Devil and using counter-magic against the *Maleficia* of other witches. Nor was the Valais panic the last. 110 women and fifty-seven men were executed in Dauphine for witchcraft between 1428 and 1447; three dozen people were tried in the vauderie of Arras in 1459 in Europe's first urban panic. (Monter, 1980, p. 31)

As time went by, the witch craze spread over Europe. Some typical reports about the witch craze are: "A French judge boasted that he had burned 800 in 16 years . . . In Geneva . . . 500 persons were burned in 1515 . . . In Trevez 7,000 were reported burned during a period of several years" (Bromberg, 1959). Or, from the *Malleus* itself (1968, pp. 220–1): "1,000 persons were put to death in one year in the district of Como. Remigius, an authorized Inquisitor, boasted of having burned 900 in fifteen years . . . 500 were executed in Geneva in three months in 1515."

Midelfort (1981, p. 28) lists some of the results of the witch-hunts:

> Between 1587 and 1593 the Archbishop-Elector of Trier sponsored a witch-hunt that burned 368 witches from just twenty-two villages. So horrible was this hunt that two villages in 1585 were left with only one female inhabitant apiece. In the lands of the Convent of Quedlinburg, some 133 witches were executed on just one day in 1589. At the Abbey of Fulda, Prince Abbot Balthasar von Dernbach . . . boasted of having sent over 700 witches to the stake . . . At the Fürstprobstei of Ellwangen, ecclesiastical officials saw to the burning of some 390 persons between 1611 and 1618 . . . the Teutonic Order of Mergentheim executed some 124 in the years 1628–30 . . . In just eight years Bishop Philipp Adolf von Ehrenberg executed some 900 persons including his nephew, nineteen Catholic priests and several small children. In the Prince Bishopric

of Eichstatt some 274 witches were executed...The Duchy of Braunschweig-Wolfenbuttel executed fifty-three between 1590 and 1620, while Duke August of Braunschweig-Luneberg eliminated seventy between 1610 and 1615...the Duchy of Bavaria probably executed close to 2,000 witches.

In the Continental witch-hunts, children, women, indeed entire families, were sent to be burnt. The historical sources are full of the most horrible, diabolic stories of the tortures these witches endured, the lies they were told by judges and inquisitors. Whole villages were exterminated. As Hughes (1952) reports, the area we call Germany was covered with stakes, where witches were burning alive. "Germany was almost entirely occupied in building bonfires . . . Travellers in Lorraine may see thousand and thousands of stakes." Bogue, a noted cruel inquisitor cried that "I wish they [the witches] had but one body, so that we could burn them all at once, in one fire!" (Trevor-Roper, 1967, p. 152).

> During the 1580's when the Catholic Counter-Reformation began to reconquer the territories they had lost to the Protestants a decade or two earlier, the Catholics became dedicated witch-hunters too. Many of the persons accused were Protestants who refused to flee or convert. In France, witches were found primarily in Huguenot areas such as Orleans, Languedoc, Normandy and Navarre. In Lorraine, Judge Remy boasted of having executed over a thousand witches. Along the Rhine in the 1590's whole villages were depopulated. (Trevor-Roper, 1967, pp. 142–5)

Toward the later stages of the witch craze, cruelty increased again. As many as 50 to 100 were burned each year in villages in Bavaria (Lea, 1957, pp. 1088–117, 1228–51). And, as Trevor-Roper (1967, p. 157), Robbins (1959) and Lea (1957, 1901) report, the worst persecution of them all was probably in Bamberg.

In Bamberg, the witch craze reached unimaginable peaks. It was not only Prince-Bishop von Dornheim who committed atrocities. His cousin, Prince-Bishop Philipp Adolf von Ehrenberg (1623–31) also burned 900 witches. Strasbourg, Breslau, Fulda, and Würzburg were also places where witches were severely persecuted at this time. The witch craze reached Bamberg fairly late but the persecution there were most horrible. It started with Bishop Johann Gottfried von Aschhaused (1609–22), who burned about 300 witches, and continued under von Dornheim. Small towns in the area did not lag behind. Places like Zeil, Hallstadt, and Kronch were persecuting witches too. In Bamberg there were evidently cases of political executions as well, for some of the accused were clearly from the town's elite (for example Dr Haan, Johannes Julius, and other prominent officials). The pace of the trials was shocking. Frau Anna Hansen was arrested on June 17, 1629, put to torture between June 18 and June 28, and on July 7 (less than a month after her arrest) was beheaded and burned. It seems clear that the prince-bishop of Bamberg ignored orders from the emperor to release some of the witches. Ferdinand's order to release Dorothea Block, for example, was disregarded as was his order to release Dr Haan and his family because "their arrest was a violation of the law of the Empire not to be tolerated." Bamberg's witch craze ended when King Gustavus of Sweden threatened the city (he invaded Leipzig in September 1630). This, along with the death of the prince-bishop in 1631 and local opposition to the torture ended the mania (Robbins, 1959, pp. 35–7).

In Bamberg, the prince-bishop, Johann George II Fuchs von Dornheim, known as the *Hexenbischof* or "witch bishop," built a "witch house," complete with torture chamber adorned with appropriate biblical texts. In his ten-year reign (1623–33) he is said to have burnt 600 witches. It is interesting to note that one of the victims was the bishop's chancellor, Dr Haan, who was burnt in 1628 as a witch for showing leniency as a judge. Here we have one of the most touching stories of that witch craze. Under torture, Dr Haan confessed to having seen five members of the city elite at the Sabbath – all of whom were duly burnt. One of them, Johannes Julius, under fierce torture confessed that he had renounced God, given himself to the devil, and seen 27 of his colleagues at the Sabbath. But afterwards, from prison, he contrived to smuggle a letter out to his daughter, giving a full account of his trial: "Now my dearest child," he wrote, "you have here all my acts and confessions, for which I must die. It is all falsehood and invention, so help me God . . . They never cease to torture until one says something . . . If God sends no means of bringing the truth to light our whole kindred will be burnt" (cited in Trevor-Roper, 1967, p. 157; see also Robbins, 1959).

As Trevor-Roper (1967, p. 145) points out, the wars of religion in the seventeenth century added fuel to the five of the witch craze, and introduced the worst period of persecution. Protestants and Catholics zealously accused one another of witchcraft, and the witch craze reached an unprecedented climax in the early decades of the 1600s. It also seems that the Thirty Years War (1618–48) brought with it a renewed and vicious wave of witch-hunting, what Trevor-Roper (1967, pp. 161–2) called the "épidémie démoniaque." In their most devastating form the witch-hunts ceased after the ending of the Thirty Years War, with the Peace of Westphalia (1648). While we can mark the beginning of the terror in the 1490s with the publication of the *Malleus Malificarum*, so we can, symbolically, date its end when the Thirty Years War ended. During this period, between 200,000 and half a million people were tortured and executed by burning, drowning, hanging, and the like (Currie, 1968; Kittredge, 1972; Robbins, 1959). Hsu (1960) estimates a minimum of 30,000 victims and a maximum of several millions. For a significantly lower estimate see Levack (1987, pp. 19–22).

Evidence indicates that the majority of the witch craze's victims were women (Garrett, 1977; Andreski, 1982; Heinsohn and Steiger, 1982). In one specific area in southwest Germany, females constituted 85 percent of all victims (Midelfort, 1972, pp. 179–80). Monter (personal communication) claims that nearly 90 percent of the hunts' victims were women. Lea (1957, p. 1079) reports that in Switzerland "almost every woman" was considered a witch. In Weisensteig and Rothenberg "we find overwhelming proportions of women (90–100 percent)" (Midelfort, 1972, p. 179). While at the beginning of the witch craze we often find that accused witches were widows, spinsters or "strange" old women. Later on, married women and young girls were persecuted as well. The various historical sources on the European witch craze suggest that neither social status nor age made a significant difference; rather, this crucial variable was gender: most of the victims were women. Jaquerius in 1458 stated that witches were women and the *Malleus* associated witchcraft specifically with women because, as we saw, "All witchcraft comes from carnal lust, which is in women insatiable." The association of witchcraft was thus with women, not with poor, elderly, impoverished widows or those of rich, gentle of noble birth. Monter (1976, p. 110) notes that "sex seems to have been more important than wealth." His data clearly undermine the notion that poor, widowed or otherwise strange women were persecuted. Monter also notes (1976, p. 124) that "compared to sex, poverty and other factors seem to be secondary." The major weight of empirical data supporting the inaccurate view that witches were old, deviant women, comes mainly from British cases (specifically from Keith Thomas, 1971). But the British witch craze was unlike what happened in Continental Europe.

The witch-hunts did not affect all the countries or areas of Continental Europe in the same way, and showed a number of differences from area to area. The English witch craze is notably different from that which occurred in Continental Europe (Anderson and Gordon, 1978; Currie, 1968; Keith Thomas, 1971; Macfarlane, 1970). In contrast, the witch craze in Scotland resembled more closely the Continental than the English pattern (Robbins, 1959).

In England, the witch-craze started and ended later than in Continental Europe and was much milder. A demonological ideology did not prevail there, and persons accused of witchcraft were considered to have committed crimes against men and not against God. It is very likely that the lack of inquisitorial machinery, the clear-cut relationship between church and state, and a strong monarchy rendered less painful the English struggle with the problems Europe faced. Furthermore, in England the judicial system was more humane than in Europe. It appears that during the late Middle Ages England was in many respects outside the dispute which tore Europe apart. Scotland, however, experienced much more religious turmoil, which affected the judicial foundations of the law and – together with King James I's personal encouragement – enabled the occurrence of a virulent witch craze there. Larner says: "The Scottish witch-hunt was arguably one of the major witch-hunts of Europe. During its peak it was matched only by those of the German principalities and Lorraine" (1981, p. 197).

From the sources available it appears that the worst European witch-hunts occurred in Germany, Switzerland, and France, and only to a much lesser extent in other areas (see Cohn, 1975; Hughes, 1952; Kieckhefer, 1976; Lea, 1957; Monter, 1969, 1976; Robbins, 1959; Russell, 1972; Trevor-Roper, 1967; Williams, 1959; Midelfort, 1972).

It has also been observed that the witch-hunts were conducted in their most intense form in those regions where the Catholic church was weakest and most threatened (Lea, 1957), that is, in Germany, Switzerland, and France. In those areas with a strong church, such as Spain, Poland and eastern Europe, the witch-craze phenomenon was negligible (Lea, 1957; Robbins, 1959; Henningsen, 1980a, 1980b; Monter, 1980, p. 33). By this time, the church was no longer a single unit, as evidenced by the religious turmoil in Switzerland and France. Nonetheless, when using the term "the church," we refer specifically to Catholicism as the religious social structure that in essence held Europe together over an extended period of time.

The Scandinavian countries (Robbins, 1959; Midelfort, 1981) and Russia (Zguta, 1977) present us with an interesting additional dimension. In these areas, a strong supernaturalistic, pagan belief system existed alongside the church. Witch-hunt patterns in those countries were truly negligible. Thus, in Russia and in the Scandinavian countries belief in sorcery and demons was well established, which partly explains why there was such a low rate of witchcraft cases there. Taken together, these points imply that the coexistence of Christianity with widespread popular beliefs in demons and paganism could conceivably counteract the persecutions, prevent them, or have a strong moderating effect on them. This conclusion contradicts the view that in the witch-hunt, sorcerers and practices and beliefs associated with paganism were and eradicated. The evidence strongly supports the view that the witchcraft ideology, that is demonology, was invented and was not necessarily aimed against existing, popular cults or pagan groups. In sum, then, where the church was strong, witchcraft cases were rare.

The European Witch Craze: The Unanswered Questions

There can hardly be a doubt that the European witch craze constitutes a classical illustration of intermittent but continuous moral panics. The European witch craze of the fifteenth to the seventeenth centuries was a historically unique combination of accusations against people, especially women, of whom the overwhelming majority were almost certainly completely innocent, and the creation of a theological-moral system in which witchcraft became a phenonemon of central importance.

The craze's extended length of time and the large number of victims it affected are very disturbing issues. Why did no one successfully challenge the basic moral theory, that is, its demonology, which lay behind the witch-craze for nearly three centuries? Many researchers rightly insist that without widespread popularity and intellectual support, the craze would neither have begun nor have lasted so long. How do we explain this widespread popularity? Why did people – who for centuries had rejected demonological theories – suddenly lend their support to the demonological claims of the Dominicans and others? What in those theories captured contemporary minds? This issue of *timing* and the related popular acceptance of the witch myth are crucial for an understanding of the nature of the witch craze.

A second issue is that of *content*. Why witchcraft, why witches? While there is little doubt that the inquisition was very influential in producing the form that witchcraft took in the fifteenth to the seventeenth centuries, why did it divert its attention from more traditional scapegoats, such as the Jews, Moors, or heretical movements, such as the Cathars or Waldensians to witchcraft and witches? Why did Catholics and Protestants persecute witches with equal zeal? Why were witches persecuted so mildly in Spain or Portugal and so severely in Germany and France? In short, how can we explain the *content* on which the hunts were based?

A third issue focuses on the direction and *target* of the witch-hunts. Nearly all scholars agree that most victims of the hunts were women; why? While women occupied an inferior status relative to men, they had never before been hunted *as* women. This link between womanhood and demonology has to be explained.

Timing: Why Did the Witch-hunts Begin?

The witchcraft myth was largely created and crystallized by a number of Dominican friars. Until the thirteenth century, the Catholic

Church's official policy regarding witchcraft was summarized in the aforementioned *Canon Episcopi* which regarded beliefs in witchcraft as mere illusions.

The Inquisition was founded in the thirteenth century in order to combat heresy – primarily that of the Cathari and, to a lesser extent, that of the Waldenses (see Lea, 1901, vol. 1, p. 2; Madaule, 1967; Sumption, 1978; Nelson, 1971; Wakefield and Evans, 1969).

In 1216, Pope Innocent III formally sanctioned the Dominican order, which was established with the express hope that it would successfully win back various groups of heretics to the church – the Albigensians, the Waldenses, and most important – the Cathari (Hinnebusch, 1966; Mandonnet, 1944). The Pope's expectations were never realized, however: the lost sheep were not brought back to the fold (see Madaule, 1967; Puech, 1974; Turberville, 1964; Cohn, 1975, p. 58; Rose, 1962). Between 1208 and 1213, Innocent III started a military crusade against heretics in southern France in general, and the Cathari in particular (Madaule, 1967). The swift and bloody battle at Montsegur in 1245, for all practical purposes, marked the end of the Cathari movement as a serious threat to the church. Most of the Cathari who remained were driven underground, and many of the French Cathari fled to Italy. Although the heresy lingered through the fourteenth century, most of it faded in 1270s and finally disappeared altogether in the fifteenth century (Puech, 1974; Turberville, 1964). The Waldenses (see Rose, 1962, p. 235) received almost the same treatment. By the end of the thirteenth century, it was clear that persecution had virtually eliminated the sect, and by the end of the fifteenth century the survivors were segregated, for the most part, in the Italian and French valleys of the Alps (Cohn, 1975).

Although the Cathari and Waldenses were probably the most visible and important heretics at the time, they were not the only ones (Loos, 1974; Russell, 1971; Runciman, 1955; Turberville, 1964). Other heretical movements, prophets and religious dissent groups were also present during the late Middle Ages (Lerner, 1970). For example, there were the Hussites who flourished from the end of the thirteenth century to about 1430, the Lollards (extinguished in 1431), the Flagellants who flourished from about 1260 until the mid fifteenth century – their last persecutions and trials being in 1446–81 (Leff, 1967), and the dancing manias (Rosen, 1969). However, by the 1250s practically no heretics were left to be pursued by the Inquisition (Lea, 1901; Nelson, 1971; Trevor-Roper, 1967; Turberville, 1964). The two major heretic factions – the Cathari and Waldenses – were virtually eliminated, while other groups were either too small or were controlled with an iron hand. In order to justify the existence of the Inquisition's machinery, the inquisitors began to search for new apostates. "When the Inquisition had crushed the religious deviation . . . it had little justification to continue to exist. Its work was done. The Inquisition, however, set about to introduce and develop the parallel heresy of witchcraft, thereby widening its scope" (Robbins, 1959, pp. 107–208). A campaign was initiated in Rome to extend their jurisdiction to the infidel Jews and the Moors of Spain. The Inquisition continued to persecute the Jews of Spain and Portugal until the seventeenth century (Roth, 1971), which explains in part the virtual absence of witch-hunting there.

While the inquisitors immediately began a campaign to extend their jurisdiction to the more traditional scapegoat, the Jews, they simultaneously demanded, from the thirteenth century on, that their authority be expanded to include the witches they claimed to have found in the Pyrenees and the Alps. As early as 1257, the Inquisition pressed the papacy, specifically Pope Alexander IV, to extend its jurisdiction to sorcery (Trevor-Roper, 1967, p. 103). The papacy resisted; indeed in the same year, Pope Alexander replied with the Bull *Quod super nonnullis*, reaffirming that the *canon episcopi* was still church policy and urging the inquisitors not to be diverted from their real task, the retrieval of heretics to the church (Lea, 1901, vol. 3, pp. 452–3). The Bull was later reissued by Nicholas IV, and in response to similar petitions from inquisitors, it became canon law under Boniface VIII in 1303. Its intent was to discourage the inquisitors from hunting witches (although Boniface himself believed in them). However, inquisitors did not rest their case and proposed that all witchcraft and sorcery were, by their very nature, heretical. Their efforts were yielding results early in the fourteenth century with Pope John XXII's help. A fervent believer in the power and reality of magic, the pope himself gave the European witch craze its impulse when he encouraged the Dominicans and inquisitors to persecute all sorcerers, magicians and other heretics (Lea, 1901, vol. 3, pp. 450–4). In effect, however, as Lea (1901) notes, the actions of Pope John XXII merely reinforced already-growing fears about witchcraft. In 1326 he issued his *Super illius specula* which "authorized the full use of inquisitorial procedure against witches" (Trevor-Roper, 1967, p. 103). There he specifically stated that: "Some people, Christian in name only, have forsaken the first light of truth to ally themselves with death and traffic with hell. They sacrifice to and adore devils; they make or obtain figurines, rings, vials, mirrors . . . by which they command demons . . . asking their aid [and] giving themselves to the most shameful subjection for the most shameful of ends (Robbins, 1959, p. 288).

This document declared that all who used the services of sorcerers were to be punished as heretics, and all books on the subject were to be burnt (Lea, 1901, vol. 3, pp. 452–3).

The pope's efforts resulted in a small scale witch-hunt in the Alps and the Pyrenees for more than a century and a half. Although individual, scattered trials of witches were carried out in 1245 and 1275 (Robbins, 1959, pp. 107–209, 287–8), the early decades of the fourteenth century witnessed a tremendous intensification of attempts to stifle witchcraft practices especially in France. The fifteenth century was also a witness to the beginnings of many writings about witchcraft. Robbins (1959, pp. 145–6) reports on the writing of about 16 different books about witchcraft in the fifteenth century. Midelfort (1972, p. 70) reports on the publication of 37 such books in the sixteenth-century in Germany alone.

However, the most important and interesting book which appeared in this period, prior to the publication of the *Malleus Maleficarum*, was Jacquier's *Flagellum Haereticorum Fascinatiorium* (published in 1458) which proved to be something of a turning point. Jacquier defined witchcraft – for the first time – as a new, evil form of heresy (Lea, 1901, vol. 3, p. 497; Robbins, 1959), claiming that witches were qualitatively different from the rest of humanity. It should be recalled that until this time the Catholic church's official position toward witchcraft was based upon the *Canon Episcopi*, which pointed out that beliefs in witchcraft were mere fantasies. Jacquier's problem was how to cope with this statement in terms of his own beliefs in witchcraft. His solution was swift and clear. Jacquier suggested that the existence of the witch sect indicated witches which were qualitatively different from the ones to which the *Canon Episcopi* alluded. Thus he stated that contemporary witches were unlike their traditional counterparts, which paved the way for a new, different conception of the witch. All this, however, was only the beginning. When the *Malleus Maleficarum* was printed, between 1487 and 1489, with the blessings of Pope Innocent's witch Bull *Summis desiderantes* – the "art of witchcraft" had reached its peak, and the inquisitors' desire to control witchcraft was almost totally realized.

The *Malleus* appeared about 30 years after Jacquier's book and it was to become the most influential and widely used book on witchcraft. It was written by two Dominican friars – Sprenger and Kramer. Monter (1976, p. 24) declares it to be "the single most important book in the history of European witchcraft." Robbins regards the *Malleus* as "the most important work on demonology ever written" and states that, "if any one work could, [it] opened the floodgates of the inquisitorial hysteria" (Robbins, 1959, p. 337).

The book is divided into three parts. The first section attempts to prove the existence of witches and devils. To be more accurate, this section proves by argumentation (rather than factual demonstration) that he who does not believe in the existence of witches is himself a victim of witchcraft practices – a clear departure from the policy of the *Canon Episcopi*. The second section tells the reader how to identify a witch – what signs, techniques, and tests to use. Before the publication of the *Malleus* there had been no readily available, easy definition of a witch. The third section of the book describes the legalities of investigating and sentencing a witch. This section goes into the details of legal technicalities and the technique of delivering a witch from the devil to the secular arm of justice for execution. The favorite way to destroy the devil was to burn his host "using green wood for the slow burning of the grossly impenitent" (Sprenger and Kramer, 1968, p. 220), and specifically encouraged the use of torture as means of eliciting confessions. The *Malleus* also explicitly connected witchcraft with womanhood. As Zilboorg (1941, p. 151) points out, this abominable creation, launched some time between 1487 and 1489, immediately became the textbook of the Inquisition.

The importance of the *Malleus* cannot be overestimated. Its enormous influence was practically guaranteed – not only because of its authoritative appearance but also its extremely wide distribution. It was one of the first books to be published on the newly invented printing press (Trevor-Roper, 1967, p. 101) and appeared in no less than 20 editions (Zilboorg, 1941). It became the textbook of the Inquisition, and, with the appendage of the *Summis Desiderantes* as its preface, the last impediment to the inquisitorial witch-hunters was removed: the moral backing had been provided for a horrible, endless march of suffering, torture, and human disgrace inflicted upon thousands, in all likelihood, hundreds of thousands, of women.

In 1484, shortly before the *Malleus* was published, Sprenger and Kramer petitioned Pope Innocent VIII to appoint them general witch-hunters in the Rhineland. In response to their petition he issued his Bull, the *Summis Desiderantes* (Lea, 1901, vol. 3, p. 540; Kors and Peters, 1972, pp. 107–13). In this Bull, the pope asserted official church belief in witchcraft and the church's duty – with the help of its tool, the Inquisition – to exterminate it. The *Summis Desiderantes* itself explains the nature of witchcraft as follows:

> It has come to our ears ... that ... many persons of both sexes, unmindful of their own salvation and straying from the Catholic Faith, have abandoned themselves to devils, incubi and succubi, and by their incantations, spells, conjurations, and other accursed charms and crafts, enormities and horrid offences, have slain infants yet in the mother's womb, as also the offspring of cattle, have blasted the produce of the earth, the grapes of the vine, the fruits of the trees, nay, men and women, beasts of burthen, herd-beasts, as well as animals of other kinds, vineyards, orchards, meadows, pastureland, corn, wheat, and all other cereals; these wretches furthermore afflict and torment men and women, beasts of burthen, herd-beasts, as well as animals of other kinds, with terrible and piteous pains and sore diseases, both internal and external; they hinder men from performing the sexual act, women from conceiving, whence husbands cannot know their wives nor wives receive their husbands; over and above this, they blasphemously renounce that Faith

which is theirs by the Sacrament of Baptism, and at the instigation of the Enemy of Mankind they do not shrink from committing and perpetrating the foulest abomination and filthiest excesses to the deadly peril of their own souls, whereby they outrage the Divine majesty and are a cause of scandal and danger to very many. (Sprenger and Kramer, 1968, pp. XLII–XLV)

Lea (1957, vol. 1, pp. 338–45) and Zilboorg (1941, p. 151) both provide vivid and accurate descriptions of the various techniques of deception used by Sprenger and Kramer in order to authenticate their book. Apparently, the authors did not take for granted the general acceptance of their demonology, especially by the academic community, and were therefore eager for the *Malleus* to appear authoritative. Before releasing the handbook, the authors sought the endorsement of the entire faculty of the theological school at Cologne, one of the most prominent schools of theology in Europe at the time. Lea (1957, vol. 1, pp. 338–45) reports that nearly all of the members of the faculty refused to endorse the *Malleus* and did not want the name of the school associated with it. Sprenger and Kramer then forged the endorsement they desired and published it along with the *Summis* at the front of the book. They were careful to omit their forgery from the copies destined for Cologne, but the deception was soon discovered, and the theologians were furious. But to no avail. The book was already widely distributed and accepted as the official demonology, despite their protests. For the sake of historical accuracy, we have to consider Zilboorg's version of the matter as well:

> almost two and a half years after the issuance of the papal bull [Sprenger and Kramer] submitted the *Malleus* to the Faculty of theology at the University of Cologne. On the nineteenth of May, 1487, Dean Lambertus de Monte called a faculty meeting. The Dean affixed his signature to the indorsement of the *Malleus*. Four out of seven professors concurred in similar manner. The lack of unanimity was not acceptable to the Inquisitors. They persisted and prepared a new letter of indorsement, and, whatever their powers of persuasion, these powers must have proved sufficiently intimidating, for the remaining members of the faculty finally signed the document. The two Inquisitors were now in possession of both spiritual and academic authorization. (Zilboorg, 1941, p. 151)

In addition, they secured a special document from Maximilian, the King of Rome. The document, issued from Brussels, dated November 6, 1486 with royal signature and seal duly affixed and in perfect order, took official notice of the *Summis desiderantes affectibus* and gave official support to Sprenger and Kramer in the discharge of their sacred duty (Zilboorg, 1941, p. 151). By 1490, therefore, the Inquisition found itself in possession of potentially very powerful judicial machinery. It was authorized specifically to uncover and punish offenders whose crime was, by its nature, unobservable and unprovable except by the offenders' own confession which could be readily obtained through the use of torture. This account clearly links the beginnings of witch-hunts to the vested interest of the Dominicans and the Inquisition. They had a professional interest in the discovery of problems and populations on which to exercise their specialized theological expertise in heresies and their investigative skills. The fact that they showed much less interest in witches in such places as Spain and Portugal than in other countries of western Europe is consistent with this hypothesis of professional interest. In the Iberian peninsula the persecution of Jews and Moors provided them with plenty of intellectual challenge and employment.

The End of the Medieval Order

The professional and organizational interest of the inquisitors explains why they began to take interest, as moral entrepreneurs, in the witches as early as the thirteenth century. But the transformation of this interest into an elaborate demonological theology took place only in the fifteenth century, and only at that time did the general public begin to share the interest of professional inquisitors in witches.

During the thirteenth to the seventeenth centuries in general, and the fifteenth to the seventeenth centuries in particular, medieval social order underwent a series of significant changes, which, over the course of a few centuries, completely transformed European culture and society.

According to Pirenne (1937), the growth of cities and an industrial form of production started in the Low Countries and in England in the twelfth century, and from there reached down the Rhine in the thirteenth century. Among the changes that took place in the economic expansion of the thirteenth century was the development of numerous cities in Flanders (Nicholas, 1976) and England; a significant increase in population size, improvement of the monetary system, and the mapping of new lands (Pirenne, 1937, pp. 189–90; Thrupp, 1972; Le Goff, 1972; Bernard, 1972). The expansion of commerce was not limited only to central Europe, as ore-mining began in Poland (Molenda, 1976), and Mediterranean trade flourished at the same time (Ashtor, 1975, 1976; Abulafia, 1981).*

---

* Pirenne's account is corroborated by many other scholars: Earle, 1969; Lane, 1932, 1933; Lopez, 1972, 1976; Hicks, 1969; Carus-Wilson, 1941; Van der Wee 1975; Stromer, 1970; Irsigler, 1977; Nate, 1975; Malawist, 1974; Postan and Rich, 1972; Pounds, 1979. Cipolla (1976, 1978, p. 32) referred to these changes as a "Commercial

This economic development brought with it increased trade, expanded urban industry, standardization, exports, division of labor and specialization (Bernard, 1972; Griggs, 1980; Thrupp, 1972; Le Goff, 1972, 1980, pp. 43–52). By the end of the thirteenth century and the beginning of the fourteenth: "the development of industry and commerce completely transformed the appearance and indeed the very existence of society . . . continental Europe was covered with towns from which the activity of the new middle class radiated in all directions . . . the circulation of money was perfected . . . new forms of credit came into use" (Pirenne, 1937, pp. 189–90).

All this was only the beginning of a process the peak of which was reached in the fourteenth, fifteenth and sixteenth centuries. These centuries proved not only a turning point in commerce (Bogucka, 1980; Lane, 1932), but also in geographical discoveries and their utilization (Postan and Rich, 1952; Pounds, 1979). "The exploration and exploitation of non-European areas by Europeans during the 15th and 16th centuries form one of the greatest phenomena of the Renaissance" (Penrose, 1962, p. vii) and, no doubt, forced "a re-evaluation of the idea of Europe as a model Christian society" (Rattansi, 1971, p. 7).

These extreme and relatively rapid changes in the economic, commercial, monetary, and urban spheres made deep inroads in the hierarchical structure of feudal society sanctioned and legitimized by the Catholic church. In the medieval tradition, the moral boundaries of society were clearly defined. Christendom was ruled spiritually by Rome and structured in a uniformly conceived hierarchic feudal order, firmly embedded in a finite cosmic order ruled by God. This order was threatened by the heretic Jews and Moslems, but their heresies were already related to the Christian tradition, and the relationship to them was clearly defined: they had to be converted and saved and, if recalcitrant, fought and suppressed.

This order became increasingly threatened by the rise of an urban society that did not fit into the feudal hierarchy, by the growth of contact with non-Christian people, which did not fit the conversion–conflict model, and by the resultant autonomy of economic and political transactions from theological guidance. Furthermore, Brown

Revolution" and "a sort of Industrial Revolution." Other sources corroborate the fact that Europe in the period 1100–1200 experienced intensive industrial, commercial, and monetary developments. Within the general economic development of Europe at that time (Hicks, 1969), we have what Carus-Wilson (1941) labeled "An Industrial Revolution in the 13th Century." His focus was England, but his findings are very instructive as to Continental Europe as well. Van der Wee (1975) reports on industrial developments in the Netherlands; Stromer (1970) tells of the commercial development of Nuremberg; and Irsigler (1977) of Cologne. Nate (1975) reports on extensive commercial activity in Europe; and Malawist (1974) described intensive economic activity in central and eastern Europe.

(1969) points out that during the eleventh and twelfth centuries the sacred was disengaged from the profane. This is a major point in the process of the differentiation of a strong and viable secular element in the collective consciounce.

The stress and confusion created by these circumstances were further aggravated by external catastrophes, especially the devastating epidemics of plague and cholera which decimated the population of Europe and lasted throughout the fourteenth century. Furthermore, even the physical climate of Europe underwent severe changes in those fateful centuries, as evidenced by the onset of the Little Ice Age, "affecting . . . central and eastern Europe . . . by changes in temperature . . . The coldest time began in the 13th century with the onset of the Little Ice Age which, with exceptions of occasional periods of warmth, lasted until well into the 18th century" (Russell, 1972, pp. 51–2, see also Lamb, 1982; Le Roy Ladurie, 1971; Robock, 1979).

To add to the confusion and distress, in 1456 Halley's comet was clearly visible in the sky. The appearance of the comet was often interpreted as a bad omen and created much anxiety, fear, and unrest.

Furthermore, Griggs (1980) points out that the massive population growth in the thirteenth century was not paralleled by technological developments (especially in agriculture):

> all writers believe that populations had grown beyond the technology and resources of the period . . . We can conclude then that by 1300 population densities in [some parts] of Western Europe had exceeded the optimum density for the technology, resources and institutions of the time, that there may in some regions have been a Malthusian crisis . . . by the late thirteenth century symptoms of overpopulation were appearing: prices and land values were rising, in many regions there was little left to bring into cultivation, holdings were small. (pp. 81–2)

All this, obviously, created more stress and contributed to the feelings of an impending doomsday.

Rosen (1968, pp. 154–5) describes the "feeling of melancholy and pessimism which marked the period. A sense of impending doom hung over men and women, intensified by a belief that the end of time was approaching and that the last days were at hand." In such a period, Rosen (1968, p. 155) mentions that madness was not unusual:

> Within this context madness, through its linkage with the revelation of religious truth, became a means of achieving knowledge. Madness was a primitive force of revelation, revealing the depths of menace, destruction, and evil that lurked beneath the illusory surface of reality. Unreason revealed the unbearable, the things in the world upon which one could not otherwise bear to look . . . This theme of cosmic madness is a major element in the art and literature of the fifteenth and sixteenth centuries.

Foucault (1967, p. 15) adds a most picturesque description: "Up to the second half of the 15th century, or even a little beyond, the theme of death reigns alone. The end of man, the end of time bear the face of pestilence and war. What overhangs human existence is this conclusion and this order from which nothing escapes."

Stress and confusion, however, were only one aspect of these developments (Holmes, 1975). There was confusion about the moral boundaries of society and the cognitive map of the world; frequently there was fear of impending doom. But there was also an opening up of new possibilities and a rise in standards of living in the wake of the great catastrophes of the fourteenth century. Those who survived the epidemics inherited the wealth of the deceased, and even those who had to maintain themselves by their work could obtain far better wages than before because of the shortage of manpower.

Thus the fifteenth century was a time of great enterprise, bold thought, innovation, as well as one of deep confusion and anomie, a feeling that society had lost its norms and boundaries and that the uncontrollable forces of change were destroying all order and moral tradition. These developments allowed many contemporary thinkers to overstep the boundaries of reality and enter the realm of magic, fancy, and makebelieve. "The disengagement of the sacred from the profane opened up a whole middle distance of conflicting opportunities for the deployment of human talent compared with which the society of the early Middle Ages appears as singularly monochromatic" (Brown, 1969, p. 135). Between the fifteenth and seventeenth centuries there was frequently no clear demarcation between rational science and magic.

The inquisitors were forming their demonological theories in the early years of the Scientific Revolution (Ben-David, 1971; Rattansi, 1972), when pseudo-science was rarely distinguished from other forms of science (Thorndike, 1941; White, 1912; Shumaker, 1972). There was great preoccupation with so-called "secret (or esoteric) knowledge," namely the Hermetica which "focused attention on . . . extraordinary and marvelous virtues . . . The aim was to grasp the hidden powers of nature and the mysterious forces" (Rattansi, 1972, p. 5). This explains why "The growth of demonology and of the witch-hunt mania paralleled that of the scientific revolution" (Kirsch, 1978, p. 152) as well as the rise of interest in social utopias and "ideal societies" in the early decades of the fifteenth century (Cohn, 1961; Graus, 1967), which was another reaction to the dissolution of the cognitive and moral boundaries of the medieval world. The anomie resulting from the uncontrolled changes called forth positive, as well as negative reactions. The expansion of horizons and the instability of social conditions, the Reformation, the beginnings of the Scientific Revolution, and Renaissance art and humanism took advantage of the disappearance of traditional norms and boundaries for the creation of greater cultural diversity and freedom, giving rise to a new, infinitely more differentiated culture than that of the Middle Ages. The witch craze was a negative reaction in the sense that its purpose was to counteract and prevent change, and to reestablish traditional religious authority.

Parsons (1966, 1971) contends that the traditional feudal system began to differentiate during the eleventh century, starting a process which led – by the seventeenth century – to an increasing autonomy of the religious, governmental, and economic institutions. The new social order, based on relatively autonomous institutions, replaced a previous rigid, religiously defined, and more or less unified social system (Parsons, 1971). The social change affected the very "center," or the "collective conscience," of society (Durkheim, 1964; Shils, 1970), or, to use Parsons's own term, the definition of the "societal community" (which, for him, was "the salient foci of tension and conflict, and thus of creative innovation" [1971, p. 121]). Parsons (1971, p. 45) notes that the Renaissance was the first era which gave rise to a highly developed secular culture which was differentiated from the previous primarily religious matrix. In simpler terms this means that there was a newly felt need for the definition of the moral boundaries of society. The European witch-hunts should be considered in this context. By persecuting witches, this society, led by the church, attempted to redefine its moral boundaries. This was one of the numerous instances in which deviance served the social functions of emphasizing and creating moral boundaries and enhancing solidarity. In fact, this was fictitious deviance, created for those purposes.

Until the Renaissance, the Catholic church was at its peak of power. All problems were treated as theological or theosophical, and moral boundaries of society were well defined with no serious threat to them. This is why during the so-called "dark" or Middle Ages we have hardly any record of a witch craze.

Once the results of the differentiation process became visible in the fifteenth century, and a sharp decline in the church's authority was noticeable "the church began to need an opponent whom it could divinely hate" (Williams, 1959, p. 37), so that a redefinition of moral boundaries could take place. During the Renaissance, the process of the differentiation of the societal community began to take a visible shape – vibrating the structure of medieval society. This process directly threatened the church's authority and legitimacy. For a highly rigid social and religious system one can hardly imagine a greater threat. Thus the major social stress was what Parsons conceptualized as the differentiation process. Given this background, it becomes clearly obvious why the church "needed" an opponent it could "divinely hate." A redefinition of moral boundaries was necessary, but using deviants in order to redefine moral boundaries meant that a very special type of deviant had to be produced, one who would be perceived as directly threatening the differentiating, disintegrating, religiously defined societal community and the Christian worldview. What, other than witchcraft would better serve this need? This helps us to understand why only the most rapidly developing countries, and where the Catholic church was weakest, experienced a virulent witch craze (Germany, France, Switzerland). Where the Catholic church was strong (Spain, Italy, Portugal) hardly any witch craze worth mentioning occurred. Although this was not the first time that the Catholic church was threatened, this development, culminating in the Reformation, was definitely the first time that the church had to cope with a large-scale threat to its very existence and legitimacy (Elton, 1963).

For this reason, Protestants persecuted witches with almost the same zeal as the Catholics, despite many objective differences between them. Protestantism might have resulted from a process of differentiation, but Protestants, as much as Catholics, felt threatened by the process, and by each other. "The Reformation shattered the unity of Christendom, and religious conflicts . . . the Wars of Religion . . . destroyed the illusion of the perfect Christian societies" (Rattansi, 1972, p. 7). Luther himself believed in witches and believed that his mother had been bewitched. He "often felt sick when he visited Wartburg and attributed this to spells cast by his adversaries there" (Lea, 1957, vol. 3, p. 417). Calvin was more skeptical of the Dominican witch beliefs than was Luther. He believed that the devil could do nothing without the permission of God and that he could never conquer the faithful. Nevertheless, he was an alert and an energetic enemy (Lea, vol. 1, p. 428). In 1545, Calvin led a campaign against witchcraft in Geneva that resulted in the execution of 31 witches (Szasz, 1970, p. 296). Calvinist missionaries succeeded in spreading the craze to Scotland in 1563. When James VI of Scotland, a Cavinist, became king of England, he revised the lenient statutes dealing with witchcraft and wrote his own handbook for witch-hunters, *Damonologie* (Trevor-Roper, 1967, p. 142; Robbins, 1959, p. 277).

This interpretation makes plausible why such a strange and esoteric phenomenon as witchcraft was chosen for elaboration into a myth, and why it was so widely accepted at the dawn of the modern era in Europe. Dominican theory portrayed witchcraft and witches as the negative mirror-image of the true faith. As Clark (1980) pointed out, in a social world characterized by dualism, the Dominican theory made a great deal of sense. This made it possible to attribute all the undesirable phenomena associated with the anomie of the age to the conspiracy of Satan and the witches against Christianity. By associating everything negative, bad, and vicious with witchcraft, the ideal components of the true faith were positively highlighted. In his 1597 *Damonologie*, King James gave this idea a direct expression when stating "since the Devil is the verie contrarie opposite to God, there can be no better way to know God, than by the contrarie" (quoted in Clark, 1980, p. 117). In this sense, the witch craze could be called a "collective search for identity" (Klapp, 1969) and the authors of the *Malleus Maleficarum* can be seen as "moral entrepreneurs" (Becker, 1963, pp. 147–63), taking part in a "moral crusade" (Gusfield, 1963), striving to restore the integrity of the old religious–moral community. Witches were the only deviants who could be construed as attacking the very core of the social system, through anti-religion.

This explains why a number of theologians and intellectuals found in the demonology of witches a cognitively satisfactory diagnosis of the moral ills of their time. It still has to be explained how and why this abstruse theory was (apparently) accepted by the masses.

As a result of the severe socioeconomic stress, the entire feudal social order crumbled and "immense sadness and a feeling of doom pervaded the land" (Anderson, 1970, p. 1733), intensified and aggravated by the severe climatological changes, demographical revolutions and the disruption of family and communal life, all of which were perceived as signs of impending doom. Furthermore, "the individual was confronted with an enromously wider range of competing beliefs in almost every area of social and intellectual concern, while conformity-inducing pressures of a mainly ecclesiastical sort were weakened or discredited" (Rattansi, 1972, pp. 7–8). The existential crisis of individuals expressed in terms of anomie, alienation, strangeness, powerlessness (O'Dea, 1966) and anxiety – created a fertile soil in which the Dominican solution could flourish.

What could better explain the strain felt by individuals than the idea that they were part of a cataclysmic, cosmic struggle between the "sons of light" and the "sons of darkness?" Their personal acceptance of this particular expalnation was further guaranteed by the fact that they could assist the "sons of light" in helping to trap the "sons of darkness" – the despised witches – and thus play a real role in ending the cosmic struggle in such a way that would bring salvation nearer. Thus the differentiation process not only threatened the macroinstitutional level, but also the microlevel – each person's individual cognitive map. In such a case, a redefinition of moral boundaries and a restructuring of cognitive maps would be more than welcome: For this reason the moral panic that was based on a new demonology and expressed in a witch craze won such extensive popular support.

Witchcraft as an Ideology: The Question of Content and Target

The aspects of the demonological theory which made it so attractive to the masses was that it had all the characteristics of what would be considered today as an effective ideology (Geertz, 1964). Although

Geertz limits his discussion to situations in which the need for cognitive and moral reorientation is the result of the emergence of "autonomous polity," namely the differentiation of the political from the religious sphere, widespread need for such reorientation is caused by every process of significant institutional differentiation. Such process creates a disturbing discrepancy between what reality is believed to be and reality as it actually is. Consequently, a fertile soil for the creation of moral panics is invoked. The function of ideology is to provide authoritative and credible concepts capable of rendering the situation explicable and meaningful, and "suasive images" by which this meaning can be "sensibly grasped," and which can arouse emotions and direct mass action towards objectives which promise to resolve existing strain.

The existence of widespread strain due to the inadequacy of traditional concepts, especially in the religious–moral sphere has been documented above. However, it is possible to show that much of this strain became particularly focused on women, which explains why witches – usually female ones – could become such effective symbols in a new ideology.

How women became such a symbol can be explained through three events: structural and functional changes in the family; changes in the status and role of the woman; and demographical changes.

Structural and Functional Changes in the Family

Ariès (1962) points out that the medieval family was a property-holding unit, and "the home of the early Middle Ages was the heart of the industrial life of the community" (Goodsell, 1915, p. 207). In this home, the woman possessed a central role, both as a housekeeper and mother, and as a breadwinner (Chojnacki, 1974; Herlihy, 1971). For example, "in the 7th century the textile industry was wholly carried on by wives and daughters of the family . . . Such was the case prior to the 12th century when weaving [increasingly became] a skilled craft in the hands of the men" (Goodsell, 1915, p. 208). Goodsell's book leaves the reader with a firm impression of the medieval wife's hard life.

According to Jarrett (1920), the main functions of married women were to provide male heirs for the family's property and to make her husband richer by the treasures she was supposed to bring as her dowry and to work (see also Bullough and Bullough, 1974; Goodsell, 1915). Jarrett's main theme is the emphasis on the subordinate status of medieval women.

The social position of medieval women is a problematic issue, and researching it is still a new area (see, for example, Bridenthal and Koonz, 1975; Gies and Gies, 1978; Herlihy, 1971; Morewedge, 1975; Power, 1975; Stuard, 1976). Power (1926, 1975) states that the social position of medieval women was far from clear in that it was the subject of an ongoing dispute between the church and the aristocracy. She claims, however, that everyone seemed to accept the subordination of women, and that the prevailing attitude toward women was one of possession. Women, thus, had very little control over their fate. There were also those who regarded women as superior beings (as in the Virgin Mary cult; see Warner, 1976), or even as seductive and dangerous. Lemay (1978) reports that in the thirteenth and fourteenth centuries it was taught in universities that women were biologically inferior to men and extremely dangerous. The lecturers emphasized that menstruating women kill little children, that they insert chemicals in the vagina in order to wound the penis of their sexual partner, that they feign virginity and conceal pregnancy. Herlihy (1971) pointed out that the general inferior status of women was changed many times due to the frequent absence of men who went to fight wars. This process, peaking in the eleventh century, enabled many women to gain almost total control over the family property and thus improve their status. Furthermore, as the Gieses (1978, p. 29) point out, the later rapid growth of commerce and city life added to women's status. It is also important to notice that several studies generally tend to corroborate the conception of the subjugation of medieval women (Bainton, 1973, 1971; Bridenthal and Koontz, 1977; Chojnacki, 1974; Coleman, 1971; Gies, 1978; Herlihy, 1971; Morewedge, 1975; O'Faolain and Martines, 1972; Stuard, 1976), but also point to specific instances, periods, and situations in which women successfully raised their status. (Policelli [1978] even points to a case where an influential Franciscan friar preached that women should have more rights than they did.)

Toward the end of the thirteenth and the beginning of the fourteenth century, a time ripe with economic upheavals and changes, many families moved from the rural areas to towns, changing their economic outlook and shifting from producing and exchanging goods to a purely cash economy. This shift had a number of consequences: first, the family could hardly afford to support ill, unemployed, or unproductive members; second, it changed from a property-holding, working unit to a consuming unit; and third, as a result of the great number of peasants coming to town, the worker's real wages remained very low, and any fluctuation in business caused severe survival problems (Garraty, 1978). This situation understandably produced considerable insecurity among the new city dwellers (Cohn, 1961; Helleiner, 1967); consequently, male employees in large-scale enterprises (textile, flour mills, mining) subsisted close to the starvation level and could not afford marriage. Moreover, guild members who had not reached master status were forbidden by the guild to marry (McDonnell, 1954, p. 84; see also Wrigley, 1969). This rule was an attempt by those in power to keep it. As Marx pointed out, this development, together with the insecurity of the new city dwellers, also gave rise to a permanent proletariat.

Changes in the Status and Role of Women

The changes described above created very strong pressures on women to enter the job market, either to support their families, if they had any, or to support themselves, if they were alone. The fate of the unmarried girl was more or less sealed (Goodsell, 1915, p. 210). Some were sent to convents, an alternative provided "for those women who were prevented from fulfilling their natural calling" (McDonnell, 1954, p. 83). In Germany and Belgium, for example, these convents "were charitable houses for unmarried and widowed women" (McDonnell, 1954, p. 88). Unmarried women could also stay with their families and help with the work. In the cities, however, women without mates, without families to support them, or with no chance of entering a convent usually worked in spinning and weaving. Some also resorted to prostitution (McDonnell, 1954). Some documentation indicates that the number of prostitutes increased quite significantly at the very beginning of industrial development, especially in growing cities. Other sources (Bullough, 1964; Henriques, 1963; Sanger, 1937; Scott, 1936) attest to the sharp increase in the number of prostitutes in the urban industrial centers of the fourteenth and fifteenth centuries. La Croix (1926, vol. 2) points out that cities along the Rhine and in Alsace Lorraine (where new industries were developing) had instituted numerous laws against prostitution by the end of the fourteenth century. (These places, incidentally, were also characterized by a high degree of witch-hunting.) It hardly seems coincidental that Sprenger – one of the authors of the *Malleus* – came from Cologne, the principal industrial and commercial city on the Rhine (Nelson, 1971, p. 25). During this period, numerous rich families attempted to establish secular convents to which they could send their unwed daughters, but they deteriorated rapidly and were later turned into hospitals and poorhouses (McDonnell, 1954, pp. 82, 84; Nelson, 1971, p. 25). Women responded to these pressures by entering various newly industrialized spheres. Consequently, during the thirteenth and fourteenth centuries, the woman's dual role as part of the traditional family structure and as an unmarried worker became very problematic.

Demographic Changes in the Fourteenth Century

During the fourteenth century, Europe experienced severe demographical changes that bore directly on the concentration on women as victims of witch-hunts. In particular, the Black Death (1347–51) had devastating and far-reaching effects. Although the major epidemic abated in 1350, the disease reappeared intermittently in various localities until the end of the century. The mortality rate was particularly high in cities because of the density of population and the absence of hygienic conditions. Those who ran from the afflicted cities back to the villages only spread the disease to the rural areas as well (Helleiner, 1967). Lea (1901, vol. 2) reports of certain places where, out of every 1,000 people, barely 100 survived. McNeill (1967, p. 149) estimated that at least one-third of the total population died.

This constituted a turning point in the demography of Europe (Russell, 1972; Borrie, 1970; Wrigley, 1969). The population had grown with relative rapidity since the tenth century (Griggs, 1980). Various cities had reached populations of 50,000 to 100,000. "Central and northern Europe . . . saw a threefold growth in the pre-plague period with its most rapid advance from about 1150–1200 to 1300" (Russell, 1972, p. 40). Griggs (1980, p. 77) adds that "in the early fourteenth century the populations of Florence and Venice were not far short of 100,000, of Paris about 80,000, of London and Ghent about 50,000. North of the Alps and the Danube, Europe's urban population had probably reached 2 million" (1980, p. 77). J. B. Russell (1972) also indicates that until the fourteenth century, there had been more males than females in the population, although it is not clear exactly when a more favorable female/male ratio was achieved later. Griggs indicates that: "There is . . . some evidence of over-population in some parts of Western Europe by the end of the thirteenth century" (1980, p. 70). The effect of the plague on the population was thus devastating. "Two thirds or three quarters or five sixths of the inhabitants of Europe fell victim to the pest" (Lea, 1901, vol. 2, pp. 378–9). It can be assumed with a fair degree of certainty that between 30 and 50 percent of the population was annihilated by this disaster (Bridbury, 1973; Cipolla, 1974; Griggs, 1980, p. 54; Langer, 1964; Russell, 1972; Usher, 1956; Ziegler, 1971). Postan (1950), for example, reports that the decrease in population size was so sharp, with no corresponding increases during following centuries, that almost 60 percent of the land was deserted in Denmark, Sweden, Norway, and Germany (in this regard, the situation in England was different, see Bridbury, 1973, 1977; Postan, 1950; Usher, 1956; Gottfried, 1978).

While Griggs indicates that parts of Europe "must have had a very low standard of living in the early fourteenth century" (1980, p. 67) after the major plagues had passed, the peasant and wage-laborer survivors found themselves in a highly favorable and advantageous position. As a direct result of the shortage in manpower (Spengler, 1968, p. 433), their real income was tremendously increased, food supplies improved, and job security magnified. In addition, many survivors had inherited large amounts of wealth from their deceased relatives (Langer, 1964). Chojnacki (1974) notes in particular that women enjoyed increased economic success, and wealth also increased (p. 198). Thus he documents the fact that following the end of the plague, women became increasingly active in the economy and gained much economic power.

Under such favorable conditions, one might expect an increase in the population size, but this did not occur (Nelson, 1971; Spengler, 1968; Deevey, 1960; Helleiner, 1957). The real increase in population did not take place before the sixteenth or seventeenth centuries (Helleiner, 1957; Langer, 1964; Wrigley, 1969). This phenomenon can be explained in part by the sporadic, unpredictable reappearance of disease, as well as by the continuation of the Hundred Years War. But the essential reason lies elsewhere. The fact that the population did not increase and the birth rate decreased in the second half of the fourteenth century was due to the massive use of contraception and infanticide (Helleiner, 1967, p. 71). Why these techniques were used can be easily understood.

Because part of the population was – quite suddenly – exposed to a high standard of living because of an increase in real income, these people did not want to undermine their new prosperity by raising large families. Moreover, in the fourteenth century, life expectancy rose sharply for women, so that it is possible that they also outnumbered men and marriage became even more difficult (Geis and Geis, 1978, p. 230). Furthermore, the economic, monetary, commercial, and urban revolutions that accompanied the Renaissance and Reformation probably also gave a powerful stimulus to the rise of individualism and egoism (Brown, 1969; Colin, 1972). Those who married took care to limit the number of their offspring, while those who did not marry made efforts to prevent pregnancy (Spengler, 1968, pp. 436–7, 440). The church bitterly complained of the widespread use of coitus interruptus, by married and single persons alike, as a means of preventing pregnancy (Himes, 1936; Noonan, 1965; Wrigley, 1969, p. 124). Although historical research on infanticide is still in its infancy and cannot yet provide us with reliable numbers concerning the actual scope of the phenomenon in the twelfth through the fifteenth centuries, a growing number of scholars have suggested that the rate and scope increased sharply and significantly during the period under question. "Widespread infanticide and abandonment of children were responsible for the spread of foundling homes in the late Middle Ages" and for extensive legislation by the church to fight this practice (Trexler, 1973, p. 99).

This problem began before the fourteenth century. By the end of the twelfth century, Innocent III had established a hospital in Rome "because so many women were throwing their children into the Tiber" and "there were as many infanticides as there were infants born out of wedlock" (Trexler, 1973, p. 99).*

Coleman notes that "many children were left abandoned at a church's door; and they were accepted in order to prevent their death at the hands of their parents" and that "the purpose of . . . infanticide was to regulate children, not eliminate them" (1976, pp. 57, 69). It was exceedingly difficult to prove the crime of infanticide; indeed, "the unwed mothers and the presumed witches . . . were to bear the brunt as examples and admonitions" (Langer, 1974b, p. 350).

It is quite clear that the fifteenth and sixteenth centuries brought with them one of the most severe demographic changes Europe had ever experienced. Hajnal demonstrates how the patterns of European marriage date roughly from this time: "The marriage pattern of most of Europe as it existed for at least two centuries up to 1940 was, so far as we can tell, unique . . . in the world . . . The distinctive marks of the 'European Pattern' are (1) a high age of marriage and (2) a high proportion of people never marry at all" (1965, p. 101; see also Spengler, 1968, p. 1433, and Wrigley 1969, p. 90). Hajnal notes in particular that

> the proportion of singles among women [was] high . . . The marriage pattern is tied in very intimately with the performance of the economy as a whole [and] wealth may . . . cause late marriage. It was suggested . . . that people married late because they insisted on a certain standard of living . . . as a prerequisite of marriage. More single men married late because they could not "afford" to marry younger. (1965, pp. 117, 132–3)

He suggests that the origin of this marriage pattern lies "somewhere about the sixteenth century [and] became quite widespread . . . in the general population . . . in the seventeenth century" (Hajnal, 1965, p. 134; see also Russell, 1972, p. 60). Litchfield (1966) gives us additional figures that exemplify changes in family structure and functions. He reports that the age of marriage for males rose to 25 and over. He also indicates that among the upper middle class in Florence in the sixteenth century, larger dowries were required for marriage. This both delayed marriages and motivated more of the ruling classes in Catholic countries to send their daughters to convents, which required smaller dowries (pp. 202–3). The rise of the Beguines reflected new arrangements concerning marriage and the status of women in the fifteenth and sixteenth centuries. The parallel development in Protestant coun-

---

* See also Spengler, 1968; Himes, 1936; Noonan, 1965; Wrigley, 1969; Coleman, 1971; Davies and Blake, 1956; De Mause, 1974; Goodsell, 1915; Helleiner, 1967; Helmholtz, 1975; Langer, 1974a, 1974b; Radbill, 1974; and Webster, 1979.

tries was an increased number of spinsters. Midelfort reports similar facts, and he adds that in some places, the age of marriage for women rose to 23 and even 27. He also reports that the proportion of those remaining single rose from 5 to 15 or even 20 percent (1972, p. 184). Wrigley notes that "between two fifths and three fifths of the women in childbearing age 15–44 were unmarried" (1969, p. 90). These changes took place progressively over Europe. In many areas they began in the fifteenth and sixteenth centuries; in others, they may have been present as early as the fourteenth century (Wrigley, 1969; Herlihy, 1965).

These figures indicate a definite shift to late marriage which was the focus for the crystallization of the nuclear family on the one hand, and the marriage by choice on the other (Noonan, 1968, p. 468). The significance of a high proportion of unmarried is tremendous in a society that attaches a stigma to being single. In particular, the appearance of a large number of unmarried women produced serious problems, and it is probably no coincidence that a significant number of the witches were either widows or spinsters (at least when the persecutions started). Later on, however, married women and young girls were persecuted as well (Midelfort, 1972).

It is evident from all this that, beginning in the twelfth century and throughout the entire period with which we are concerned, the social role of women was in constant flux. Urban industrial life compelled them to step outside their traditional roles. Women entered a market characterized by lack of manpower. Their assumption of traditionally male employment, particularly in cities, where the job market was tighter, helped to produce an apparently dangerous misogyny (Bainton, 1971, pp. 9–14; Kelso, 1956; Midelfort, 1972, p. 183). Two centuries earlier many women could not get married because many men could not afford marriage; in the fifteenth century, they were unable to marry because of many men's reluctance to marry.

There were other deep changes in women's social roles as sexual partners and mothers. As we have seen, there was widespread use of contraception and infanticide, which the church strongly and fiercely denounced as evil. Trexler notes that "child-killing has been regarded almost exclusively as a female crime, the result of women's inherent tendency to lechery, passion, and lack of responsibility . . . Infanticide was . . . the most common social crime imputed to . . . witches . . . by the demonologists" (1973, pp. 98, 103; See also Lea, 1957, vol. 1; Murray, 1918; Sprenger and Kramer, 1968). Moreover, Piers (1978) notes that as large waves of immigrants came into the newly established towns, many of them extremely poor, women had no choice but to sell themselves. Many times, they also followed armed forces who traveled throughout Europe fighting numerous wars. Because of the low pay, prostitutes had to have many customers. They thus became bearers of veneral diseases. Even the higher-status job of a servant meant that a woman was at the disposal of her master's (or his friend's) sexual appetite. Piers points out that the servant's unquestioning sexual availability was often the only thing that stood between her and plain starvation. All these conditions obviously created countless cases of pregnancy, which many times ended in infanticide.

But infanticide was not only a result of the fact that many children were born out of wedlock. Many rich women either could not breast-feed their offspring or did not want to. Consequently, wet nurses were sought. There are indications that many wet nurses were poor women who hired themselves after their infants either died naturally or were killed (Piers, 1978). Trexler suggests that it is quite possible that in many cases, becoming a wet nurse was a planned course of action. It was a safe, comfortable living. No wonder, then, that midwives were among the chief suspects of witchcraft (Forbes, 1966; Heinsohn and Steiger, 1982). The Dominicans suspected – and probably rightly so – that midwives were experts in birth control and no doubt helped and cooperated in infanticide. This suspicion was explicitly voiced in the *Malleus*: "No one does more harm to the Catholic Faith than midwives" (reported by Parrinder [1958, p. 109], who quotes from the 1928 English translation of the *Malleus*).

Under the chaotic circumstances described above – large numbers of unmarried men and women, sexual license, sinful contraception, infanticide – the relationship between the sexes must frequently have been one of mutual exploitation fraught with deep feelings of guilt and resentment (see also Payer, 1980). Because of the powerlessness of women under secular and religious law, and their inferior status, it was convenient to project on them all the resentment and guilt. The ideology of the witch-hunt made use of these emotions. It made it possible for men who indulged in sex that proved unhealthy for them to accuse women of taking away their generative powers. Those who were party to contraception through coitus interruptus could project their guilt on women for stealing their seed. The fantasies about the unlimited sexual powers and depravity of women might have been a reflection of the fear engendered by the large number of unmarried women not subject to the authority of fathers or husbands, as, according to prevailing standards, they ought to have been.

It is thus clear why women were the principal victims of witch-hunts. The witch craze paralleled profound changes in women's roles and in the structure of the family. The tensions reflected in the images of demonology must have been very widespread among men, who presumably in large numbers took advantage of the prevailing sexual freedom. Among married women, who probably did not or could not indulge in illicit sex, there must have been strong feelings against "bad women" who might have "bewitched" their husbands and sons. Therefore, the female witch, using sex to corrupt the world, was a "suasive image" of great power in an ideology that aimed to rid the world of Satan's power, of all the effects of social change, and to restore its moral boundaries.

Timing: Termination of the Witch Craze

How did the European witch craze end? In their most devastating form, the witch-hunts lasted until the seventeenth century, or to be more accurate, until the end of the Thirty Years War. Several factors contributed to the end of the craze. First, the invasion of foreign armies from the north halted the persecution of witches in many cases (Nelson, 1971; Robbins, 1959). Second, the sheer terror, scope and nature of the witch craze helped undermine the process itself.

The terrible persecution of the 1620s caused a crisis within the very order which did so much to direct it: the Jesuits. "Already in 1617, Tanner, a Jesuit of Ingolstadt [had raised] very elementary doubts ... Another Jesuit, Friedrich Spee, was more radically converted by his experience as a confessor of witches in the great persecution at Würtzburg. That experience ... turned his hair permanently white [and] convinced him that all confessions were worthless" (Trevor-Roper, 1967, p. 158).

Third, the number of executions and the organization they demanded represented an enormous burden, both economically and socially. The witch craze caused havoc in Europe, whole villages were destroyed, commerce was inhibited. "Germany was almost entirely occupied in building bonfires ... Switzerland had had to wipe out whole villages in order to keep them down" (Trevor-Roper, 1967, p. 152). It seems very clear that the cost of the craze began to be too high, too many people were burned, a substantial part of the population was eliminated, and the atmosphere it created was increasingly unbearable.

Solzhenitsyn (1975) and Connor (1972) point out that in a similar craze, the Stalinist persecutions in the USSR between 1936 and 1938, the economic problem was solved by the slave work the prisoners did. In the Russian case, the patterns of repression were successfully constructed so as to decrease the economic pressure associated with the persecutions. The witch craze, on the other hand, was – economically and socially speaking – disastrous (see also Oplinger, 1990).

Fourth, although there were critics of the witch craze, such as Weyer, Scot, Spee, Tanner, and Paracelsus, none doubted the existence of the devil and witches. Their main criticism was leveled against the use of torture. During the sixteenth century, it was understood that the church was engaged in a life-and-death struggle with Satan. In the seventeenth century, this central dogma was under attack. By 1624, such people as Episcopius and Greve had begun to doubt the central dogma and persecutions. "Men revolted against the cruelty of torture, against the implausibility of confessions, against the identification of witches" (Trevor-Roper, 1967, p. 172).

The witch craze was thus attacked at its foundation. As Midelfort (1972) shows, the fact that secular courts were used for judging witches also undermined the craze. This happened mainly because of changes in the law itself in the seventeenth and the eighteenth centuries. It included breaking accusations of witchcraft into parts. For example, poisoning was viewed as a different kind of murder, and infanticide was separated – legally – from witchcraft. Eventually, witchcraft as a category for trial disappeared.

Thus, the ideological basis for the witch-hunts was clouded by growing doubts as to its legitimacy, and the various technologies and tortures used to hunt and isolate witches were meeting with severe criticism. Eventually, power was taken away from the courts, the inquisitorial machinery was dismantled, and the persecution of witches came to an end. This is consistent with the idea that once the differentiation process was well under way and people had begun adjusting to the new situation, the persecutions ceased.

The coincidence of the termination of the worst of the craze with the close of the Thirty Years War is not just a chance occurance. The Peace of Westphalia gave official recognition and legitimacy to religious pluralism and symbolically ended the struggle to redefine the moral system of Europe. The stresses, insecurity, and instability experienced by persons living in war-stricken areas provided fuel to the burning furnace of the final phase of the witch craze. But once stability was achieved and religious pluralism accepted, the witch-hunts weakened, finally disappearing altogether.

It is thus evident that by the seventeenth century, new cognitive maps and new institutional arrangements had emerged. There was a demarcation between science, magic, and religion, recognition of autonomy of government and economy in England, and settlement of secular and spiritual relationships elsewhere in a way that recognized supremacy of the political sphere. A new social order had visibly and triumphantly been created. The Age of Reason was at hand within its model of the "rational man." It was the era of emerging nation states, where people's loyalty was beginning to shift from the church to the state. This was part of a more general secularization of society. When the differentiation process came so far, the basis for the moral panic embedded in the witch craze was, in fact, eliminated. The reasons for its beginning and duration, as well as for the popular support in it, ceased to exist. A new definition of societal borders was taking shape, the societal community was already fractured, and the witch-hunt had no purpose whatsoever.

Were the persecutions successful in restoring the religious boundaries of medieval society? Obviously, the answer to this question is negative. Medieval society was not reconstructed or restored and, in all likelihood, could not have been restored. The attempt to do so was futile, and the sacrifice of innumerable human lives could not be justified even in instrumental terms. Whether participation in witch-hunts helped people psychologically to survive the period of uncertainty and transition is a different question. Even if it did, it was at the expense of the lives of many for the passing gratification of some, and it certainly did not make the persecutors into better Christians, which was its avowed purpose.

Generally speaking, it appears, then, that when a community so vehemently and desperately tries to restore its moral boundaries, it is doomed to fail. It is possible that the very attempt is in itself a symptom that profound change is taking place, that it is impossible to "go back," so to speak. In this sense, the persecutions can be interpreted as a symbol of incapacity, of a system's failure, as death throes, if you wish, and they might be viable proof that the previous equilibrium cannot be recaptured. The European witch craze, and the witchcraft trials of Salem, Massachusetts, (especially Erikson's 1966 analysis) seem to be sound proof of this (in 1692, a witch craze broke out in Salem, Massachusetts, and lasted for about one year. Only 52 individuals were brought to trial, and only eight were convicted [see Erikson, 1966; Demos, 1982; Mappen, 1980; Weisman, 1984]).

Concluding Discussion

In the previous pages, we examined in details a specific illustration for a moral panic. We analyzed the European witch craze as a byproduct of the European transition to modernity. This craze is an example of a fabricated form of deviance within a prolonged process of social change. On the one hand, the transition period was characterized by various innovative movements in the scientific, political, and religious realms. These innovations, branded more than once as heretical and deviant, introduced essential elements of flexibility and, in the final analysis, created and reinforced a new society. On the other hand, there was the witch-hunt, a clear attempt to redefine the dissolving boundaries of medieval society. This attempt introduced an element of rigidity to the system. The witch-hunt represented a futile effort to keep previous moral boundaries intact and prevent the changes that the medieval social order was going through. The dual nature of the transition and of its deviants thus fit the theoretical framework.

Within this context, we interpreted the European witch craze on several levels, suggesting that it occurred because of the convergence of a few key factors. Having described the elements of the craze, we isolated the following questions:

1   *Timing*   Why did the witch craze start when it did, why did it end when it did, why was it so widely accepted, and why was it distributed the way it was? The witch craze began in the late fourteenth century because the inquisitors and the Dominicans as the relevant moral entrepreneurs had a vested interest in it. They either had to find new goals for themselves or remain without purpose and slowly lose power and disintegrate. However, that in itself is not enough of an explanation. During the fifteenth and sixteenth centuries, Europe experienced the painful birth pangs of a new social order. We referred to this as a differentiation process. The confusion and sense of powerlessness and anomie experienced by contemporary individuals were further aggravated by severe climatological and demographic changes and by hitherto unimagined geographical discoveries. Nevertheless, the dissolution of the medieval cognitive map of the world also gave rise to utopian expectations and bold scientific explorations. These conditions created a widespread need for a redefinition of moral boundaries. This need explains the popular acceptance of the craze, as a desperate attempt to recapture and restore the previous moral social order.

2   *Content*   Why a witch craze and not something else? How do we explain the emergence of an anti-religious ideology, focusing on the witches? The answer to this question lies precisely in the antinomian character of the ideology. By emphasizing the negative, the bad, an implicit finger was pointed at what should have been. Only demonology and witches could serve this purpose since no other heretical group – imaginary or real – threatened the Christian legitimacy. The elaboration of witchcraft theories into a complex religious ideology was a direct result of the need for a theoretical construct to explain the turmoil and anomie of the period. This ideology culminated in the actual persecution of witches, first because it was devised for that purpose, and second, because the trials and executions represented the endeavor to redefine moral boundaries. Demonology provided the theoretical justification for the craze; persecutions were its manifestation. We also examined the efficiency and success of the witch-craze ideology. Neither in early modern Europe or in seventeenth-century Massachusetts did the persecutions fulfill their primary function and prevent, or reverse, social change.

3   *Target*   Why were women the major victims of the craze? Our analysis of changes in the economy, demography, and the structure of the family, especially changes in the role of women, clarified the nature of the target of the craze, it is evident that the increased number of unmarried women, the incidence of prostitution and infanticide, and the use of contraception formed a salient complex of problems likely to

arouse strong feelings. These conditions explain the suitability of a female symbol, such as the witch, to become an effective and central element in a demonological ideology. Furthermore, women offered a safe, weak target for the emotional zeal of the craze. Women had an inferior status to begin with, and their lack of power and organization (Lewis, 1971) rendered them easy victims of widespread persecutions.

The moral panic expressed in the witch craze ended when the conditions for its inception were no longer in existence. The spatial distribution of the witch-hunts (and its termination) were direct results of the presence or absence of all or part of the conditions described above. The witch craze occurred in those countries and areas where the crisis was most deeply felt and where the church was weak. Where the church was strong or where progress was not marked (or both), hardly any witch craze occurred. The disappearance of these conditions everywhere in the seventeenth century inevitably meant the end of the craze.

11

THE ISRAELI DRUG PANIC
OF MAY 1982

Introduction

On May 13, 1982 the Israeli public learned from news stories in the media that half the students in its best high schools used illegal psychoactive drugs. These claims generated a national moral panic which, although intense, did not survive beyond the end of May. The fact that surveys conducted over the course of the previous decade revealed that between 3 and 5 percent of Israel high school students had tried illegal drugs did not seem to dim the fervor of this concern.

To understand the dynamics of this particular moral panic, it is necessary to address two key dimensions: *timing* and *content*.

First the question of timing. Why did this moral panic break when it did? Why did it end when it did? It is not enough to know what generated the panic and whose moral universes the behavior in question challenged or threatened; these matters do not explain its origin and course of development. To understand the timing of moral panics, we need to bring active, living actors into our analysis, that is, microsociological level variables, such as down-to-earth interests, in addition to our macrosociological variables, such as moral universes.

The second dimension entails explaining the *content* of the panic – in this case, one generated by adolescent drug use. Why does a particular sphere of human behavior suddenly become the target for a moral panic? Why concern over *this* particular issue and not something else? The choice of drugs for the 1982 drug panic was not accidental. The symbolic-moral universe of drug abusers has usually been portrayed as evil, inferior, dangerous, detested, and morally wrong. A clash between the negative moral universe attributed to drug abusers and the positive moral universe attributed to abstainers necessarily draws societal boundaries between those who are "morally right" and those who are "morally wrong" (see Young, 1971a). The use of illicit psychoactive drug consumption as a locus for a moral panic provides moral crusaders with an opportunity to delineate their version of a moral universe with virtually no opposition. In the Israeli case, certain interests of one party who was involved in creating and sustaining the panic – the Israeli police – dictated the choice of drugs.

Between 1979 and 1982 Ben-Yehuda directed the central Israeli drug abuse unit, the coordinating and administrative arm of the Israeli Interministerial and Interinstitutional Committee on Drug Abuse. The major task of the Committee was to crystallize a national drug abuse intervention policy and to coordinate all drug abuse intervention activities in the country. The Committee answered directly to the Israeli government, usually through the minister of social affairs. Almost everyone connected with drug abuse policy was a member of the Committee (which had 36 members in all). Ben-Yehuda attended the fateful May 12, 1982 Parliament meeting (to be described later), and all those that followed. Ben-Yehuda described the ongoing events in field notes, on a day-by-day basis.

The media played a crucially important role in this moral panic – as it did in other panics. The media, both electronic and printed, provided the information which fueled the panic; relevant media items were collected and filed.

Narrative of the 1982 Israeli Drug Panic

Public attention to the drug abuse problem in Israel began after the Six Day War in 1967. Following that war Israel was flooded with volunteers who came to Israel from Europe and North and South America to help in a variety of assignments. The perception was that many of the western volunteers brought to Israel a new form of illicit psychoactive drug use – recreational drug use, mostly of hashish. It seems that such recreational drug use spread throughout urban, middle-class youth, especially the kibbutzim (Ben-Yehuda, 1979). While virtually no systematic data exists regarding the prevalence of illicit psychoactive drug use in the general Israeli population, the prevalence of illicit psychoactive drug use among adolescents has been studied in a fair amount of detail. The available studies that were conducted on this topic between 1971 and 1983 reveal a more or less consistent picture.

These studies (Peled, 1971; Peled and Schimmerling, 1972; Shoham et al., 1974; Har-Paz and Hadad, 1976; Shoham et al., 1979, 1981; Barnea, 1978; Kandel and Adler, 1981; Kandel, Adler, and Sudit, 1981; Javitz and Shuval, 1982; Burkof, 1981; Rahav, Teichman, and Barnea, 1985) indicate that only between 3 and 5 percent of Israeli adolescents between the ages of 14 and 18 had used at least one illegal psychoactive drug (usually hashish) one or more times during their lifetimes. Not only is this finding consistent from one study to the next, the figure is also remarkably stable between 1971 and 1983. As a result of this multiple independent confirmation, we can have a great deal of confidence that drug use among Israeli youth was extremely low at the time the 50 percent figure was released.

Background: Preceding Events

In July 1980 the Israeli police supposedly penetrated a large drug smuggling organization in the northern part of the country. The activities of the police led to a large-scale mopping up operation (code named "cleaning the valleys") in September. At that time, about 70 people were arrested and charged with smuggling and selling illicit psychoactive drugs. In May 1982 a key state witness in the trials which followed this operation, one Amos Sabag, filed a statement to the Israeli supreme Court. In the statement, Sabag not only denied his September 1980 testimonies, but also claimed that he had lied in court. This revelation touched off turmoil in the prosecution camp because Mr Sabag's 1980 testimonies had helped put about 70 people behind bars. Mr Sabag appeared on the Israeli television evening new on May 9, 1982 and repeated, very dramatically, his statement to the Supreme Court. The major daily newspapers gave substantial coverage to this event. *Yedioth Aharonot* (May 9, 1984) quoted Mr Sabag in a major headline:

> "I lied," claimed the state witness who caused the arrest of 70 drug dealers. He claims that operation "cleaning the valleys" in 1980 was staged and under police pressure; that he and a police agent simply "stuck" accusations on various delinquents . . . Amos Sabag, 26, from Tveria . . . claims that he and the police agent divided the hashish into small portions and put on each portion a name of a person, as if they had bought the drug from him . . . Sabag claims that most of the portions were meant to frame delinquents whom the police wanted to get rid of. On the night of Sept. 8, 1980 all the people against whom there was "proof" were arrested . . . Sabag wrote in his statement [to the supreme court] that "I decided to reveal the truth."

The police denied Sabag's claims. *Ma'ariv* of May 10, 1982 (p. 15) told its readers that the Israeli police were very angry at Sabag and that he was going to be investigated.

In early May 1982 theaters in Israel began the premiere of the German movie *Christian F.* This movie is a shocking dramatized version of a book reputing to document the true story of a 15-year-old female heroin addict in Berlin. The atmosphere early in May 1982, it can be inferred, was highly charged with the drug abuse issue, and very conducive to a drug abuse scandal.

The Panic Begins: Discussions in the Knesset

The 1982 Israeli drug panic began with events that took place on the floor of the Israeli Parliament – the Knesset – in May 1982.

On Wednesday, May 12, 1982, Parliament Member Ora Namir convened the Knesset Committee on Education, which she chaired, for a discussion on drug abuse among youth. In May 1982 the Likud Party was leading the governmental coalition. Mrs Namir was a member of the Ma'arach, the major opposition party. It seems safe to assume that Mrs Namir had received a few leaks from some police officers prior to the fateful May 12, 1982 meeting of the Committee. The meeting was well organized, and quite a few public officials were invited to it. A number of reporters were in attendance who apparently knew that something dramatic was going to happen.

Mrs Namir opened the meeting by stating that she had received some "alarming" information about drug abuse among young people. She then gave the floor to police officer Amnon Helfer, Chief of detectives in the Tel Aviv police youth branch. Mr Helfer told the Committee that as a result of a youth drug abuse survey conducted in Tel Aviv (the largest metropolitan area in Israel), the police concluded that one out of every two elite high school adolescents had tried hashish at least once. Mr Helfer clearly implied that this situation probably characterized all of Israel. Mr Zvi Ariel, head of the drug abuse unit in the national Israeli police headquarters, followed suit. He stated that about 22 percent of all schools in Tel Aviv, and about 20 percent of the youth clubs, had a drug problem.

The police officers explicitly accused high school directors of avoiding cooperation with the police. This accusation found dramatic expression in the media when, on May 13, it was repeated on the front page of *Yedioth Ahronoth*, a widely circulated Israeli daily newspaper. There, the Hebrew headline read "Half of high school students experienced smoking hashish," and the item continued:

> One of every two high school students in Israel had tried smoking hashish . . . [this] was told by . . . Amnon Helfer, head of detectives, youth branch, Tel Aviv to the education committee of the Knesset . . . Policemen criticized high school principals for not cooperating with the police . . . Parliament member Goldstein, from the Likud, who initiated the discussion, attacked the teachers and claimed that high school principals shy away from the subject and encourage permissiveness . . . Shmuel Shimoni, principal of Tichon Hadash in Tel Aviv, attacked the media for "overblowing" the problem . . . Yoseph Mechoulam, principal of [a] high school in Yahud, admitted that he had a drug problem and asked for advice from the committee. Chairperson of the committee, Parliament Member Ora Namir, accused the Ministry

of Education of doing nothing about the problem . . . She expressed her opinion that the increase of 10 percent in juvenile delinquency in 1981 was due to the fact that adolescents burglarized houses and stores in order to finance the drugs. (Ella and Reicher, 1982)

Ha'aretz followed suit and on May 13 its major back-cover headline stated "more than 50% of high school students experience hashish."

Members of the Interministerial Committee on drug abuse (including Ben-Yehuda) were present but were permitted to question neither the data presented by the Israeli police nor the methodology used to obtain it. The apparent scale of the drug problem gave other parliamentiary members of the Committee an opportunity and a reason to attack high school principals and the Ministry of Education for their failure to address the problem of adolescents' drug abuse. One member argued that contemporary high schools were too liberal: if pupils were required to wear school uniforms (as they had in the 1960s), all would be well. The session degenerated into an attack on Israeli high schools, high school seniors, and on the Ministry of Education above all. Furthermore, a few members of the Knesset Committee suggested that the efforts of the police in curbing the drug abuse problem were hampered by "too liberal legislation." This attack clearly carried a moralistic, not a tactical message. Most speakers expressed their concern about the apparently spreading "menace" of drug abuse among elite adolescents (those who attended the best schools), supposedly the future leaders of the country. Illicit psychoactive drug use was attributed to a decay of morality, overly liberal policies and morally confused parents.

The accusations that high school principals did not help or cooperate with the police conveyed a distinct and critical message. It appeared as if the police *had* a clear and swift solution for the problem: law and order. High school principals' lack of action was interpreted to mean that they did not know what to do, or only wanted to protect their school's reputation or indulge in too much liberalism. The reporters present throughout the discussion were obviously interested in this drug scare and intensively interviewed the committee members after the session.

The Panic Develops: Media Coverage

The following day, May 13, the Israeli public was flooded with drug abuse-related media items. The major daily newspapers carried front page headlines on the drug epidemic among high school seniors. A major morning radio talk show (*All the Colors of the Rainbow*) had substantial coverage on the topic – including interviews with a number of high school students. The following two to three weeks witnessed a virtual drug "festival" in the media.

On May 12, Mrs Namir appeared on the evening television news and told the Israeli public that there was a "government conspiracy to hide the true magnitude of drug abuse among Israeli youth," specifically blaming the Ministry of Education. When the interviewer questioned the data she used, her response was that the problem was not whether 3 percent or 60 percent of the young used drugs, but that the Ministry of Education was not doing anything about the problem. (See the parallel with the estimates made by the missing children movement in Best, 1990, p. 50.)

The proposed conspiracy theory became an important issue because it contrasted two opposing symbolic-moral universes. One was portrayed as a secret governmental universe, seeking to mislead innocent citizens, hiding that which should not be hidden. The other was portrayed as non-plotting, non-secretive, open, free, democratic, populist, courageous, seeking to openly share information and cope with the problem directly.

The Panic Develops: The Police versus the Ministry of Education

As the panic developed, the Israeli police for the most part were silent on the question of drugs. The media and the Ministry of Education, however, were not. A moral panic regarding illicit psychoactive drug use by middle-class (and elite) adolescents flourished on a full scale. One school in Tel Aviv called "Tichon Hadash" ("New High School" in Hebrew) was cynically renamed by the media Tichon Hashash (Hashish High School), following accusations of a high rate of illicit drug use there. The fact that the principal of that school brought statistics showing that only one high school pupil was found using drugs there did not help.

On May 19, 1982 *Yedioth Ahronoth* (p. 4) told its readers that

> High school principals do not cooperate [with the police] in the war against drugs. A general attack on the Ministry of Education was carried out yesterday in the educational committee of the Knesset . . . A principal of a prestigious high school in Tel Aviv said that there was no drug problem in his school. A secret police unit discovered that at least 21 pupils in that school smoked drugs, almost regularly . . . All present in the meeting said that high school principals did not cooperate with the authorities in order to eradicate the drug plague . . . Mr Turgiman, chief of Tel Aviv police, said that the high schools in Tel Aviv which suffered most from the drug plague were precisely the most prestigious schools in the north. (Reicher and Tommer, 1982a)

Furthermore, on May 20, 1982, *Ha'aretz* (p. 10), a morning news-paper, claimed that principals of high schools hide, and/or camouflage, the true magnitude of the problem in order to keep the reputation of their high schools intact (Harel, 1982).

On May 17, a spokesman for the Ministry of Education accused the police of helping to create a "drug panic," and of using unreliable statistics, demanding that the police should give the Ministry a list of names of those pupils who had been suspected of drug misuse. His account was titled "The drug festival" of the police.

> Every year . . . the police conducts its "annual drug festival" on the educational system. The script almost repeats itself: police detectives discover a few adolescents who used some sort of drug, outside school, in a city . . . Later on, police officers are invited to public forums to tell the nation about the achievements of the Israeli police in capturing adolescents who use drugs . . . Suddenly we discover, God forbid, that we no longer deal with one city – but with all of Israel . . . After a few months, police notify (not always) the stigmatized schools that the investigation was finished and then . . . it is disclosed that [the problem] concerns only very few students . . . The school's name, however, remains stigmatized . . . This year, the police had gone too far . . . The percentage of drug users in the educational system is low . . . I call on the police to give us the namelists of the students who used drugs so that we would be able to treat them. (*Ma'ariv*, p. 3)

At the same time, police estimates that more than 100,000 high school pupils used hashish were widely reported in the media. The Ministry of Education demanded, again, to know who even some of them were – to no avail.

Meanwhile, anxious parents began to pressure the Ministry of Education to "do something" about the "terrible drug problem" in high schools, threatening to keep their children away from schools. High school pupils also expressed their anger and protest about the campaign, stating that all high school students – as a category – were smeared and stigmatized with no real justification. Some parents even began refusing to send their children to schools because of the "drug menace."

The Panic Continues: The Second Knesset Meeting

On May 18, the Parliament (Knesset) Education Committee had a second meeting on the youth drug abuse problem. Ben-Yehuda attended this meeting. Before the meeting began, Ben-Yehuda was asked to Mrs Namir's (the chairperson's) room. He gave her the accurate statistics and pointed out that the data used by her committee were probably biased or false, and methodologically flawed. He also protested that he was not given the right to speak in the previous session. Mrs Namir rejected Ben-Yehuda's arguments and pointed out that his turn to speak would be delayed. He was told that the scientist members of the Interministerial and Interinstitutional Committee on Drug Abuse were biased and too "liberal" and thus not really very helpful or cooperative. Furthermore, he was told again that the problem was not whether 3 percent or 60 percent of high school students were using illicit drugs, but that no one – certainly not the Ministry of Education – was doing anything about it. Mrs Namir repeated that the Israeli public had not been given accurate information about the true nature and magnitude of the problem.

By this time it was clear that accusations of "liberalism" and "lack of cooperation" had become identified with a "soft" stand on the drug issue. A "soft" stand was usually interpreted to mean not showing enough combatant and militant spirit, and the required conservatism needed, supposedly, to eradicate drug abuse. One group of policy decision-makers, Parliament Members and police officers, demanded, in the familiar rhetoric, quick, and decisive action against the supposedly spreading menace of drug abuse among middle-class and elite adolescents. Members of this conservative symbolic-moral universe spoke of their imaginary antagonists as conspirators, lacking in fighting spirit, uncooperative, soft liberals, overly permissive and morally confused. Inhabitants of this negative symbolic-moral universe, according to those in the opposing symbolic-moral universe, actually helped propagate and intensify the problem.

The atmosphere of the May 18 session was tense. Unlike the previous session, only a handful of reporters were allowed in. The session was opened very dramatically by police superintendent Mr Yehezkel Karti, national police chief of investigations, who demanded to speak. Mr Karti told the Knesset Education Committee, in a very straightforward way, that they should not invest the figures given to them only a week earlier with much credibility. He stated that the "study" was, in fact, an internal intelligence report based on an intelligence survey, and not on accepted scientific methods. The two police officers who presented the data only a week earlier were not present at the May 18 meeting. Unquestionably Mr Yehezkel Karti's speech eased the tense atmosphere considerably.

While the few reporters present started to leave the room the Police–Ministry of Education feud was not over yet. Tel Aviv police superintendent, Mr Turgiman, claimed that the youth drug abuse problems in Tel Aviv characterized mostly prestigious high schools and middle-class and elite adolescents. He stated that neither high school teachers/principals nor students cooperated with the police. Other members of the Knesset Education Committee, including some invited guests, attacked the Ministry of Education again. They pointed out that even if the problem of adolescent drug misuse was minor, the Ministry was still doing absolutely nothing about it. They indicated that teachers, principals and pupils had no place to get help to deal with the drug abuse problem. While this meeting eased the tensions and put the magnitude of the problem in proportion, the drug panic itself did not abate.

The Panic Continues: The Crystallization of the Main Themes

The following two weeks witnessed major newspaper coverage of the issue: "killer drugs" and the "white death" were two of the slogans employed. These catch phrases attributed illicit psychoactive drug use to excessive permissiveness and liberalism, and to morally confused parents. Other newspapers suggested that youth drug abuse in Israel was characterized by a "silent conspiracy," which helped inflate the real magnitude of the problem.

> Drug trafficking and drug consumption in the country are no longer a peripheral phenomenon, as they used to be . . . Today . . . crime and corruption have become accepted norms . . . Using the services of prostitutes . . . contributes in no small measure to moral deterioration, part of which is drug use. (Shamir, 1982)

Hed Hakriot implied a connection between youth drug abuse and the consequences of teenagers' promiscuous sexual practices-abortions (Abramowitz, 1982). *Yedioth Ahronoth* quoted Mrs Namir: "kids under 13 years of age sell drugs and use guns because they know that, due to their age, they cannot be prosecuted" (Ella, 1982, p. 4). The Ministry of Education was doing nothing to educate pupils, parents, and teachers about how to cope with the problem, she reiterated.

In the period, between May 12 and the end of the month, items on the "youth drug abuse plague" appeared in the national and local media (both the press and radio and television). The panic crystallized along five distinct lines.

First, the panic focused increasingly on illicit psychoactive drug consumption among middle-class and elite adolescents in middle-class and elite high schools. The danger portrayed is obvious. If these particular groups subscribed to the wrong moral values, then the future of the country was in danger. The fact that higher (and real) rates of illicit drug use existed among less privileged young people did not seem to trouble anybody very much.*

---

* Wolanski (1981) and Wolanski and Kfir (1982) asked street guides who work with youth in distress to fill out questionnaires regarding their estimate of drug abuse among

Second, accounts which leveled strong criticisms about the lack of action by governmental agencies – especially the Ministry of Education – against the spreading menace of illicit psychoactive drug use appeared in the media. These accounts typically expressed shock and amazement at the nature and scope of the problem among young people. They frequently associated adolescent drug abuse with general societal processes such as permissiveness, the guest for new experiences, sensation-seeking, lack of parental guidance and control, and general alienation. These popular analyses tended to acknowledge that while the Ministry of Education should "get its act together" regarding drug misuse, the Ministry was only one agency in "combatting" drug misuse. It was pointed out that parents, family, and peers should take equal part in coping with the problem. (Examples of letters of this sort can be found in, for instance, *Yedioth Ahronoth*, June 6, 1982, p. 19; June 7, 1982, p. 11; and *Ha'aretz*, May 23, 1982, p. 9.) A few, however, warned that a whole generation of youngsters should not be stigmatized, and insisted that the police were to be blamed equally for the fact that drugs were so easily available. (See, for example, *Ha'aretz*, May 23, 1982, p. 16; and Donevitz's column, p. 9.)

Third, the media offered advice to adults on "how to tell" and "what to do" if their children were using drugs. These articles included information about the dangers and hazards associated with the abuse of various chemical substances (for example, *Yedioth Ahronoth*, June 7, 1982, p. 18, "How to Behave with a Drug Abusing Adolescent," and *Yedioth Ahronoth*, May 24, 1982, "The Dangers of Hashish"). In a perusal of the daily newspapers for 1981 and 1983 (that is, May to May the year before and the year following the 1982 panic), no such items on drug abuse could be found.

Fourth, toward the end of the panic, some items appeared in the media in which the public was informed that alcohol abuse, not hashish use, among youth was the real problem. These articles pointed out that alcohol abuse was far more dangerous than marijuana/hashish abuse (see, for example, *Yedioth Ahronoth*, June 6, 1982, p. 5).

Fifth, there was a discussion as to whether *religious* adolescents used illicit psychoactive drugs, and whether religious belief could be considered as a "good immunization" against the danger of illicit use of

their clinets. In 1981 the estimated rate of use was reported as 14.2 percent and in 1982 as 23 percent (the daily estimated use in the last survey was 5.5 percent). From a personal communication with Menachem Horowitz, Chief of Corrections (Youth and Adults) in Israel until January, 1986, we learned that his indirect estimate (based on reports from his probation officers) was that about 50 percent of his clients used drugs (mostly hashish). However, one has to take these estimates with great caution, due to the indirect, crude measurements used (see also Ben-Yehuda, 1989). Barnea, Teichman and Rahav's recent study (1991) corroborates this observation.

psychoactive drugs. *Yedioth Ahronoth*, a secular daily newspaper, took one side of the argument. For instance, its June 3, 1982 issue (p. 4) carried the headlines: "Drug Abuse Is Prevalent among Religious Youth Too," Drug Use Is Prevalent among Religious and Traditional Youth" (Reicher and Tommer, 1982b). The news item also quoted Parliament Member Rabbi H. Druckman as protesting the statement. Rabbi Druckman argued that research proved that the prevalence of illicit psychoactive drug abuse among religious adolescents was about half that of the prevalence among non-religious adolescents. On the same day, *Hatzophe*, a daily Jewish religious newspaper, published a front-page account, entitled "Religious Education Prevents Drug Abuse," which read:

> Rabbi Parliament Member Druckman said that the claim that religion "does not protect against the use of drugs" has no basis in reality. In a study that was published a year ago . . . in *Ma'ariv*, it was proven that drug use among religious youth is about 50% less than among non-religious youth . . . This study proved that as the religious education runs deeper, and is more intensive, it provides a better protection against drug abuse.

This last argument is particularly interesting because it confronted the accounts given by two different moral universes – secular and religious – regarding the abuse of illicit psychoactive drugs by adolescents, its causes and the methods of coping with it.

As time passed, it became clear that the sides of the argument were losing their initial zeal and vigor. The event which really stopped the drug panic, however, was the tension that was building up on Israel's northern border in late May and early June 1982. The Israeli invasion into south Lebanon on June 6, 1982, and the combat which followed between Israeli forces and the PLO and Syrian forces put the moral panic regarding adolescent drug abuse to an end. One media item which illustrates this appeared in *Yedioth Ahronoth*, June 18, 1982, which published a picture of a group of tired and proud young Israeli soldiers near their armored vehicle; the caption read: "Until a year ago, this generation was defined as the one who [uses] drugs" (p. 6 of the "7 Days" supplement). Hilgartner and Bosk's contention (1988) that there is a limited "carrying capacity" in major social problems in a given country at a given time is born out by the media's switch from drugs as a problem to the conflict in Lebanon. Moreover, *within the context of the military campaign*, in which Israeli youth redeemed their virtue as clean-living, hard-fighting patriots, the previous attribution of (presumed) heavy indulgence in recreational drugs was regarded as a closed book, a thing of the past, a dead issue.

Discussion

Moral panics and crusades are inevitably and intimately linked to politics and deviance. They revolve around negotiations of power and morality, and they typically include campaigns which are aimed to deviantize (Schur, 1980) specific subpopulations. They are also linked to the processes through which societal control agents and agencies create or amplify deviance.

The historical record makes it evident that the May 1982 Israeli drug scare was, in fact, a moral panic, as we have characterized it. Adolescent drug abuse appeared to emerge in May 1982 as a threat to societal values and interests. This threat was presented in a stylized and stereotypical fashion by the mass media by actors with high credibility and perceived morality. Actors announced diagnoses, solutions, and ways of coping. The panic ended in short order. The moral entrepreneurs were successful in creating the panic because they had power and were considered credible; the perceived threat potential of drug abuse was high; the moral entrepreneurs involved were successful in using the media and creating awareness of the drug problem; they encountered very little opposition, and they suggested a clear and acceptable solution for adolescent drug abuse. The nature of the panic and its historical development correspond to similar moral panics described by Cohen (1972), Dickson (1968), Ben-Yehuda (1985, pp. 23–73), Johnson (1975), and Fishman (1978).

The Israeli May 1982 moral panic provides a golden opportunity for analyzing the panic using the interest perspective. The panic had at least two interested and powerful advocates: the Israeli police and Ora Namir, chairperson of the Committee on Education of the Knesset. Both are located in the higher echelons of the hierarchy of credibility and morality.

The police had two types of interests in creating the panic. The first, a general background factor, is a long-standing vested interest to press the legislators into allocating more resources to the police fight against the "drug menace." The Israeli police is a centralized force and local city units are all directed from the national headquarters in Jerusalem. In reality, the police control fairly tightly what it leaks to the press or to other interested parties. The two young police officers who appeared before the parliamentiary committee in its first meeting did so with the fullest approval of their superiors at the national police headquarters. Although their superiors knew fairly well that the scientific quality, validity, and accuracy of the supposed study they brought was doubtful, they nevertheless encouraged their appearance. The fact remains that they did not attend the second meeting, in which Mr Yehezkel Karti, National Police Chief of Investigations, withdrew endorsement of the study's supposed findings. The police interest in receiving more funds, however, is long-standing and did not have to be timed specifically to May 1982. Reporters receive information from the police year round about various and grandiose drug raids made every now and then. Indeed, Conklin (1986, p. 51) notes that: "Rising crime rates have been used to justify higher police salaries and increases in police personnel, although police chiefs often acknowledge that police efficiency cannot be evaluated by crime data or arrest statistics."

The second, much more immediate interest of the police was to deflect the public's attention away from the fact that a key state witness withdrew his testimony implicating some 70 drug users and dealers and thus both called into question the methods used by the police, and raised serious questions regarding the legality of the arrest of these 70 suspects. It was this second interest which, from the police point of view, was the most important. Regardless of the outcome of this dispute, the diversion of attention from the state witness problem to the broader drug panic was, one has to admit, very successful.

The second interested party, Ora Namir, then chairperson of the Committee on Education of the Knesset, was not only a member of the major opposition party, which at that time had some bitter arguments with Begin's coalition government; she had, in addition, always had very strong and explicit aspirations to become Minister of Education herself. Mrs Namir gave these aspirations clear expression in interviews she eagerly gave to reporters, to the media, and in informal interviews. Obviously, before election time these aspirations frequently found expression in the media. Being part of the major opposition party, Mrs Namir could not become the Minister of Education. She was appointed instead by her party to the position of the chairperson of the committee on education of the Israeli Parliament. There can hardly be a question that Mrs Namir had a strong vested interest to attack the Ministry of Education. This interest was first to attack the coalition party and thus to maintain a traditional opposition watchdog role. Second, through these attacks Mrs Namir was not only pointing out that there was something basically wrong with the way the Ministry of Education was functioning, but that she had some better ideas as to what ought to, and could, be done regarding the problem of adolescent drug abuse. Furthermore, this moral panic gave Mrs Namir a most convenient media opportunity to present to the public the moral universe she believed in, and contrast it with another moral universe which she portrayed as evil. This is an excellent example of how symbolic-moral universes clash and negotiate, how sympathy and power can be generated, and how one can legitimize one's own moral universe by portraying a counter imaginary evil, antagonistic and dangerous moral universe. In this way moral boundaries could be sharply drawn.

Thus, the interests of two parties which helped to create the May 1982 moral panic coincided almost perfectly. Drug abuse professionals who could, perhaps, cool the panic were divided among themselves and incapable of genuine coordinated action. Furthermore, those who were present in the discussion at the Knesset were prevented from stating their views, and reporters were not especially interested in what they had to say. The analysis of the actions taken by the different parties points to their specific political/economic interests which led to creating and maintaining the May 1982 drug moral panic in Israel. One is, of course, left puzzled about the dubious role the media played in helping this moral panic come about. There can hardly be a question that the media helped construct the social reality (Adoni and Mane, 1984) where the panic flourished.

Morality, Deviance, Ideology, and Moral Panics: The Question of Content

Lofland (1969, p. 14) focused on the "threat potential" in various deviant acts. We have also noted Schur's (1980) term "deviantization process" referring to a process through which specific groups of social actors become deviantized. Schur stated that "stigma contests" are the major mechanism for such processes: "partisans in collective stigma contests are widely engaged in the use of propaganda: the manipulation of political symbols for the control of public opinion" (1980, p. 135). Moral entrepreneurs, moral crusades, and panics therefore involve processes of "stigma contests" which focus on various and competing definitions of the boundaries between different symbolic-moral universes. The area of illicit psychoactive drug use includes deviantization processes *and* a significant threat potential.

The choice of a topic for a moral panic is not governed by a random process. Moral panics are aimed at deviantizing entire subpopulations, and provide vivid illustrations of the clash of different moral universes. Moral panics, therefore, are intimately linked to the basic nature of various cultures.

According to Lidz and Walker (1980, pp. 251–2) the drug crisis in the United States was "a phony creation of a variety of powerful people who felt threatened by the growth of expressive passivist beliefs in the youth culture and revolutionary politics among Blacks. It seems that there was little reality to the belief that large sectors of the American population were about to become addicted to heroin." Their conclusion is therefore that the drug crisis "was a smoke screen for the repression of political and cultural groups" (see also Helmer, 1975). In his work on the prohibitionist movement, Gusfield states that:

What prohibition symbolized was the superior power and prestige of the old middle class in American society. The threat of decline in that position had made explicit action of government necessary to defend it. Legislation did this in two ways. It demonstrated the power of the old middle class by showing that they could mobilize sufficient political strength to bring it about, and it gave dominance to the character and style of old middle class life in contrast to that of the urban lower and middle classes. (1963, p. 122)

As Gusfield points out, the symbolic message carried out by the end of Prohibition meant the end of the dominance of old middle-class virtues and the end of rural, Protestant dominance (1963, p. 126). In the United States, many anti-drug campaigns can be traced to ideological and moral issues.* Indeed, Goode (1993, p. 59) states: "Much of the drug legislation passed in this century was motivated by political and moral reasons rather than by a genuine concern for the health and welfare of vulnerable members of the society." At different times and in different cultures, drugs have traditionally been associated with moral-ideological issues. The choice of drugs for the creation of a moral panic is, obviously, not an Israeli invention.

In the 1982 Israeli moral panic over drugs, the choice of drugs, while perhaps not necessarily consciously planned, was also no mere coincidence. Capitalization on the drug menace as a societal threat has at least two important aspects. First is the fact that drug scares, especially those concerning youth, are very attractive to both the media and the public. It is relatively easy to use this issue in order to generate a moral crisis. Ideologies provide, and help construct, the boundaries of symbolic-moral universes. In this specific respect, ideologies and morality share a common denominator: they help social actors to utilize ideologically given rationale and justifications.

An analytical conceptualization of ideology which is consistent with the terminology we use here was suggested by Geertz (1964), and which we used in the context of the European witch craze as well. According to Geertz, the function of ideology is to provide authoritative concepts capable of rendering situations meaningful, and "suasive images" by which their meaning can be "sensibly grasped," and which can arouse emotions and direct mass action. That drugs can be used as a "suasive image" for corrupting youth and thus destroying the country's future seems clear. Thus, we find such expressions as "drugs destroy young minds," "drugs destroy the future of the country," and the like. When these phrases are used by Parliament, the press, and by high-ranking officials, an effective anti-drug ideology is activated. Fur-

---

* See Anderson, 1981; Ashley, 1972; Conrad and Schneider, 1980; Dumont, 1973; Duster, 1970; Klerman, 1970; Kramer, 1976; Morgan, 1978; Musto, 1973; Trebach, 1982; Young, 1971a.

thermore, as Thomas Szasz (1975) Nils Christie (1984) and Christie and Bruun (1985) as well as others have shown, drugs represent an easy and safe enemy to create, magnify, portray in evil colors and focus hatred on.

The second aspect of drug abuse as the content of panics is the fact that the moral statements used in the anti-drug ideology help to draw and maintain moral boundaries, especially between those who use drugs and those who do not, those who are morally right and those who are morally wrong. A typical example is the argument that was waged toward the end of the panic as to whether orthodox Jews were somehow more resistant to (and perhaps even "immunized" against) drug abuse in comparison with secular Jews. In this sense, two opposing symbolic-moral universes were sharply and visibly contrasted. Berger and Luckmann argue that when two such contradictory symbolic-moral universes meet, a conflict is indeed unavoidable: "heretical groups posit not only a theoretical threat to the symbolic universe, but a practical one to the institutional order legitimated by the symbolic universe in question" (1966, p. 124). In the moral panic described here one symbolic-moral universe fabricated a negative, morally evil symbolic universe of drug users, and successfully campaigned against some of the arch-enemies who supposedly helped support this deviant, heretical symbolic-moral universe.

The symbolic-moral universe which stated that it valued the work ethic, coping with everyday life problems and maximum self control, claimed moral superiority. It portrayed an opposing negative symbolic-moral universe of drug users who supposedly symbolized moral degeneracy, loss of control, danger, lack of correct ideas, irrationality, and so on.

The above situation is not unique. Elsewhere in this book we argue that when the medieval Inquisition found itself without heretics to pursue, it had an interest in finding, or inventing, a new type of heretic to justify the continued existence of the Inquisition's machinery. Thus, the Inquisition set out to introduce and develop a new form of heresy – that of witchcraft. A few Dominicans, and the Inquisition, fabricated a negative, detested, and fearsome moral universe – that of demonic witchcraft. That symbolic-moral universe was described as diametrically opposed to the positive moral universe of the true believers. There can be little doubt that based on this negative moral universe the Inquisition was very successful in creating a devastating moral panic which lasted for a very long period of time. Gusfield also showed that the development of the "myth of the Killer Drunk" (1981, pp. 151–4) helps American society maintain the illusion of moral consensus about such positive values as being sober, in control, rational, hardworking, and the like. This point refers to the "boundary maintenance" function of deviance in moral panics (see, for example, Durkheim, 1938; Erikson, 1966; Lauderdale, 1976; Ben-Yehuda, 1985).

The way various organizations, and the government, in Israel coped with what they perceived as the "drug menace," and the generalized accounts they chose to present their stance, are instructive as to the underlying moral tone of the drug abuse issue in Israel. For example, AL SAM, the only Israeli voluntary citizen's association against the use of drugs, states officially on its letterhead that it has declared "war on drugs." In a country that has fought six wars in the last 40 years (apart from anti-terrorist battles and activities) this slogan carries a heavy moral tone.

Some of the motivational accounting systems which were used in governmental publications from the late 1960s and early 1970s were almost consciously intended to create moral panics. For example a poster published in 1971 by the Israeli government used a very interesting vocabulary of motives: "the number of hashish users in Egypt is approximately five million. In the Six Day War everyone could see the type and quality of the Egyptian soldiers. Don't delude yourself that there is no connection between these two facts." (This particular reasoning must have made sense in post-1967 Israel, when its youngsters might very well have felt like supermen. In the 1973 war the Egyptian soldiers proved to be of a higher quality than in 1967, so that today when this poster is shown to Israeli students they usually roar with laughter.) Another poster from the early 1970s stated that: "if being a man means to have a strong and stable character, those who use drugs prove the opposite: apathy, lack of initiative and ambition, in difference." Obviously, these statements clearly and explicitly contrast morally desirable qualities with morally undesirable ones. In this context, it is not difficult to see why it is so easy to use drugs as corrupting the innocent, perhaps morally confused, youth on behalf of those who are morally perceived to be actually wicked, corrupt, and even evil.

In Israel, therefore, as in the United States, the drug issue has always been intimately associated with various moral and ideological issues. Thus, the rhetorical devices used in official publications on drug abuse reflect the struggle between different symbolic-moral universes. The reasoning used in these publications is not strictly technical, for they do not restrict themselves to the obvious medical or physical dangers of drug abuse; instead, they focus on the type of person who, supposedly, chooses to use drugs, and the social and moral implications of such use. "The sale and use of marijuana remain illegal, however, primarily because most of the older adult public are ideologically opposed to decriminalization. Use of the drug is symbolically associated in much of the public mind with many kinds of activities, life styles, and moral and political beliefs these dominant groups find repugnant, for example, hedonism, sexual promiscuity, altered states of consciousness, radicalism, irreverence towards authority, and so on" (Hills, 1980, p. 38).

The drug abuse issue symbolizes something crucial regarding the nature of the Israeli collective conscience. In the Israeli context this issue represents something which is very alien to the Israeli ethos of trying to create a new society, based on industriousness, asceticism, activism, bravery, and technical expertise. Drug users, in this cultural context, are typically portrayed as *folk devils* (Cohen, 1972).

In Israel, there might have also been an added factor helping the May 1982 moral panic to flourish. The educational system in Israel seems, somehow, to be prone to various moral panics. For example, in 1979 and again in 1981, the Israeli public learned, through the media, about terrible problems of violence and vandalism in Israeli schools. Horowitz and Amir (1981) indicated that the reports on violence and vandalism in schools were widely exaggerated. Ajzenstadt (1984) pointed out that the panics about violence and vandalism in Israeli schools probably began, and were fueled by, the different groups whose interest it was to create such panics: for example the teacher's union, which was negotiating for the annual salary raises of teachers, wanted to show how hard their job was; and parents who were against integrating schools with students from different sex and ethnic groups, had an interest in showing that this integration had disastrous outcomes. Thus, another moral panic located within the educational system was associated in the public mind with what it felt were endemic problems to this system.

The May 1982 Moral Panic: Morality and Interests

The questions of the specific *timing* and of the specific *content* of the panic need now to be addressed directly.

What the May 1982 drug moral panic in Israel suggests is that it is quite possible for the relevant interested parties to capitalize on existing diversity and animosity between various symbolic-moral universes and exploit this situation for their own benefit. This does not imply that the interested parties do not happen to believe in a specific moral universe. Rather, that they work within the existing context of moral divisions by using the media to exploit that factor.

The argument so far explains why illicit psychoactive drug use is an almost natural topic for a moral panic. Drug abuse is an easy target (Christie, 1985; Dumont, 1973; Szasz, 1975), and can be used in a moral panic as a boundary maintenance device in a clash between opposing symbolic-moral universes. The Israeli police, however, had a much more specific interest in using this topic for a moral panic. The state witness who retracted his testimonies in early May challenged the morality, integrity – indeed, the legitimacy – of the police anti-drug abuse action. Mr Sabag's statement implied that the police used deliberately doubtful methods. The police denied Mr Sabag's claims – and was stuck with the account. It had either to justify what it did, neutralize Mr Sabag's account, or divert attention from this challenge. It appears that the police decided to pursue the third alternative. The choice of the police of drugs for a moral panic was not coincidental. Since the challenge to the police was raised within the context of drug law enforcement, the proper reaction had to take place within that area. There were three major messages that the police delivered during the drug moral panic it helped to create. First, the prevalence of drug abuse is very high, much more serious than what we assume. When the accusation about governmental conspiracy was made, the police did nothing to negate this obviously wrong accusation. Second, middle-class adolescents in what are considered good, even elite, high schools are those that are massively involved in this dangerous illicit drug use. Thus, the cream of Israel's young minds are in danger. Third, while the police have the solution to this problem, lack of cooperation and permissiveness undermine its efforts.

The police used a vocabulary of motives which projected an image of being engaged in a battle with an arch-enemy that corrupted and destroyed the morality of Israel's finest minds. Clearly, when such a battle is waged, a very specific charge, such as the claim made by Mr Sabag about illegal arrests, tends to disappear. At this point even if the police had admitted to having made a mistake in the Sabag affair, the mistake would have to be regarded as trivial, technical, of little importance. After all, on the one hand, we have a symbolic-moral universe which claims to have Israel's future best interests at heart; and, on the other hand, only a questionable character making a niggling claim. Diversion of attention here seemed to be very sucessful. After May 12 no one seemed even to remember the state witness problem.

We can see why drugs were an almost natural choice for a moral panic and why scientists, and especially members of the Inter-ministerial Committee, were hardly heard. While most of them knew what the actual facts were, neither the parliamentary committee nor the press seemed very interested in these views, since these facts did not seem to help understand the drug menace. Furthermore, contrary claims were cast into the opposing symbolic-moral universe as overly permissive; they did not seem to care about Israel's youth and therefore its future. Such claims seemed to question the authority and legitimacy of the instigators of the moral panic. The above-mentioned challenge assumed one of two forms. The first was the fact that opponents to the moral panic were prevented from expressing their view both to the parliamentary committee and to the media. The second was a claim that there was a governmental conspiracy to hide the true magnitude of the problem and that scientists were too liberal. Thus, opponents to the panic always found themselves in the uncomfortable position of having to apologize and cope with either the problem of the conspiracy theory or with the accusation of being too liberal. Thus, aside from the two contrasting symbolic-moral universes, two hierarchies of credibility were contrasted here as well. On the one hand, we had the police and the politicians, on the other hand, the scientists. This analysis also helps us to understand why, in other similar situations, the voices of those who had accuarte information about the nature and extent of the problem were not given a full hearing.

The May 1982 moral panic focused not only on drugs but on drug abuse among middle-class and elite adolescents, in middle-class and elite high schools. The threat potential and the degree of dangerousness of illicit psychoactive drug use among this particular group is obvious, and magnifies the intensity and impact of the moral panic. The fact that drug abuse among non-elite, peripheral, and problematic adolescents is probably much higher than among elite adolescents did not seem to bother the moral crusaders one bit.

Hence, the danger in widespread illicit psychoactive drug use is that of a *moral revolution* (see Lidz and Walker, 1980), where the symbolic moral universe of users would gain legitimacy, power and credibility and its boundaries would expand to include members that previously inhabited other, perhaps opposing, symbolic-moral universes.

The issue of whether moral panics represent exaggeration of existing problems, or fabrication of nonexisting issues is an important one. Clearly, the May 1982 moral panic represented the exaggeration of an existing problem, not a complete fabrication. Studies by Erikson (1966), Bergesen (1978), Ben-Yehuda (1980), Victor (1993), and Richardson, Best, and Bromley (1991), in contrast represent fabrications of nonexistent conditions. As to whether fabrication or exaggeration takes place depends on the specific case.

Thus, while the explanation of the *timing* of the May 1982 drug panic links it to the different interested parties which created and fueled the panic, the explanation of the *content* of the panic is linked most strongly to the issue of morality.

12

THE AMERICAN DRUG
PANIC OF THE 1980S

Over the decades of the twentieth century, drug use has gone through cycles of intense public awareness and concern and relative indifference. For some of these decades, reformers, the public, the media, or legislators focus on a specific drug which stands in for or represents the drug problem generally. The late 1980s witnessed a drug "panic," "crisis," or "scare" (Levine and Reinarman, 1988, 1987; Reinarman and Levine, 1989; Goode, 1990). Public concern about drug use, although it had been building throughout the 1980s, fairly *exploded* late in 1985 and early in 1986. And the drug that was the special target of public concern was cocaine, more specifically, crack, a cocaine derivative. Drug use generally came to be seen as a – some say *the* – social problem of the decade. Drug use, abuse, and misuse emerged into the limelight as perhaps never before. It is possible that in no other decade has the issue of drugs occupied such a huge and troubling space in the public consciousness. And it is possible that no specific drug has dominated center stage in this concern as crack cocaine did between 1986 and, roughly, late 1989 to early 1990.

In many ways, the drug panic of the late 1980s is interesting because it was so unexpected. The 1970s represented something of a high water mark in both the use and the pubic acceptance and tolerance of illegal drugs. Consider that:

• During the decade of the 1970s, eleven states, encompassing one-third of the population of the United States, decriminalized small-quantity marijuana possession.
• In 1978, only a third (35 percent) of American high school seniors believed that people who smoked marijuana *regularly* risked harming themselves (Johnston, O'Malley, and Bachman, 1989, p. 129).
• Only a quarter (25 percent) of high school seniors said that private use of marijuana should be against the law (p. 141).
• In 1979, six out of ten American high school seniors (60 percent) had used marijuana at least once during their lifetimes (p. 48).

- Half (51 percent) had used it during the previous month (p. 49).
- Over a third (37 percent) had used it during the previous month (p. 50).
- One out of ten used marijuana every day (p. 51).
- In 1979, one quarter of Americans aged 12 to 17 (24 percent), nearly half of 18 to 25 year olds (47 percent), and nearly one in ten of those age 26 and older (9 percent), had used marijuana at least once during the previous year (NIDA, 1989).
- Tolerance and use of a number of the other illegal drugs, while not nearly so widespread as with marijuana, were at unprecedented levels.

The Decade of the 1980s: Measures of Public Concern

Something began happening in 1980 or thereabouts – for some indicators, give or take a year or so – that reversed this trend. Beginning roughly in the first year of the decade of the 1980s, public tolerance of the use of illegal drug use declined, belief that the use of illegal drugs is harmful increased, belief that use, possession, and sale of the currently illegal drugs should be decriminalized or legalized declined, and the use of these illegal drugs declined.

Periodically, the Gallup poll asks a sample of Americans the question, "What do you think is the most important problem facing this country today?" Drug abuse declined among the most important problems named by the public in Gallup polls between the early 1970s (February 1973, 20 percent) and the late 1970s (February, May, and October 1979, no mention at all), a period, ironically, as we saw, when drug use among the American public was at an all-time high. This set of circumstances represents a constructionist's dream: a condition that increased markedly in objective seriousness was one which manifested a decreasing measure of social concern. Between 1979 and 1984, drug use and abuse did not appear at all in the Gallup polls among the most often mentioned problems facing the country, indicating a relatively and consistently low level of concern about the issue.

This changed in the mid 1980s. In January, May, and October of 1985, the proportion of those polled mentioning drug abuse as the nation's number one problem fluctuated from 2 to 6 to 3 percent. In July 1986, this figure increased to 8 percent, which placed it fourth among major American social problems. In a set of parallel polls, conducted by the *New York Times* and CBS News in April 1986, only 2 percent named drug abuse as the nation's number one problem; by August, the figure had increased to 13 percent (Clymer, 1986; Jensen, Gerber, and Babcock, 1991). The figure continued to grow through nearly the remainder of the 1980s until, in September 1989, a whopping 64 percent of the respondents in the *New York Times*/CBS News poll said that drug abuse represented the most important problem facing the country; this response is one of the most intense preoccupations by the American public on any issue in polling history. The concern at that time had been fueled by a barrage of network news programs on drug abuse and a major speech by President George Bush declaring a "war on drugs" (Kagay, 1990; Oreskes, 1990). In short, by the late 1980s, drug abuse had attained what Hilgartner and Bosk refer to as a "celebrity" status (1988, p. 57).

The social construction of social concern and therefore, from a constructionist perspective, social problems, is revealed as much by the rise as the *demise* of drug abuse as the nation's number one problem. The 64 percent figure for September 1989 proved to be the apex of public concern about drugs; it is unlikely that a figure of such magnitude will be achieved for drug abuse again. After that, said one media expert, intense public concern simply "went away" (Oreskes, 1990). By November 1989, again, according to a *New York Times*/ CBS News poll, the figure had slipped to 38 percent; in April 1990, it was 30 percent; in July 1990, 18 percent; and in August 1990, only 10 percent (Kagay, 1990; Oreskes, 1990; Shenon, 1990). After that, according to the Gallup polls that continued into the 1990s, the figure remained in the 8 to 12 percent range. Why? There is something of a social problems marketplace (Hilgartner and Bosk, 1988; Best, 1990, pp. 15–16), in which different issues must compete for public attention and concern; there is something of a "carrying capacity" or saturation point of public attention: Only so many issues can rank near the top, and, obviously, only one can be number one. Late in 1989 and into the early 1990s, two additional problems overshadowed the drug issue in the public consciousness – the economic recession and the crisis and war in the Persian Gulf. By the early 1990s, "other issues [aside from drugs] came in. The media stopped covering it [the drug story], and the public stopped thinking about it as much" (Oreskes, 1990). Just as social problems can be constructed, they can also be "deconstructed"!

Another concrete measure of how certain conditions or phenomena are perceived as burning issues at a particular time is the focus of the media on them, one specific and concrete indicator of which is the number of articles published on those subjects in magazines and newspapers. The *Reader's Guide to Periodical Literature* indexes all the articles that appear each year in the United States and Canada. In 1979 to 1980 (March to February), only 15 articles were published nationally on the subjects of "Drug Abuse," "Drugs and Youth," "Drugs and Sports," "Drugs and Employment," "Drugs and Celebrities," "Drugs and Musicians," and "Drug Education." (New topics in addition to these continue to appear over the years in the *Reader's Guide* under the general topic of drugs; these were selected as indicative of the total volume of drug-related articles.) In 1980–1, the tally was 37; in 1981–2, 29; in 1982–3, 38; in 1983–4, 48; and in 1984–5, 76. In 1985, the *Reader's Guide* changed the time period include in the count to coincide with the calendar year; in that full year, there were 103 articles devoted to the above-mentioned drug-related topics. In 1986, the number of articles published on these subjects totaled 280 – between a two- and a threefold increase in only a year, and a sixfold increase in less than three years. But in 1987, drug use received strikingly less attention in national magazines: Only 116 articles were listed in the *Reader's Guide* on these drug-related topics. In 1988, 133 articles appeared; and in 1989, there was something of a rebound of interest in the subject: 222 articles on these drug subjects were listed in the *Reader's Guide*. But in 1990, only 128 articles on these topics appeared. It seems that the early 1990s (as with the public opinion polls) witnessed a diminution of interest in the drug problem.

As we saw, not only is media attention to a given condition one measure of the moral panic – relative to its threat – but exaggerations of the seriousness of the condition by media or movement representatives can also be taken as an indicator of whether a society is in the throes of a moral panic. As Best says, the media and movement representatives "tend to use big numbers when estimating the scope of a social problem" – after all, they reason, "big numbers are better than little numbers" (1990, p. 147, 1989b, pp. 21, 32). The same applies, with even greater force, to moral panics. Orcutt and Turner (1993) demonstrate how, through "shocking numbers" and "graphic ac-counts," newspaper and magazine articles distorted the extend of drug abuse in the United States in the 1980s by making it appear to be considerably more extensive than it actually was. By truncating the bottom of his graph and sqeezing the *Y*-axis into a tighter, narrower space, the graphic artist who designed the layout of a major *Newsweek* article "transformed statistically nonsignificant [year-by-year] fluc-tuations" in a high school survey "into striking peaks and valleys" (p. 194). In this way, seeming increases in the yearly use figures were transfigured "into a tangible and threatening social fact" (p. 195). Other articles presented estimates of lifetime prevalence – or use by age 27 – implying that they covered the period of use during high school (p. 198). These graphic and statistical techniques contributed to the media "feeding frenzy" that characterized the drug panic of the mid to late 1980s.

Another indication or measure of the degree of felt concern about an issue is the legislation proposed to deal with a given condition, phenomenon, or problem – both seriously and rhetorically – by politi-cians and lawmakers. In June 1986, Ed Koch, then mayor of New York

City, urged the death penalty for any drug dealer convicted of possessing at least a kilogram (2.2 pounds) of either cocaine or heroin. Two months later, Mario Cuomo, governor of New York State, regarded as a more temperate politician than Koch, called for a life sentence for anyone convicted of selling *three vials* of crack – at that time, a quantity of the drug which sold on the street for $50. In September, during the debates over a new federal drug bill, Claude Pepper, a Florida representative (now deceased) said cynically, "Right now, you could put an amendment through to hang, draw, and quarter" drug dealers. "That's what happens when you get an emotional issue like this," he added (Kerr, 1986).

In a series of speeches between June and September, 1986, President Ronald Reagan called for a "nationwide crusade against drugs, a sustained, relentless effort to rid America of this scourge." His proposed legislation first added then, strangely, partly rescinded) $2 billion in federal monies to fight the problem, including $56 million for drug testing for federal employees. In many ways, Reagan's speeches were not only a measure of concern over drugs – they also played on and exacerbated that concern. In September 1986, the House of Representatives approved, by the overwhelming vote of 393 to 16, a package of drug enforcement, stiffer federal sentences, increased spending for education, treatment programs, and penalties against drug-producing countries which do not cooperate in US-sponsored drug eradication programs. Approved by the Senate in October, the drug bill, ultimately costing $1.7 billion, was signed into law by President Reagan. In it, a death penalty provision (unlikely ever to be carried out) was included for drug kingpins. Although legislation that had been enacted in 1984 included some anti-drug provisions, the 1986 legislation represented the first effort by Congress in 15 years to enact a major anti-drug law (Stolz, 1990, p. 8). In short, in 1986, the drug question preoccupied numerous politicians and lawmakers at the municipal, state, and federal levels, all "scrambling to put their imprint on the issue." For all, "politics have become as important as the [objective harm of the] substance" (Fuerbringer, 1986).

But by the early 1990s, the issue had cooled down among politicians. Reports emanating from Washington indicated that by 1993, the administration of Bill Clinton (elected President in 1992) had downscaled the war on drugs from "one of three top [national] priorities to Number 29 on a list of 29" priorities (Schneider, 1993, p. 1). One indicator of this scaling down of priorities: in 1993, Clinton's director of national drug control policy (the so-called drug "czar"), Lee Brown, headed a staff of 24 aides, compared with 146 who worked in George Bush's drug office. In short, from the late 1980s to the early 1990s, fear of drug abuse ceased to be a moral panic; as a social problem, drug abuse lost its "celebrity" status. In that respect, it was similar to an even more extreme case, global warming (Ungar, 1992, p. 493), which, within a matter of less than a year in the late 1980s, moved from being a "celebrity" social problem to one that generated relatively little concern in the public and was rarely mentioned any longer by officials.

Other indicators, measures, or manifestations of the intense concern felt in the United States about the drug issue on a wide range of fronts include the following:

- During the 1970s, as we saw, 11 states decriminalized small-quantity marijuana possession. During the 1980s, the marijuana decriminalization intiative ground to a complete standstill; not one state decriminalized marijuana possession, and in the late 1980s and early 1990, as a result of popular referenda, two states – Oregon and Alaska – recriminalized the possession of small quantities of marijuana.

- Drug testing emerged as a major issue; by 1988, a majority of the Fortune 500 corporations required drug testing for their employees (Anonymous, 1987). In the armed services, where drug use became cause for dismissal for all officers for the first offense, and cause for compulsory treatment for enlisted men and women, the proportion testing positive dropped from 27 in 1980 to 3 percent in 1986 (Halloran, 1987).

- Celebrities such as the First Lady Nancy Reagan, comedian Bob Hope, and politician Jesse Jackson, acted as moral entrepreneurs, joining forces in "speaking out against drugs." Nancy Reagan claimed that every casual recreational drug user was an "accomplice to murder," that "Drug use is a repudiation of everything America is."

- Anti-drug propaganda proliferated. The slogan for the 1980s (issuing from the First Lady's office) became "Just say no," that is, say "no" to drug use. "Don't even try it," we were warned. "If you're going to die for something," a spokesperson for an anit-drug campaign said, "this [meaning drugs] sure ain't it." One ad suggested that taking drugs has the same effect on one's brain as frying does on an egg. Another claimed that snorting cocaine is equivalent to putting a revolver up one's nose and pulling the trigger.

- Organizations designed to deal with drug abuse sprang up in great profusion as well, with names such as College Challenge, World Youth Against Drug Abuse, the Just Say No Club, PRIDE, STOPP, Responsible Adolescents Can Help, Youth to Youth, and partnership for a Drug-Free America. (It should come as no surprise that most of these organizations have since folded.) Pamphlets, books, newsletters, and videotapes were offered for sale to concerned parents, teachers, and youth organizers who wanted to put a stop to drug use and abuse in their schools and communities. We were warned of glassy-eyed zombies high on marijuana, of cocaine sprinkled into popcorn at teen parties, of junkies nodding out on every street corner, crack addicts invading every neighborhood *en masse*. Every drug user "is a scourge and a bum," declared one police officer in an op-ed piece in a major newspaper (Williams, 1986), and a chorus of concerned citizens nodded in approval.

In short, the 1980s witnessed an enormous increase in public concern about drug use and abuse; all the actors in Stanley Cohen's drama of the moral panic – the public, the media, politicians and lawmakers, action groups, and law enforcement – expressed *strikingly* and *measureably* greater concern about the issue between 1986 and 1989 than they had previously and than they did afterward. By nearly every conceivable subjective criterion, drug use and abuse emerged as a major social problem – perhaps *the* major social problem – during the late 1980s. So intense and widespread was this concern, it would seem safe to say, the United States was experiencing something of a drug "panic" at that time.

Why the Drug Panic?

The question is, Why? What generated such intense public concern about drug abuse between 1986 and 1989? Did this issue emerge as a consequence of objective factors – that is, did changes take place late in 1985 or early in 1986 to make drug use even more threatening, dangerous, or damaging than it had been prior to that period? Had even more dangerous drugs emerged and come to be used more frequently in the mid to late 1980s than was true in the late 1970s and early 1980s? Were they used via more damaging and dangerous methods or routes of administration? Were more people dying during the "panic" period than before and after?

Or, on the other hand, was this concern solely a consequence of subjective factors – an illusory issue, perhaps, generated by politicians to get elected in the 1986 campaigns? If so, why in 1986, but not in 1984 or 1982? As we saw with the Renaissance witch craze and the Israeli drug panic of 1982, an investigation of moral panic entails investigating the question of its timing. Did the panic erupt as a result of a few moral entrepreneurs who wished to condemn and eliminate an activity they deemed immoral and damaging? Or a product of the schemes of organizational empire-builders who wished to create or expand their realm of supposed expertise? Who, exactly, was involved in the "claims-making activities" that held drug use and abuse to be a major social problem? What was it, exactly, that generated the extremely widespread and intense public concern over drug use that emerged, even erupted, in the mid 1980s?

Kerr (1986) falls just short of declaring the intense concern over drug abuse which had begun building throughout the first half of the 1980s, and fairly exploded in 1986, "all hype." "Why now?" he asks. After all, levels of drug use fell in the United States throughout the 1980s; why was drug use seen as a problem when it was at practically a decade-long low? Some form of social construction can only account for the concern, Kerr argues.

Levine and Reinarman (1987, 1988; Reinarman and Levine, 1989) take the argument a step further and claim that in the late 1980s, America was "in the throes of a drug scare . . . [that] takes a kernel of truth and distorts and exaggerates the facts for political, bureaucratic, or financial purposes. During a drug scare all kinds of social problems are blamed on the use of one chemical substance or another – problems which have little to do with the drug" (1987, p. 1). Citing the surveys conducted by the National Institute on Drug Abuse (NIDA), which show tens of millions of Americans to have used illegal drugs once or more, they argue that the "vast majority" of individuals who try drugs "do not become addicts – they do not end up in emergency rooms, or on the streets selling their mother's TV for a fix" (p. 10). They conclude that there are many problems that are objectively far more important than the illegal use of drugs. The "just say no" administration, Levine and Reinarman argue, "has just said no to virtually every social program aimed at creating alternatives for inner city youth." The drug scares of the twentieth century, they conclude, "do not aid public health; they may actually hurt it, and they give a very distorted sense of priorities and problems. This drug scare, like the others before it, is drug-abuse abuse" (Levine and Reinarman, 1987, p. 10; see also Levine and Reinarman, 1988).

Again, the question is, Why? Why a scare about a virtually nonexistent threat – or, more precisely, why a scare about a threat whose current and potential damage is less than other, far more serious, conditions? And, presumably, which causes significantly fewer deaths than it did a decade earlier, when drug use was at a strikingly higher level?

The "latest drug scare," Levine and Reinarman say, "has been concocted by the press, politicians, and moral entrepreneurs to serve other agendas" (Reinarman and Levine, 1989, p. 127); it is, "quite simply, scapegoating" (Levine and Reinarman, 1988, p. 258). It appeals to "racism, bureaucratic self-interest, economics, and mongering by the media." In addition, "the issue of illicit drug use . . . focuses attention away from structural ills like economic inequality, injustice, and lack of meaningful roles for young people. A crusade against drug use allows conservative politicians to be law-and-order minded; it also permits them to give the appearance of caring about social ills without committing them to do or spend very much to help people" (Levine and Reinarman, 1988, p. 255). The social construction of drug abuse as a major problem in the late 1980s, Levine and Reinarman argue, serves a political agenda for the powers that be (including the media): maintain the status quo and profit from doing it.

Some additional factors that have been cited by others as contributing to the construction of drug abuse as the major social problem in the mid to late 1980s include:

The Explosion of Crack Cocaine Use

At the beginning of 1985, crack, a potent crystalline form of cocaine, was practically an unknown – and unused – drug in the United States. By late 1985, the drug was beginning to be used extensively in urban areas, and the press accorded prominent coverage to it. Its previous obscurity, the seeming suddenness of its widespread use – although it had been used on a smaller scale since the early 1980s – and the degree to which it caught on in some neighborhoods made the crack story newsworthy and gave the public the impression that a major drug crisis had erupted practically overnight. Actually, the drug was and is used in large numbers only in some urban areas and, in those, only in certain neighborhoods. The 1986 national high school senior study asked a question about crack cocaine for the first time; about 4 percent in the study said that they had used the drug at least once (Johnston, O'Malley, and Bachman, 1987, pp. 16–17, 45). Thus, it was not simply the greater danger than new patterns of crack used posed but the drama of a new, previously almost unknown, and potentially destructive, drug type on the drug abuse stage that helped generate the panic.

The Death of Athletes from Cocaine Abuse

In June 1986, barely a week apart, two popular young athletes died of a cocaine overdose – on June 19, University of Maryland basketball forward Len Bias, and on June 27, Cleveland Browns' defensive back Don Rogers. Bias's death was felt to be especially devastating, to some degree, because of the proximity of Maryland's campus to the nation's capital. Said one member of the House of Representatives, "Congress is predominantly male and very sports-minded." With Bias's death, he said, "you were hit with a devastating blow" (Kerr, 1986, p. B6). More generally, a nation, such as the United States, that glorifies sports figures is one which will tend to treat the death of a famous athlete as not only a catastrophe, but will see the source of that athlete's death as more *common* and *representative* than it actually is.

The Role of the Media

The drug-related events or developments mentioned above, which would have received a great deal of media attention in any case, were even more nationally prominent because they occurred in close proximity to major media centers – Bias's death in the Washington area, and the emergence of crack cocaine use specifically in neighborhoods in New York City and Los Angeles, "only blocks from the offices of major national news organizations" (Kerr, 1986, p. B6).

The General Political Climate

Although not specific only to the 1986–9 period, one factor that helped to highlight the drug issue as a major social problem was the generally conservative political climate of the 1980s. Whether a cause or a consequence of this climate, the election of Ronald Reagan as President of the United States in 1980 set the tone for much of what was to follow throughout the decade, especially in the areas of sex, family, abortion, pornography, homosexuality, civil rights and civil liberties, and, of course, drugs. We have mentioned several of these developments on the drug front – the emergence of drug testing as a major issue, the cessation of the marijuana decriminalization movement (and the recriminalization of small-quantity marijuana posession in two states), the "just say no" campaign, the emergence of scores of anti-drug organizations, and so on. In short, "it was in this general setting of conservativism that drugs could emerge as the leading social problem" facing the country in the 1980s (Jensen, Gerber, and Babcock, 1991, p. 657).

The 1986 Congressional Election

The 1986 elections must be counted as a source of heightened concern about the drug issue (Kerr, 1986; Jensen, Gerber, and Babcock, 1991), and the 1988 election, too, must be mentioned as a factor stirring up end-of-the-decade concerns as well. There is something of a dialectic or give-and-take relationship between public concern and attention by politicians to a given issue. On the one hand, we see a "bandwagon" effect here: politicians sense that public concern about and interest in a given topic are growing and they exploit this – in other words, "Congress smells an issue . . . When the media started talking about it, it lit a fire . . . Senators, once they started talking, realized they were all hearing similar things from their local officials" (Kerr, 1986, p. B6). On the other hand, while politicians took advantage of an issue that was in the incipient problem stage, once they got on the bandwagon, public concern escalated even further (Jensen, Babcock, and Gerber, 1991, p. 660). We need not accuse politicians of being scheming Machiavellians on the drug issue. It is their job to get elected, and they try to do it the best way they know how. Moreover, they would argue, it is their job to address the needs and concerns of their constituencies; dealing with the drug issue, or seeming to – that is, only in speeches – is one way of doing just that. This also does not mean that the drug crisis was "fabricated," "engineered," or "orchestrated" by politicians who stirred up an issue in the face of public indifference. The public is not that gullible, and politicians cannot usually create feverish concern where none previously existed simply by making speeches. Many political campaigns have fallen flat, failing completely to capture the public imagination – witness the stress on the "family values" theme which was unsuccessfully touted by the 1992 election campaign of President Bush. In contrast, the drug issue tapped genuine widespread (though, in large part, erroneously based) concerns on the part of the American public, even though they were helped along by politicians who "smelled an issue."

The Role of Prominent Spokespersons

Soon after Ronald Reagan took office in 1981, his wife, Nancy Reagan, began making speeches stressing the anti-drug theme. It was from her office as First Lady that the "Just say no" slogan emerged. Some observers (Beck, 1981) have suggested that Mrs Reagan chose the issue in part out of public relations considerations. Initially, she had been portrayed by the media as a "cold and insensitive person, whose chief concern seemed to be her wardrobe" (Jensen, Babcock, and Gerber, 1991, p. 657). Her choice of the drug issue could very well have been made to boost her public image, to suggest that she was a compassionate and concerned human being. Regardless of her initial motivation, her campaign, while, again, little more than words, bore fruit some five years after it was launched. The drug crisis of the late 1980s has to be set in the context of Mrs Reagan's immensely publicized campaign. It was she who took the first steps toward galvanizing public concern and media attention. While other spokespersons, before and since, have "spoken out against drugs," she, possibly more than any single individual, is responsible for the success of the drug panic.

Crack Babies: A Panic-driven, Mythical Syndrome?

A specific moral panic arose *within* the broader panic over drugs, although it peaked at a time when the more general panic had already subsided. This was the scare that arose over crack and cocaine babies. This panic illustrates Stanley Cohen's concept of *sensitization*, that is, harm is attributed to a specific condition that tends to be ignored if caused by other, more conventional conditions. After 1964, the police were on the lookout for violence committed by Mods and Rockers, and they reacted to extremely minor offenses as if they were a major threat to the security of the community. With crack babies, what we saw was pathological conditions *associated with* the use of cocaine that was automatically *assumed to have been caused* by the drug which later, careful research indicated, were in fact caused by very conventional conditions *about which there was very little subjective concern.*

Babies are society's future, its most precious and valuable commodity – and they make up its most vulnerable members. Nothing generates more anger and outrage than the physical abuse of tiny, helpless infants. With the emergence of the use of crack cocaine after late 1985, and the upsurge of heavy, chronic cocaine abuse in the late 1980s, speculation arose as to what crack and powdered cocaine do to the offspring of dependent, using, and abusing mothers. If a mother uses either crack or powdered cocaine during pregnancy, what happens to her baby? Does the infant have more medical problems than babies born of mothers who do not use cocaine? If so, how long do these problems persist? For instance, do children entering the first grade suffer medical problems as a consequence of the cocaine use of their mothers more than six years before?

The findings of the initial studies on babies born to mothers dependent on cocaine were extremely pessimistic. Babies whose mothers were exposed to crack and powdered cocaine were, compared with those whose mothers were not exposed to drugs during pregnancy, more likely to be born premature, have a significantly lower birth weight, have smaller heads, suffer seizures, have genital and urinary tract abnormalities, suffer poor motor ability, have brain lesions, and exhibit behavioral aberrations, such as impulsivity, moodiness, and lower responsiveness (Chasnoff et al., 1989).

Findings such as these were picked up by the mass media extremely quickly and just as quickly were transmitted to the general public. Soon after a critical mass of articles on the crack-baby syndrome was published, it became an established fact that crack babies make up a major contemporary medical and social problem. William Bennett, then federal drug "czar," claimed that 375,000 crack babies were being born in the United States in the late 1980s – one out of 10 of all births! – a figure that was echoed by respected *Washington Post* columnist Jack Anderson and *New York Times* editor A. M. Rosenthal (Gieringer, 1990, p. 4). The medical care of crack babies, stated one of the most widely quoted articles to appear in a mass magazine on the subject, is 13 times as expensive as that of normal newborns (Toufexis, 1991). In New York City, the annual number of children placed in foster care in the early 1990s, compared with the number before the crack epidemic, was said to have increased five times. The New York State comptroller's office estimated that New York City alone will spend three-quarters of a billion dollars over the next decade on special education for crack children. There is fear that these youngsters will become "an unmanageable multitude of disturbed and disruptive youth, fear that they will be a lost generation" (Toufexis, 1991, p. 56).

A Pulitzer Prize-winning journalist describes the crack-baby crisis in the following dramatic, heart-wrenching words: "The bright room is filled with baby misery; babies born months too soon; babies weighing little more than a hardcover book; babies that look like wizened old men in the last stages of a terminal illness, wrinkled skin clinging to chicken bones; babies who do not cry because their mouths are full of tubes . . . The reason is crack" (Quindlen, 1990). According to common wisdom that sprang up in the late 1980s and early 1990s, cocaine abuse among pregnant mothers causes serious, in all likelihood, irreparable, medical problems in their babies. This condition is extremely widespread, many said, and will be extremely costly to the society.

The appearance of the crack-babies story in the media was not lost on law enforcement or public attitudes toward law enforcement. In a 15-state survey sponsored by *The Atlanta Constitution*, over 70 percent of the respondents polled favored criminal penalties for pregnant women whose drug use harmed their babies. Mothers in some 20 states have been arrested for the crime of "transferring" illicit drugs to a minor; that is, because of their own drug use, they caused the passage of said controlled substance through the placenta to the fetus they were carrying (Hoffman, 1990). No question about it: the illicit drug use – and more specifically, the crack cocaine use – of pregnant mothers emerged as an important social issue and problem some time in the late 1980s, and it continued to haunt us into the early 1990s.

Even from the beginning, some experts challenged the validity of the crack-baby syndrome. But it was not until the early 1990s that enough medical evidence was assembled to indicate that the syndrome is, in all likelihood, mythical in nature (Neuspiel et al., 1991; Richardson and Day, 1991; Coles, 1991; Coles, 1992; Richardson, 1992; Day, Richardson, and McGauhey, 1992). The problem with most of the early research of the babies of mothers who used powdered and crack cocaine was that there were no *controls*. Many of these women also drank alcohol, some heavily – and medical science knows that alcohol abuse is causally linked with at least one *in utero* medical problem: the fetal alcohol syndrome. In addition, no controls were applied for cigarette smoking (associated with low infant birth weight), nutritional condition, medical condition of the mother, the presence of absence of sexually transmitted disease, medical attention (getting checkups, following the advice of one's physician – or even going to a physician during pregnancy), and so on. In other words, factors that vary with cocaine use are known to determine poorer infant outcomes; mothers who smoke crack and use powdered cocaine are more likely to engage in other behaviors that correlate with poor infant health. Mothers who smoke crack are also more likely to drink; is the condition of their children due to the alcohol or the cocaine? Mothers who smoke crack are also more likely to suffer from sexually transmitted diseases; Such mothers are also less likely to eat a nutritious, balanced diet, get regular checkups, and so on. Was it these other factors, or was it the independent effect of the cocaine itself, that produced the negative outcomes?

When the influence of these other factors is held constant, "it becomes clear that cocaine use per se does not affect infant outcomes. Rather, the lifestyle and covariates of cocaine use combine to affect the infant's status" (Richardson, 1992, pp. 11–12). While much more study is needed before a definitive conclusion can be reached, current medical opinion is leaning toward the view that "the effects of prenatal cocaine exposure that have been reported to date reflect the impact of polydrug use and a disadvantaged lifestyle, rather than the effects of cocaine" (pp. 11–12). In short, it is entirely possible that the crack-babies issue will turn out to be a "hysteria-driven" rather than a "fact-driven" syndrome. While, in the late 1980s and the early 1990s, the public, the media, and even the medical profession, were sensitized to the possible harmful effects of cocaine abuse in babies, the more conventional factors were normalized, that is, their possible influence was ignored. Such processes are characteristic of the moral panic.

Interestingly, while the media were quick to pick up on and publicize the early research that seemed to show that powdered and crack cocaine caused medical harm in newborns, infants, and even school-age children, very little media attention has been devoted to correcting this – in all likelihood – mistaken view. One rare exception is *Boston Globe* columnist Ellen Goodman. Says Goodman, "It turns out that 'crack babies' may be a creature of the imagination as much as medicine, a syndrome seen in the media more often than in medicine" (1992). Dr Ira Chasnoff, whose work originally pointed in the direction of indicating medical problems for these kids, was quoted by Goodman as saying: "Their average developmental functioning is normal. They are no different from other children growing up." Says Dr Claire Coles, another researcher cited by Goodman, the myth of the crack baby became a "media hit," in part, because crack is not used by "people like us." "If a child comes to kindergarten with that label [crack baby] they're dead. They are very likely to fulfill the worst prophecy" (Goodman, 1992). It is likely that, because of this sensitization process and because the media rarely correct distorted, sensational stories, much of the public will continue to believe in the "crack-baby" myth for some time to come.

Is the Objectivist Perspective Irrelevant?

As we see, the drug panic was constructed for a variety of reasons; a number of these reasons are subjective factors and have little, if anything, to do with the concrete damage or harm inflicted on the society by the use of illegal psychoactive substances. In this sense, the constructionists are correct; the 1986–9 outbreak of concern over drugs was a moral panic. On the other hand, we should not dismiss the objective dimension as completely irrelevant. Simply because a problem or crisis is constructed does not mean that it is imaginary. Because the media, politicians, and the public do not necessarily react to the objective features of a particular condition does not indicate or imply that they do not exist. (Levine and Reinarman [1988, pp. 255–6] make essentially the same point.) As measured by the human toll, drug use was *not* the most serious condition facing the country in the late 1980s. And recreational illegal drug use was actually declining at the precise period when public hysteria reached an all-time high. These things are true, interesting, and they verify the constructionist's position. At the same time, while *occasional recreational* drug use declined throughout the 1980s, heavy, frequent, chronic use – specifically of powdered and crack cocaine – during this period actually increased. And it is among heavy users that major medical and social damage is most likely to occur, such as lethal and nonlethal overdoses and violent crime (Goode, 1990).

The valid insights of the constructionist argument should not blind us to the concrete seriousness that drug use confronts us with. While drug use may not be the number one problem in American society by any conceivable measure – nor, possibly, among the top ten problems – its contribution to the devastation of some neighborhoods and communities, and victimizing behavior of users and dealers cannot be denined. (It is entirely possible, as some critics stress, that criminalization and vigorous enforcement have actually *contributed* to the harm that drugs do [Nadelmann, 1989], but that is another matter and it is, in principle, an empirical question – one, moreover, that has not yet been demonstrated to the satisfaction of most observers of the drug scene.) Moreover, by any conceivable criterion, the contribution that the use of powdered and crack cocaine made to these problems was *growing*, not increasing.

By standardizing overdose measures and keeping the locales from which the data were drawn, the Division of Epidemiology and Prevention Research of the National Institute on Drug Abuse prepared two reports (DAWN, 1987; Adams et al., 1989), focusing on the 1976–85 and 1984–8 periods. These researchers found that between 1979 and 1985, nonlethal cocaine overdose measures in the hospitals studied increased five times, and lethal overdoses increased six times (DAWN, 1987); between 1984 and 1988, the comparable figures were five and two-and-a-half times (Adams, et al., 1989). Thus, it is a serious distortion of the facts to argue that the drug panic was little more than a "scare" hoked up as a consequence of the scapegoating function it served. Something was happening out there; it was concrete, measureable, and objectively real, and it was almost universally regarded as undesirable.

While we may agree that social problems are "not mere objective givens," that "objective conditions alone do not constitute social problems," that value judgments are a "necessary component" of what social problems are, that social problems are "inherently political phenomena" (Haines, 1979, pp. 119, 120), we may nonetheless acknowledge the role that objective seriousness plays in definitions of and public concern over a given condition. "Claims-making" activities are more successful at defining a condition as a social problem to the extent that that condition is, or, it can be made to seem that that condition is, objectively serious. To put things another way, counting up dead bodies is a resource for the claims-maker. Too often, the radical constructionist implies that social problems can be generated out of thin air with little or no concrete basis whatsoever. While this is occasionally the case (witness the current satanism ritual child abuse scare), such problems or panics are likely to grip only a minority of the public; in any case, this is most decidedly does not characterize what happened with illegal drug use in the United States in the 1980s. As Jones, Gallagher, and McFalls put the matter: "Discarding the objective domension" in the study of social problems "is analogous to studying the issues exploding in the public mind while deliberately ignoring the weaponry" (1989, pp. 7–8). Ungar (1992, p. 496) makes essentially the same point when he argues that, in overreacting to the errors associated with the objectivist approach to social problems, social constructionists "ignore real-world factors in explaining phenomena." The claims of movement activists can, in Ungar's term, "piggyback" onto "dramatic real-world events" (p. 487);

that is, actual events, some (although not all) of them objectively harmful, can dramatize claims and heighten social concern about the general conditions that *caused* those events. Of course, those events do have to be socially interpreted as such before they can be called "dramatic."

However, this is not quite what was happening in the world of drugs circa 1986–9. Note that the overdose figures we've just cited *had virtually nothing to do* with public or official concern over drug abuse. They are not an *explanation* or even a *factor* in the drug panic. Essentially, they are *irrelevant* to the question of why this concern exploded during the 1986–9 period. These figures *do* show that any argument based on the declining objective seriousness of the drug problem between the mid to late 1980s has to be false, since the data show that, objectively speaking, the problem was not declining in seriousness in the first place. In this sense, they are relevant to the drug panic: they address the issue of disproportionality. However, they do *not* address the question of why the panic came about. It is one thing for the scholar or researcher to be aware of the fact that a given objective level of a certain condition exists. The question of whether or not that level of seriousness is *recognized* or *acknowledged* by the various parties involved is quite another matter.

To judge by the fact that anti-drug crusaders in the late 1980s made almost no use of the overdose statistics cited above, it is entirely likely that they were not even aware of their existence. Why was more attention not paid to this research when it affirmed what these crusaders were saying all along – that drug abuse is extremely dangerous and increasing in seriousness? Were the data too obscure and esoteric? Were these crusaders only interested in dissuading middle-class recreational users from drug abuse and non-users from experimentation – and not at all in the use, abuse, and addiction of heavy, chronic street heroin and cocaine-dependent abusers? These are questions for which we do not have a ready answer. What the lack of focus of anti-drug activists on data that would have made their case in a convincing fashion does indicate is that crusades do not always make the best case they can, they do not always make use of information that is available. Moreover, it means that the issue of disproportionality is more than an abstract exercise; that is, the answer to the question of the discrepancy between concern and condition may exist on at least two levels – what the available information shows and what actors in the drama of the moral panic *are aware of* or *take to be true*. These two levels may be quite different from each other. In a moral panic, activists and crusaders assemble their arguments about the seriousness of the conditions they denounce with any arguments, claims, or supposed facts at their disposal. They may either not have definitive facts at hand to demonstrate their case, or they may not even be attuned to the same sorts of arguments or evidence that experts use to demonstrate a case.

1986–1989: A Moral Panic over Drug Abuse?

Was the concern generated by illegal drug use, especially crack, in the United States in the late 1980s a moral panic? Our answer to that question has to be a qualified yes. In the sense that an increase in this concern actually was accompanied by an increase in measurable harm (caused in part by an increase in heavy, chronic use), this concern cannot be referred to as a panic. On the other hand, crusaders and activists did not make a sober or systematic assessment of the facts; the concern over drugs in the late 1980s *was* a panic in the sense that claims-makers made use of arguments and facts that *were, in fact,* in excess of the available facts. (An example: the famous "This is your brain. This is your brain on drugs. Any questions?" ad campaign.) The fact that overdoses increased during this period, while relevant to the *drama* of the drug panic, was irrelevant to *whether or not* the concern constituted a moral panic, since the data to demonstrate that fact were ignored by major claims-makers in this drama. Moreover, this increase did not *cause* the concern – indeed, had nothing to do with it – because, again, key actors seemed to be unaware of their existence (or relevance to their arguments). They were not reacting to simple matters of body count and overdoses but to the usual array of constructionist factors discussed earlier – the novelty of crack, its seeming powers of enslavement, the overdoses of a few prominent athletes, the role of prominent moral entrepreneurs, and so on. Thus, the fact that some measures of concrete harm rose in concert does not deny the existence of a moral panic over drugs in the United States in the late 1980s. Indeed, a close inspection of its dynamics emphasizes its panic-like quality.

Moreover, in the sense that drug use skyrocketed to become the number one problem in the country, as measured by public opinion polls, while the actual harm it caused was very far down on the list of harmful conditions, this concern most decidedly can be referred to as a panic. In addition – and this is a matter for debate, not one of clearly verified fact – it is entirely possible that both a law enforcement crackdown and the crisis mentality that such concern generates may actually have contributed to the seriousness of the problem, rather than alleviated it (Levine and Reinarman, 1988, pp. 257–8). In this sense, too, we observed a drug panic between 1986 and 1989. And in the sense that the concern was so volatile – that it was pushed off center-stage among the country's major problems in the short span of time between September 1989 and early 1990 – likewise, indicates its panic status. Illegal drug abuse is still regarded as a major American social problem, but its precipitous fall from the problem of the decade to one problem among many, likewise, indicates that factors other than an objective assessment of the harm that it caused were at work. While the American drug panic of the late 1980s was not a classic or perfect case of a moral panic, it was a moral panic nonetheless.

EPILOGUE

THE DEMISE AND INSTITUTIONALIZATION OF MORAL PANICS

Although the rise of moral panics has received some, although insufficient, attention, their demise has been relatively neglected. The question of the demise of moral panics is linked intimately with the issue of their impact: what impact do moral panics have? Do moral panics promote substantial, long-term social change? Or is their impact much like that of fads, which flare up, are popular for a time, and then disappear without a legacy or, seemingly, a trace?

In raising this issue, our investigation parallels Max Weber's concept of the "routinization of charisma" (1968a, pp. 1111–57, 1968b). Charisma, meaning the "gift of the spirit" in ancient Greek, refers to the extraordinary quality that some leaders possess to their followers and by which they rule. Followers do not obey their commands because they inherited a position by birth (as is the case with kings and queens), or because they occupy bureaucratic positions of authority (as is the case with presidents and prime ministers), but because of this special, almost magical, sacred, and supernatural quality. Fidel Castro, Martin Luther King, Jr, Mao Zedong, Malcolm X, and Joan of Arc are examples of charismatic leaders. The problem with charisma is that it is unstable: it cannot be passed on to another leader who lacks it. Who is to be the movement's or government's leader? How to ensure that the leader's commands and injunctions are captured in the form of rules or laws that have power over followers even after he or she is gone? How, in other words, to capture or *routinize* that charisma – to compel followers to obey the leader's injunctions (or what is taken to be the leader's injunctions) in the absence of the leader himself or herself? Will followers obey the rules simply because they, presumably, once issued from the revered leader? How to enshrine the leader's vision into rules and organizational structures? How to succeed the leader with *bureaucratic* (rather than charismatic) authority? Leaders who govern by bureaucratic rules and laws, rather than the force of their personalities, do not generate as much excitement, but their reign tends to be far more stable. Often, when charismatic leaders die, the movement (and, occasionally, a government) with which they are associated dies, too.

The excitement stirred up during a moral panic is similar to the charisma possessed by certain leaders. This excitement, like charisma, is volatile and unstable. The feelings that are generated during its period of influence are intense, passionate. But they do not last. How to ensure that the willingness of individuals gripped by this temporary fervor to follow certain rules or pursue certain enemies continues over time? How to translate the vision stimulated during the moral panic into day-to-day, year-by-year normative and institutional policy? How to continue the aims and goals of moral entrepreneurs, action and interest groups, leaders – and much of the public – in "doing something" about the threat that seems to be posed during the moral panic *after* the emotional fervor of that panic has died down? What we are suggesting is that, as with charismatic leaders, some moral panics are, almost unwittingly, more successful in routinizing the demands for action that are generated during these relatively brief episodes of collective excitement.

Let us be more specific about our investigation. Four questions can help sharpen our inquiry. First, do moral panics have an impact on the society in which they take place by generating formal organizations and institutions; do they, in other words, leave an institutional legacy – in the form of laws, agencies, groups, movements, and so on? Second, if so, what specifically is the nature of that institutional legacy? Third, do moral panics transform the informal normative structure of a society? And fourth, if so, what is the nature of that transformation?

With respect to the first question, then, in principle, moral panics can have two potential outcomes: they can end leaving little or no long-term institutional legacy, disappearing, as with fads, without a trace – they may generate or stimulate no new laws, no lasting social movements, no government agencies. On the other hand, the intensity of the concern that was expressed at the height of moral panics can, in principle, become captured, routinized, or *institutionalized* into ongoing, long-lasting organizational structures. In other words, one possibility is that moral panics can, in principle, generate social change; they can either leave a substantial institutional legacy, or none. And with respect to the second question, these institutional structures can be a diverse lot: laws but no social movements; social movements but no government agencies; and so on.

What is the impact of moral panics on a society's informal normative structure, views of right and wrong? Visions of reality? On its storehouse of myths, legends, tales, and stories? Again, do moral panics comes and go without leaving long-lasting traces? Ben-Yehuda (1985, pp. 1–20) discusses the Durkheimian "double bind": does deviance, on the one hand, promote stability or, on the other, does it encourage flexibility and hence, prepare the way for social change? He suggests that the answer is dependent on which sorts of deviant behaviors are under discussion in which sorts of social systems. The same question may be raised for moral panics: does a sudden, relatively brief outburst of fear, concern, and anger over a given condition, threat, or behavior rigidify the moral boundaries of the society – or segments of the society – and hence, promote stability? Or does it transform the norms and institutions of the society in such a way as to make it a different place from what it was before?

As we have seen throughout this book, moral panics make up an extremely diverse collection of events. We do not find that they go through specific, predetermined stages, with a beginning, a middle, and a predictable end. (For a description of the sequence of stages that social problems go through, see Peyrot, 1984.) Their locus may be society-wide, or local and regional; more specifically, and broad, so-ciety-wide panic may be evident in all or nearly all communities nation-ally, or may or may not explode in certain specific locales, or, alternatively, a panic may break out entirely on a local or community-wide level. Panics may be extremely brief, lasting as little as a month or two – as with the 1982 Israeli drug panic or the "sexual slavery" panic in Orléans, France. Or they may be more long term and run their course only after several years. Some of the longer panics may represent the temporally limited portion of a much longer-range concern, as we saw with the drug panic in the United States, which is in fact a series of moral panics that have come and gone over a hundred-year period. It should come as no surprise that the outcomes of moral panics vary as much as their nature.

Some panics seem to leave relatively little institutional legacy. As we saw, the furor generated by the Mods and Rockers in England in the 1960s resulted in no long-term institutional legacy; no new laws were passed (although some were proposed), and the two germinal social movement that emerged in its wake quickly dissipated when the excite-ment died down.

In contrast, other panics result in laws and other legislation, social movement organizations, action groups, lobbies, normative and behavioral transformations, organizations or governmental agencies, and so on, which are set up or which arise to sustain some of the fervor that prevailed earlier. For example, the periodic drug panics that have washed over American society for over a century continue to deposit institutional sediment in their wake. President Nixon's mini-drug panic of the late 1960s and early 1970s hugely expanded the federal drug budget, placed the drug war on a firm international footing, and created several federal agencies empowered to deal with drug abuse in one way or another, most notably NIDA, the National Institute on Drug Abuse. The latest, 1986–9, drug panic left a substantial legacy in the form of two packages of federal legislation, passed in 1986 and 1988, a substantially larger federal budget, dozens of private social movement organizations, and a public sensitization to the drug issue. (Recall that the "crack-babies" mini-panic arose at the very time – 1989, 1990 and 1991 – that the larger drug panic was declining. If crack cocaine had been as "normalized" as alcohol, it is unlikely that this later panic would have taken hold.) In this way, not only are successive moral panics built on earlier ones, but even in quieter, non-panic periods, the institutional legacy that moral panics leave attempts to regulate the behavior that is deemed harmful, unacceptable, criminal, or deviant. Thus, the earliest drug panics – those that emerged in the late nineteenth and early twentieth centuries – *redefined* drug abuse as deviant and, eventually, criminal; in this sense, they *generated* social change. The later drug panics, in contrast, *reaffirmed* the deviant and criminal status of drug abuse after a period of drift toward normalization and thus, *prevented* social change.

Thus, we argue that moral panics may produce both effects – toward social stability and social change – under specific circumstances. Moreover, we argue, even seemingly inconsequential panics leave behind some sort of legacy. To put the issue another way, the question of the legacy of moral panics is a matter of degree. The impact of a seemingly inconsequential panic, one which produces no new laws or organizations to deal with the supposed threat it addresses, is likely to be felt, at the very least, in the informal or attitudinal realm. With the eruption of a given moral panic, the battle-lines are redrawn, moral universes are reaffirmed, deviants are paraded before upright citizens and denounced, society's moral boundaries are solidified; in Durkheimian terms, society's collective conscience has been strengthened. The message of the moral panic is clear: this is behavior we will *not* tolerate. Through the extreme reactions manifested in panics, a loud and clear moral message is sent and received. In this sense, even relatively transitory panics that do not lay down an organizational legacy, from the point of view of deviance and morality, are not "wasted": they draw precise moral boundaries. The panics which are about imaginary threats emphasize the *contrast* between the condition or behavior that is denounced and the correctness of the righteous folk engaged in the denunciation. The satanic ritual abuse scare, for example, reaffirms the moral correctness of the fundamentalist Christian way of life. The outbreak of a moral panic may result in a legacy so prosaic or mundane as a newspaper file or archive that can be dug up by reporters when, in the future, a string of stories on the same topic begins to break. Though, in the later panic, stories are unlikely to represent a mechanical repetition of stories reported in the earlier one, the very existence of such an archive may help shape later ones.

Even the stir over the Mods and Rockers, a relatively inconsequential moral panic, reminded conventional, lawabiding, middle-aged, middle and lower-middle class segments of English society in the 1960s of the moral correctness of their way of life. Indeed, it is entirely possible that some of the collective excitement generated by the Mods and Rockers was trasferred to juvenile delinquents, the basis of a later, early 1970s moral panic in Britain (Hall et al., 1978). Even extremely short-lived panics may leave some attitudinal legacy that may lie dormant, ready to fuel a later panic under the right conditions. As we saw, in Orléans, France, in 1969, though the furor over "sexual slavery" died down after its initial eruption, many citizens continued to think that something peculiar was going on that was being kept hidden from them. Under the right conditions – for example, an economic depression resulting in the need for a scapegoat, the rise of an anti-Semitic, xenophobic candidate, the eruption of a sex scandal – the sensitization resulting from this nonexistent threat could very well aggravate a new moral panic. Thus, even though moral panics may leave no organizational or institutional legacy, the collective excitement that citizens experience when it lasts prepares them for future panic-like experiences. They may reshape the normative, attitudinal, and value landscape of a society.

The more longer-lasting panics that do set up an institutional and organization structure to deal with the issue, problem, threat, or behavior under attack are clearly more consequential in their impact than those whose impact is confined mainly to the informal realm. To many observers, the 1960s and 1970s represented a drift toward permissiveness and moral laxity, especially with respect to drug use; as we saw, the late 1970s witnessed an all-time high in illegal drug use, tolerance and acceptance of drug use, and support for the decriminalization of at least one illegal substance, marijuana. The drug panic that was set in motion in the early 1980s and exploded in the late 1980s, in a sense, "brought the country back" from the drift toward accepting, and using, illegal drugs. In this sense, then, the American drug panic of the 1980s prevented social change and acted to preserve social stability.

While the impact of more short-term panics is most likely to be restricted to reaffirming moral boundaries, a series of panics focused on the same threat over a long period of time is likely to bring about institutional change as well. The dramatic change over the past century with respect to how American society controls, or attempts to control, the use – and users – of psychoactive substances represents an outstanding example of the latter process. These changes have ramified into institutional spheres as diverse as the criminal justice system, health and medicine, the family, politics, government, and the military, the economy, and education. In the United States, a hundred years ago, psychoactive substances were freely available; today, access to certain categories of drugs is tightly controlled. Over the past century, some drug panics have left a strong institutional legacy, as we saw, in the form of laws, government agencies, social movements, and so on; once these institutional structures were in place, the moral panics that followed typically strengthened the status quo. In short, the many moral entrepreneurs who have played a role in this drama needed a century, and at least a half-dozen discrete panics, to reach the current state of affairs.

A similar process occurred with witchcraft: the early panics transformed the very definition of witchcraft; once that transformation was achieved, later moral panics resulted in preventing changes in existing moral boundaries. It is important to stress that, in discussing moral panics, we are not focusing on a single, brief, discrete episode lasting a few months or a year or two. We are, in fact, discussing a series of events – a process. In the case of witchcraft, clusters of panics stretched out over several centuries. Moral entrepreneurs needed an entire decade to convince the papacy to support the anti-witchcraft campaign, and the impact of that decision stretched out for centuries afterwards.

In short, panics are not like fads, trivial in nature and inconsequential in their impact; they do not come and go, vanishing, as it were, without a trace. Even those that seem to end without impact often leave informal traces that prepare us for later panics. A close examination of the impact of panics forces us to take a more long-range view of things, to look at panics as social process rather than as separate, discrete, time-bound events. Moral panics are a crucial element of the fabric of social change. They are not marginal, exotic, trivial phenomena, but one key by which we can unlock the mysteries of social life.

REFERENCES

Abramowitz, Shlomo. 1982. "The drugs – 'a conspiracy of silence' or 'an inflated baloon'." *Hed Hakriot* (Haifa), May 21, p. 1 (Hebrew).

Abulafia, David. 1981. "Southern Italy and the Florentine economy 1265–1370." *Economic History Review*, Second Series, 34(3): 377–88.

Adams, Edgar H., Ann J. Blanken, Lorraine D. Ferguson, and Andrea Kopstein. 1989. "Overview of selected drug trends." Rockville, MD: The Division of Epidemiology and Prevention Research, National Institute on Drug Abuse, unpublished paper.

Adoni, Hanna and Sherill Mane. 1984. "Media and the social construction of reality. Toward an integration of theory and research." *Communication Research*, 2(3): 323–40.

Ajzenstadt, Mimi. 1984. "The Israeli treatment of 'deviant behavior' in schools as a 'social problem'." Jerusalem, unpublished MA thesis. Institute of Criminology, Hebrew University (Hebrew).

——. 1989. "An historical analysis of a moral panic: perceptions of excessive drinking in British Columbia." Paper delivered at the meetings of the American Society of Criminology, November 1989, Reno, Nevada.

Allport, Gordon W., and Leo Postman. 1946–7. "An analysis of rumor." *Public Opinion Quarterly*, 10 (Winter): 501–17.

Ammerman, Nancy Tatum. 1987. *Bible Believers: Fundamentalists in the Modern World*. New Brunswick, NJ: Rutgers University Press.

Anderson, Alan and Raymond Gordon. 1978. "Witchcraft and the status of women – the case of England." *British Journal of Sociology*, 29(2): 171–82.

Anderson, Patrick. 1981. *High in America. The True Story behind NORML and the Politics of Marijuana*. New York: Viking Press.

Anderson, Robert D. 1970. "The history of witchcraft: a review with some psychiatric comments." *American Journal of Psychiatry*, 126(12): 1727–35.

Andreski, S. 1982. "The syphilitic shock." *Encounter*, (May) 58(5): 7–26.

Anonymous. 1985. "P&G drops logo from its packages: Satan rumors are blamed." *The New York Times*, April 25, pp. D1, D8.

——. 1987. "Graduates face drug tests in joining job market." *The New York Times*, June 21, p. 29.

Anslinger, Harry, with Courtney Ryley Cooper. 1937. "Marihuana: assassin of youth." *American Magazine*, July, pp. 19, 150.

Ariès, Philippe. 1962. *Centuries of Childhood: A Social History of Family Life*. New York: Knopf.

Aronson, Naomi. 1984. "Science as claims-making activity: implications for social problems research." In Joseph W. Schneider and John J. Kitsuse (eds), *Studies in the Sociology of Social Problems*. Norwood, NJ: Ablex, pp. 1–30.

Ashley, Richard. 1972. *Heroin: The Myths and the Facts*. New York: St Martin's Press.

Ashtor, Eliyahu. 1975. "The volume of Levantine trade in the later Middle Ages 1370–1498." *Journal of European Economic History*, 4(3): 573–612.

——. 1976. "Observations on Venetian trade in the Levant in the XIV century." *Journal of European Economic History*, 5(3): 533–86.

Bainton, Ronald H. 1971. *Women of the Reformation in Germany and Italy*. Boston: Beacon Press.

——. 1973. *Women of the Reformation in France and England*. Boston: Beacon Press.

Barlow, Hugh D. 1993. *Introduction to Criminology* (6th edn). New York: Harper Collins.

Barnea, Zippora. 1978. "A multidimensional model of young people's readiness to use drugs." Tel Aviv, unpublished MA thesis, Institute of Criminology, Tel Aviv University (Hebrew).

Barnea, Zippora, Meir Teichman, and Giora Rahav. 1991. "The use of alcohol and drugs among Israeli youth 1989–1990" *Hevra Urevacha*, October, pp. 3–24 (Hebrew).

Baroja, J. C. 1965. *The World of the Witches*. Chicago: University of Chicago Press.

Bartholomew, Robert E. 1990. "Ethnocentricity and the social construction of 'mass hysteria.'" *Culture, Medicine and Psychiatry*, 14 (December): 455–94.

Barton, Allan H. 1969. *Communities in Disaster: A Sociological Analysis of Collective Stress Situations*. Garden City, NY: Doubleday.

Beck, Melinda, with Gerald Lubenow and Martin Kasindorf. 1981. "Nancy: searching for a role." *Newsweek*, February 22, p. 54.

Becker, Howard S. 1963. *Outsiders: Studies in the Sociology of Deviance*. New York: Free Press.

——. (ed.). 1966. *Social Problems: A Modern Approach*. New York: John Wiley.

——. 1967. "Whose side are we on?" *Social Problems*, 14 (Winter): 239–47.

Ben-David, Joseph. 1971. *The Scientist's Role in Society*. Englewood Cliffs, NJ: Prentice-Hall.

Ben-Yehuda, Nachman. 1979. *Drug Abuse in Israel – A Survey*. Jerusalem, Interministerial Committee on Drug Abuse, Ministry of Social Affairs (Hebrew).

——. 1980. "The European witch craze of the 14th to 17th centuries: a sociologist's perspective." *American Journal of Sociology*, 86(1): 1–31.

——. 1985. *Deviance and Moral Boundaries: Witchcraft, the Occult, Science Fiction, Deviant Sciences and Scientists*. Chicago: University of Chicago Press.

——. 1986. "The sociology of moral panics: toward a new synthesis." *The Sociological Quarterly*, 27(4): 495–513.

——. 1989. "The Prevalence of drug abuse in Israel – is it expanding or is it static? A sociological hypothesis." *Delinquency and Social Deviance*, 17: 85–75 (Hebrew).

——. 1990a. *The Politics and Morality of Deviance: Moral Panics, Drug Abuse, and Reversed Stigmatization*. Albany: State University of New York Press.

——. 1990b. "Positive and negative deviance: more fuel for a controversy." *Deviant Behavior*, 11(3): 221–43.

Berger, Peter L. and Thomas M. Luckmann. 1966. *The Social Construction of Reality*. Baltimore: Penguin.

Bergesen, Albert J. 1978. "A Durkheimian theory of 'witch hunts' with the Chinese Cultural Revolution of 1966–69 as an example," *Journal for the Scientific Study of Religion*, 17(1): 10–29.

Berk, Richard A. 1974. "A gaming approach to crowd behavior." *American Sociological Review*, 39 (June): 355–73.

Bernard, J. 1972. "Trade and finance in the Middle Ages, 900–1500." pp. 274–329, in Cipolla, C. M. (ed.), *The Fontana Economic History of Europe*, vol. 1, *The Middle Ages*. New York: Fontana.

Best, Joel. 1988. "Missing children, misleading statistics." *The Public Interest*, no. 92 (summer): 84–92.

——. (ed.). 1989a. *Images of Issues: Typifying Contemporary Social Problems*. New York: Aldine de Gruyter.

——. (ed.). 1989b. "Dark figures and child victims: statistical claims about missing children." In Joel Best (ed.), *Images of Issues: Typifying Contemporary Social Problems*. New York: Aldine de Gruyter, pp. 21–7.

——. 1990. *Threatened Children: Rhetoric and Concern about Child-Victims*. Chicago: University of Chicago Press.

——. 1991. "'Road warriors' on 'hair-trigger highways': cultural resources and the media's construction of the 1987 freeway shootings problem." *Sociological Inquiry*, 61 (August): 327–45.

——. 1993. "But seriously folks: the limitations of the strict constructionist interpretation of social problems." In James A. Holstein and Gale Miller (eds), *Reconsidering Social Constructionism: Debates in Social Problems Theory*. New York: Aldiue de Gruyter, pp. 129–47.

Blumer, Herbert. 1939. "Collective behavior." In Robert E. Park (ed.), *Principles of Sociology*. New York: Barnes & Noble, pp. 221–79.

——. 1969. "Collective behavior." In Alfred McClung Lee (ed.), *Principles of Sociology* (3rd edn). New York: Barnes & Noble, pp. 67–120.

——. 1971. "Social problems as collective behavior." *Social Problems*, 18 (Winter): 298–306.

Bogucka, Maria. 1980. "The role of Baltic trade in European development from the XVI to the XVIII centuries." *The Journal of European Economic History*, 9(1): 5–20.

Bonnie, Richard J., and Charles H. Whitebread II. 1970. "The forbidden fruit and the tree of knowledge: an inquiry into the history of American marihuana prohibition." *Virginia Law Review*, 56 (October): 971–1203.

——. 1974. *The Marihuana Conviction: A History of Marihuana Prohibition in the United States*. Charlottesville: University of Virginia Press.

Borrie, W. D. 1970. "The population of the ancient and medieval world." pp.

40–57 in *The Growth and Control of World Population*. London: Weidenfeld & Nicolson.

Braden, William. 1970. "LSD and the press." In Bernard Aaronson and Humphrey Osmond (eds), *Psychedelics*. Garden City, NY: Doubleday Anchor, pp. 400–18.

Brecher, Edward M., et al. 1972. *Licit and Illicit Drugs*. Boston: Little, Brown.

Bridbury, A. R. 1973. "The Black Death." *Economic History Review*, 2nd series 26(4): 577–92.

Bridenthal, R. and Koontz, C. (eds). 1977. *Becoming Visible: Women in European History*. Boston: Houghton Mifflin.

Britannica. 1975. "Witchcraft." *The New Encyclopedia Britannica*. Chicago, vol. 19, pp. 895–900.

Bromberg, W. 1959. *The Mind of Man*, New York: Harper & Row.

Bromley, David G. 1987. "Subversion mythology and the social construction of social problems." Paper presented at the Annual Meeting for the Scientific Study of Religion, Lexington, KY, November.

——. 1991. "Satanism: the new cult scare." In James T. Richardson, Joel Best, and David G. Bromley (eds), *The Satanism Scare*. New York: Aldine de Gruyter, pp. 49–72.

Bromley, David G., Anson Shupe D., and Ventimiglia J. C. 1979. "Atrocity tales: the Unification Church and the social construction of evil." *Journal of Communication*, 29(3): 42–53.

Brown, Peter. 1969. "Society and the supernatural: a medieval change." *Daedalus*, 104: 133–51.

Brownmiller, Susan. 1975. *Against Our Will: Women, Men, and Rape*. New York: Simon & Schuster.

Brunvand, Jan Harold. 1981. *The Vanishing Hitchhiker: American Urban Legends and their Meanings*. New York: W. W. Norton.

——. 1984. *The Choking Doberman and Other "New" Urban Legends*. New York: W. W. Norton.

——. 1986. *The Mexican Pet: More "New" Urban Legends and Some Old Favorites*. New York: W. W. Norton.

——. 1989. *Curses! Broiled Again!* New York: W. W. Norton.

Buckner, H. Taylor. 1965. "A theory of rumor transmission." *Public Opinion Quarterly*, 29 (Spring): 54–70.

Bullough, Vern L. 1964. *The History of Prostitution*. New Hyde Park, New York: University Press.

Bullough, Vern L., with Bonnie L. Bullough. 1974. *The Subordinate Sex*. New York: Penguin.

Burkof, Haim. 1981. *Use of Drugs and Alcohol among Youth in Ramat Hasharon – an Epidemiological Survey*. Jerusalem: An Interim Report No. 1. The Interministerial Committee on Drug Abuse, Ministry of Social Affairs (Hebrew).

Carus, Paul. 1974. *The History of the Devil and the Idea of Evil*, La Salle, IL: Open Court.

Carus-Wilson, E. M. 1941. "An industrial revolution in the thirteenth century." *Economic History Review*, 11: 39–60.

Chambliss, William, and Milton Mankoff (eds). 1976. *Whose Law? What Order?* New York: John Wiley.

Chasnoff, Ira J., et al. 1989. "Temporary patterns of cocaine use in pregnancy." *Journal of the American Medical Association*, 261 (March 24/31): 1741–4.

Chojnacki, S. 1974. "Patrician women in Renaissance Venice." *Studies in the Renaissance*, 21: 176–203.

Christie, Nils. 1984. "Suitable enemies". Paper given at the Howar League Second Annual Conference, The Individual and the State: The Impact of Criminal Justice. Oxford, September 10.

Christie, Nils and Kettil Bruun. 1985. *Den Gode Fiende*. Oslo, Norway: Universitetsforlaget As. (Norwegian).

Cipolla, Carlo M. 1974. "The plague and the Pre-Malthus Malthusians." *Journal of European History*, 3(2): 277–84.

——. 1976. *Before the Industrial Revolution*. London: Methuen.

——. 1978. *Economic History of World Population*. Baltimore: Penguin.

Clark, A. J. 1921. "Flying ointments." In M. A. Murray, *The Witch Cult in Western Europe*. London, Oxford University Press (appendix 5).

Clark, Stuart. 1980. "Inversion, misrule and the meaning of witchcraft." *Past and Present*, 87: 98–127.

Clymer, Adam. 1986. "Public found ready to sacrifice in drug fight." *New York Times*, September 2, pp. A1, D16.

Cohen, Israel. 1982. "'The drug festival' of the police," *Ma'ariv*, May 17, p. 3 (Hebrew).

Cohen, Maimon M., Michelle J. Marinello, and Nathan Back. 1967. "Chromosomal damage in human leukocytes induced by Lysergic Acid Diethylamide." *Science*, 155 (17 March): 1417–19.

Cohen, Stanley. 1967. "Mods, Rockers, and the rest: community reactions to juvenile delinquency." *Howard Journal*, 12(2): 121–30.

——. 1972. *Folk Devils and Moral Panics: The Creation of the Mods and Rockers*. London: MacGibbon & Kee.

——. 1988. *Against Criminology*. New Brunswick, NJ: Transaction.

Cohn, Norman. 1961. *The Pursuit of Millennium*. New York: Harper Torchbooks.

——. 1975. *Europe Inner Demons. An Inquiry Inspired by the Great Witch Hunt*. New York: Basic Books.

Cole, Stephen. 1993. *Making Science: Between Nature and Society*. Cambridge, MA: Harvard University Press.

Coleman, Emily. 1971. "Medieval marriage characteristics: a neglected factor in the history of medieval serfdom." In T. K. Rab and R. I. Rothberg (eds), *The Family in History*. New York: Harper & Row, pp. 1–15.

——. 1976. "Infanticide in early Middle Ages." In Susan M. Stuard (ed.), *Women in Medieval Society*. Philadelphia: University of Pennsylvania Press, pp. 47–70.

Coleman, James W. 1989. *The Criminal Elite: The Sociology of White Collar Crime* (2nd edn). New York: St. Martin's press.

——. 1993. *The Criminal Elite: the Sociology of White Collar Crime* (3rd edn). New York: St. Martin's Press.

Coles, Claire D. 1991. "Substance abuse in pregnancy: the infant's risk: how great?" Paper presented at the Symposium on Pregnant Drug Abusers: Clinical and Legal Controversy, American Psychiatric Association Annual

Meeting, New Orleans, LA, May 15.

——. 1992. "Effects of cocaine and alcohol use in pregnancy on neonatal growth and neurobehavioral status." *Neurotoxicology and Teratology*, 14 (January–February): 1–11.

Colin, Morris. 1972. *The Discovery of the Individual*. London.

Conklin, John E. 1986. *Criminology* (2nd edn), New York: Macmillan.

Connor, J. 1975. "The social and psychological reality of European witchcraft beliefs." *Psychiatry*, 38: 366–80.

Conrad, Peter and Joseph W. Schneider. 1980. *Deviance and Medicalization*. St Louis: C. V. Mosby.

Cromer, Gerald. 1988. "'The roots of lawlessness': the coverage of the Jewish underground in the Israeli press." *Terrorism*, 11(1): 43–51.

Currie, Elliott P. 1968. "Crimes without criminals: witchcraft and its control in Renaissance Europe." *Law and Society Review*, 3 (August): 7–32.

Davies, K. and J. Blake. 1956. "Social structure and fertility." *Economic Development and Cultural Change*, 4(3): 211–35.

Davis, Nanette J., and Clarice Stasz. 1990. *Social Control of Deviance: A Critical Perspective*. New York: McGraw-Hill.

Davison, Bill. "The hidden evils of LSD." *Saturday Evening Post*, August 12, pp. 19–23.

DAWN (see Drug Abuse Warning Network).

Day, Nancy L., Gale A. Richardson, and Peggy J. McGauhey. 1992. "The effects of prenatal exposure to marijuana, cocaine, heroin, and methadone." In Herbert L. Needleman (ed.), *Prenatal Exposure to Pollutants and Development of Infants*. Baltimore: Johns Hopkins University Press.

Deevey, Edward S. 1960. "The human population." *Scientific American*, 203(3): 194–206.

De Mause, L. (ed.). 1974. *The History of Childhood*, New York: Harper & Row.

Demos, J. P. 1982. *Entertaining Satan: Witchcraft and the Culture of Early New England*. New York: Oxford University Press.

Diamond, Stanley. 1971. "The rule of law versus the order of custom." *Social Research*, 38 (Spring): 42–72.

Dickson, Donald T. 1968. "Bureaucracy and morality: an organizational perspective on a moral crusade." *Social Problems*, 16 (Fall): 143–56.

Dickson, Paul, and Joseph C. Goulden. 1983. *There Are Alligators in Our Sewers and Other American Credos*. New York: Delacorte Press.

Dishotsky, Norman I., William D. Loughmann, Robert E. Mogar, and Wendell R. Lipscomb. 1971. "LSD and genetic damage." *Science*, 172 (30 April): 431–40.

Donnerstein, Edward, Daniel Linz, and Steven Penrod. 1987. *The Question of Pornography: Research Findings and Policy Implications*. New York: Free Press.

Douglas, Jack D. 1967. *The Social Meaning of Suicide*. Princeton, NJ: Princeton University Press.

——. 1971. *American Social Order: Social Rules in a Pluralistic Society*. New York: Free Press.

Drug Abuse Warning Network (DAWN). 1987. *Trends in Drug Abuse Related Hospital Emergency Room Episodes and Medical Examiner. Cases for Selected*

Drugs, DAWN 1976–1985. Rockville, MD: National Institute on Drug Abuse.

Dumont, M. P. 1973. "The junkie as a political enemy." *American Journal of Orthopsychiatry*, 43(4): 533–40.

Durkheim, Emile. 1938 (1895). *The Rules of Sociological Method.* New York: Free Press.

——. 1964 (1933). *The Division of Labor in Society.* New York: Free Press.

Duster, Troy. 1970. *The Legislation of Morality: Law, Drugs, and Moral Judgment.* New York: Free Press.

Dworkin, Andrea. 1981. *Pornography: Men Possessing Women.* New York: Perigee.

——. 1982. "For men, freedom of speech; for women, silence please." In Laura Lederer (ed.), *Take Back the Night: Women on Pornography.* New York: Bantam Books, pp. 255–8.

Dye, Thomas R. 1986. *Who's Running America: The Conservative Years.* Englewood Cliffs, NJ: Prentice-Hall.

Dynes, Russell R. 1970. *Organized Behavior in Disasters.* Lexington, MA: D. C. Heath.

Earle, Peter. 1969. "The commercial development of Ancona." *Economic History Review*, 22(1): 28–44.

Eckenstein, Lina. 1896. *Women under Monasticism: Saint Lore and Convent Life Between A.D. 500 and A.D. 1500.* Cambridge: Cambridge University Press.

Eckholm, Erik. 1986. "Radon: threat is real, but Scientists argue over its severity." *New York Times*, September 2, pp. C1, C7.

——. 1992. "AIDS, fatally steady in the U.S., accelerates worldwide." *New York Times*, June 28, p. E5.

Ehrenreich, B. and English, D. 1972. *Witches, Midwives and Curses: A History of Women Healers.* New York: Feminist Press.

Ella, Sima. 1982. "Kids under 13 years of age sell drugs and use guns." *Yedioth Ahronoth*, May 23, p. 4 (Hebrew).

Ella, Sima and Gideon Reicher. 1982. "Half of high school students in Israel experienced smoking hashish." *Yedioth Ahronoth*, May 13, pp. 1, 4 (Hebrew).

Ellis, Bill. 1983. "De Legendes Urbis: modern legends in Ancient Rome." *Journal of American Folklore*, 96(2): 200–8.

Elton, G. R. 1963. *Renaissance and Reformation, 1300–1648.* New York: Macmillan.

Erikson, Kai. 1966. *Wayward Puritans: A Study in the Sociology of Deviance.* New York: John Wiley.

——. 1990. "Toxic reckoning: business faces a new kind of fear." *Harvard Business Review*, 68 (January–February): 118–26.

Ermann, M. David, and Richard J. Lundman (eds). 1990. *Corporate and Governmental Deviance: Problems in Organizational Behavior in Contemporary Society.* New York: Oxford University Press.

Finkelhor, David. 1979. *Sexually Victimized Children.* New York: Free Press.

Finkelhor, David, Gerald T. Hotaling, and Andrea J. Sedlak. 1992. "The abduction of children by strangers and nonfamily members: estimating the incidence using multiple methods." *Journal of Interpersonal Violence*, 7 (June): 226–43.

Fishman, Mark. 1978. "Crime waves as ideology." *Social Problems*, 25 (June): 531–43.

——. 1980. *Manufacturing the News*. Austin: University of Texas Press.

——. 1989. "Where do crime waves come from? Paper presented at the 41st Annual Meeting of the American Society of Criminology, Reno, Nevada, November.

Flake, Carol. 1984. *Redemptorama: Culture, Politics, and the New Evangelism*. New York: Penguin.

Forbes, T. R. 1966. *The Midwife and the Witch*. New Haven, CT: Yale University Press.

Forst, Martin L., and Martha-Elin Blomquist. 1991. *Missing Children: Rhetoric and Reality*. New York: Lexington Books.

Foucault, M. 1967. *Madness and Civilization*. London: Tavistock.

Freedman, Estelle B. 1987. "Uncontrolled desires." *Journal of American History*, 74: 83–106.

Friedmann, Wolfgang. 1964. *Law in a Changing Society*. Harmondsworth, England: Penguin.

Fritz, Noah J., and David L. Altheide. 1987. "The mass media and the social construction of the missing children problem." *The Sociological Quarterly*, 28(4): 473–92.

Fuerbringer, Jonathan. 1986. "Wide bill on drugs pressed in House." *New York Times*, September 11, p. A24.

Fuller, Richard C., and Richard Myers. 1941. "Some aspects of a theory of social problems." *American Sociological Review*, 6 (February): 24–32.

Galbraith, John Kenneth. 1990. *A Short History of Financial Euphoria*. Knoxville, TN: Whittle Direct Books.

Garb, Maggie. 1989. "Abortion foes give birth to a syndrome." *In These Times*, February 22–March 1, pp. 3, 22.

Garraty, J. A. 1978. *Unemployment in History*, New York: Harper & Row.

Garrett, Clarke. 1977. "Women and witches: patterns of analysis." *Sigma*: *Journal of Women in Culture and Society*, 3(2): 461–79.

Geertz, Clifford. 1964. "Ideology as a cultural system." In Apter, David (ed.), *Ideology and Discontent*. New York: Free Press, pp. 47–76.

Geis, G. 1978. "Lord Hale, witches and rape." *British Journal of Law and Society*, summer, 26–44.

Gentry, Cynthia. 1988. "The social construction of abducted children as a social problem." *Sociological Inquiry*, 58(4): 413–25.

Gerassi, John. 1966. *The Boys of Boise: Furor, Vice, and Folly in an American City*. New York: Macmillan.

Geschwender, James A. 1990. "Foreword." In Richard L. Henshel, *Thinking about Social Problems*. San Diego: Harcourt Brace Jovanovich, pp. v–xi.

Gibbons, Don C. 1992. *Society, Crime, and Criminal Behavior* (6th edn). Englewood Cliffs. NJ: Prentice-Hall.

Gieringer, Dale. 1990. "How many crack babies?" *The Drug Policy Letter*, II (March/April): 4–6.

Gies, Frances and Joseph. 1978. *Women in the Middle Ages*. New York: Thomas Y. Crowell.

Goldberg, Peter. 1980. "The Federal government's response response to illicit drugs, 1969–1978." In The Drug Abuse Council, *The Facts About "Drug*

Abuse." New York: Free Press, pp. 20–62.

Goleman, Daniel. 1991. "Anatomy of a rumor: it flies on fear." *New York Times*, June 4, pp. C1, C5.

Goode, Erich. 1969. "Marijuana and the politics of reality." *Journal of Health and Social Behavior*, 10 (June): 83–94.

——. 1972. *Drugs in American Society*. New York: Alfred A. Knopf.

——. 1973. *The Drug Phenomenon: Social Aspects of Drug Taking*. Indianapolis, IN: Bobbs-Merrill.

——. 1978. *Deviant Behavior: An Interactionist Perspective*. Engelwood Cliffs, NJ: Prentice-Hall.

——. 1990. "The American drug panic of the 1980s: social construction or objective threat?" *The International Journal of the Addictions*, 25(9): 1083–98.

——. 1991. "Positive deviance: a viable concept?" *Deviant Behavior*, 12 (July–September): 289–309.

——. 1992. *Collective Behavior*. Fort Worth, TX. Harcourt Brace Jovanovich.

——. 1993. *Drugs in American Society* (4th edn). New York: McGraw-Hill.

——. 1994. *Deviant Behavior* (4th edn). Englewood Cliffs, NJ: Prentice-Hall.

Goodman, Ellen. 1992. "Panic over 'crack babies' conceals real issue: neglect." *Boston Globe*, January 2, p. 69.

Goodsell, M. 1915. *History of the Family as a Social and Educational Institution*. New York: Macmillan.

Gottfried, Robert. 1978. *Epidemic Disease in Fifteenth Century England. The Medical Response and the Demographic Consequences*. Leicester, England: Leicester University Press.

Gould, Stephen Jay. 1984. *Hen's Teeth and Horse's Toes: Further Reflections in Natural History*. New York: W. W. Norton.

Graus, F. 1967. "Social utopias in the Middle Ages." *Past and Present*, 38: 3–19.

Griego, Diana, and Louis Kilzer. 1985. "The truth about missing kids." *The Denver Post*, May 12, pp. 1-A, 12-A.

Griggs, D. B. 1980. *Population Growth and Agrarian Change*. New York: Cambridge University Press.

Gusfield, Joseph R. 1955. "Social structure and moral reform: a study of the Women's Christian Temperance Union." *American Journal of Sociology*, 61 (November): 221–32.

——. 1963. *Symbolic Crusade: Status Politics and the American Temperance Movement*. Urbana: University of Illinois Press.

——. 1967. "Moral passage: the symbolic process in public designations of deviance." *Social Problems*, 15 (Fall): 175–88.

——. 1981. *The Culture of Public Problems: Drinking-Driving and the Symbolic Order*. Chicago: University of Chicago Press.

Haines, Herbert H. 1979. "Cognitive claims-making, enclosure, and the depoliticization of social problems." *The Sociological Quarterly*, 20 (Winter): 119–30.

Hajnal, J. 1965. "European marriage patterns in perspective." In D. V. Glass and D. E. C. Eversley (eds), *Populations in History*. London: Edward Arnold.

Hall, Stuart, Chas Critcher, Tony Jefferson, John Clarke, and Brian Roberts.

1978. *Policing the Crisis: Mugging, the State, and Law and Order*. London: Macmillan.

Halloran, Richard. 1987. "Drug use in military drops: pervasive testing credited." *New York Times*, April 23, p. A16.

Hansen, B. 1975. "Science and magic." In D. C. Lindberg (ed.), *Science in the Middle Ages*. Chicago: University of Chicago Press, pp. 483–500.

Hansen, C. 1969. *Witchcraft at Salem*. New York: Mentor Books.

Harel, Tzvi. 1982. "Principals against the police." *Ha'aretz*, May 20, p. 10 (Hebrew).

Har-Paz, Haim and Moshe Hadad. 1976. "Drug use." In *Studies, Employment and Leisure Time Activity Among Young People*. Survey published by the Department of Research and Statistics of Tel Aviv Municipality, pp. 58–64 (Hebrew).

Harrison, Michael. 1973. *The Roots of Witchcraft*. London: Tandem Books.

Heinsohn, G. and Steiger, O. 1982. "The elimination of medieval birth control and the witch trials of modern times." *International Journal of Women's Studies*, 5(3): 193–214.

Helleiner, K. F. 1957. "The vital revolution reconsidered." *Canadian Journal of Economic and Political Science*, 23(1): 1–9.

——. 1967. "The Population of Europe from the Black Death to the eve of the vital revolution." In *The Cambridge Economic History of Europe*, vol. 4, *The Economy of Expanding Europe in the Sixteenth and Seventeenth Centuries*, ed. by E. E. Rich and C. H. Wilson, Cambridge: Cambridge University Press, pp. 1–96.

Helmer, John. 1975. *Drugs and Minority Oppression*. New York: Continuum Press.

Helmoholtz, R. H. 1975. "Infanticide in the Province of Canterbury during the 15th Century." *History of Childhood Quarterly*, 2(3): 379–90.

Henningsen, G. 1980a. *The Witches' Advocate*, Reno, NV: University of Nevada Press.

——. 1980b. "The greatest witch trial of all: Navarre, 1609–1614." *History Today*, 30: 36–9.

Henriques, F. 1963. *The Immoral Tradition*, London: Panther.

Henshel, Richard L. 1990. *Thinking about Social Problems*. San Diego: Harcourt Brace Jovanovich.

Herlihy, David. 1965. "Population, plague and social change in rural Pistoria 1201–1430." *Economic History Review*, 2nd series. 18(2): 225–44.

——. 1971. *Women in Medieval Society*, Smith History Lecture, Houston, TX: University of St Thomas.

Hicks, John. 1969. *A Theory of Economic History*. Oxford: Oxford University Press.

Hicks, Robert D. 1991. *In Pursuit of Satan: The Police and the Occult*. Buffalo, NY: Prometheus Books.

Hills, Stuart L. 1980. *Demystifying Social Deviance*. New York: McGraw-Hill.

——. (ed.). 1987. *Corporate Violence: Injury and Death for Profit*. Totowa, NJ: Rowman Littlefield.

Hilgartner, Stephen, and Charles L. Bosk. 1988. "The rise and fall of social problems: a public arenas model." *American Journal of Sociology*, 94 (July): 53–78.

Himes, Norman E. 1936. *A Medical History of Contraception.* New York: Schocken.

Himmelstein, Jerome. 1983. *The Strange Career of Marihuana: Politics and Ideology of Drug Control in America.* Westport, CT: Greenwood Press.

Hinnebusch, W. A. 1966. *The History of the Dominican Order,* New York: Alba.

Hoffman, Jan. 1990. "Pregnant, addicted – and guilty?" *New York Times Magazine,* August 19, pp. 33–5, 44, 53, 55, 57.

Holmes, George. 1975. *Europe, Hierarchy and Revolt, 1320–1450,* New York: Fontana.

Horowitz, Tami and Menachem Amir. 1981. *Coping Patterns of the Educational System with the Problem of Violence.* Research Report no. 219, Publication no. 602. Jerusalem: The Szold Institute (Hebrew).

Hsu, F. L. 1960. "A neglected aspect of witchcraft studies." *Journal of American Folklore,* 73, 35–8.

Hughes, P. 1952. *Witchcraft.* Baltimore: Penguin Books.

Ibarra, Peter R., and John I. Kitsuse. 1993. "Vernacular constituents of moral discourse: a interactionist proposal for the study of social problems." In James A. Holstein and Gale Miller (eds), *Reconsidering Social Constructionism: Debates in Social Problems Theory.* New York: Aldine de Gruyter, pp. 25–58.

Irsigler, Frantz. 1977. "Industrial production, international trade and public finances in Cologne." *Journal of European Economic History,* 6(2): 269–306.

Jarrett, B. 1962. *Social Theories of the Middle Ages: 1200–1500,* London: Benn.

Jarvie, I. C. 1986. *Thinking about Society: Theory and Practice.* Boston: D. Reidel.

Jayyusi, Lena. 1984. *Categorization and Moral Order.* Boston: Routledge Kegan Paul.

Javitz, Rachel and Judith T. Shuval. 1982. "Vulnerability to drugs among Israeli adolescents." *Israel Journal of Psychiatry,* 19(2): 97–119.

Jenkins, Philip. 1992. *Intimate Enemies: Moral Panics in Contemporary Britain.* New York: Aldine de Gruyter.

Jenkins, Philip, and Daniel Meier-Katkin. 1992. "Satanism: myth and reality in a contemporary moral panic." *Crime, Law and Social Change,* 17(1): 53–75.

Jensen, Eric L., Jurg Gerber, and Ginna M. Babcock. 1991. "The new war on drugs: grass roots movement or political construction?" *Journal of Drug Issues,* 21(3): 651–67.

Johnson, Bruce D. 1975. "Righteousness before revenue: the forgotten moral crusade against the Indo-China opium trade." *Journal of Drug Issues,* 5: 304–26.

Johnston, Lloyd D., Patrick O'Malley, and Jerald G. Bachman. 1987. *National Trends in Drug Use and Related Factors Among High School Students and Young Adults, 1975–1986.* Rockville, MD: National Institute on Drug Abuse.

——. 1989. *Drug Use, Drinking, and Smoking: National Survey Results From High School Seniors, College Students and Young Adult Populations, 1975–1988.* Rockville, MD: National Institute on Drug Abuse.

Jones, Brian J., Bernard J. Gallagher, III, and Joseph A. McFalls, Jr. 1989. "Toward a unified model for social problems theory." *Journal for the Theory of Social Behavior*, 19: 337–56.

Kagay, Michael R. 1990. "Deficit raises as much alarm as illegal drugs, a poll finds." *New York Times*, July 25, p. A9.

Kahneman, Daniel, Paul Slovic, and Amos Tversky. (eds). 1982. *Judgement Under Uncertainty: Heuristics and Biases*. Cambridge, England: Cambridge University Press.

Kandel, Denise B. and Israel Adler. 1981. *The Epidemiology of Adolescent Drug Users in Israel and in France*. New York: Department of Psychiatry and School of Public Health, Columbia University.

Kandel, Denise B., Israel Adler, and Myriam Sudit. 1981. "The epidemiology of adolescent drug use in France and Israel." *American Journal of Public Health*, 71: 256–65.

Kapferer, Jean-Noel. 1990. *Rumors: Uses, Interpretations, and Images* (trans. Bruce Fink). New Brunswick, NJ: Transaction.

Kelso, R. 1956. *Doctrine for the Lady in the Renaissance*. Urbana: University of Illinois Press.

Kerr, Peter. 1986. "Anatomy of an issue: drugs, the evidence, the reaction." *New York Times*, November 17, pp. A1, B6.

Kieckhefer, R. 1976. *European Witch Trials*. Berkeley and Los Angeles: University of California Press.

Kilbourne, Brock K., and Maria T. Kilbourne. 1983. *The Dark Side of Science*. San Francisco: Pacific Division, American Association for the Advancement of Science.

Kimmel, Allan J., and Robert Keefer. 1991. "Psychological correlates of the transmission and acceptance of rumors about AIDS." *Journal of Applied Social Psychology*, 21(9): 1608–28.

Kindleberger, Charles P. 1987. *Manias, Panics, and Crashes: A History of Financial Crises* (revised edn). New York: Basic Books.

Kirsch, I. 1978. "Demonology and the rise of science: an example of the misperception of historical data." *Journal of the History of the Behavioral Sciences*, 14: 149 57.

Kitsuse, John I., and Malcolm Spector. 1973. "Toward a sociology of social problems: social conditions, value-judgements, and social problems." *Social Problems*, 20 (spring): 407–19.

Kitsuse, John I., and Joseph W. Schneider. 1989. "Preface." In Joel Best (ed.), *Images of Issues: Typifying Contemporary Social Problems*. New York: Aldine de Gruyter, pp. xi–xiii.

Kittredge, George L. 1972 (1929). *Witchcraft in Old and New England*. New York: Atheneum.

Klerman, G. L. 1970. "Drugs and social values." *The International Journal of the Addictions*, 5(2): 313–19.

Knopf, Terry Ann. 1975. *Rumors, Race, and Riots*. New Brunswick, NJ: Tranction Books.

Kobler, John. 1973. *Ardent Spirits: The Rise and Fall of Prohibition*. New York: G. P. Putnam.

Kors, A. C. and E. Peters (eds). 1972. *Witchcraft in Europe, 1100–1700*. Philadelphia: University of Pennsylvania Press.

Kramer, J. C. 1976. "From demon to ally: how mythology has, and may yet, alter national drug policy," *Journal of Drug Issues*, 6(4): 390–406.

La Croix, P. 1926. *History of Prostitution*, 2 vols. Chicago: Pascal Covici.

Ladurie Emmanuel Le Roi. 1971. *Times of Feast, Times of Famine: A History of Climate Since the Year 1000*. London: Allen & Unwin.

Lamb, H. H. 1982. *Climate History and the Modern World*. London and New York: Methuen.

Lane, Frederic C. 1932. "The rope factory and hemp trade in the fifteenth and sixteenth centuries." *Journal of Economic and Business History*, 4: 824–40.

——. 1933. "Venetian shipping during the commercial revolution." *American Historical Review*, 38(2): 219–37.

Langer, William. 1964. "The Black Death." *Scientific American*, 210(2): 114–21.

——. 1974a. "Further notes on the history of infanticide." *History of Childhood Quarterly*, 2(1): 129–34.

——. 1974b. "Infanticide: a history survey." *History of Childhood Quarterly* 1(3): 353–65.

Larner, Christina. 1981. *Enemies of God. The Witch Hunt in Scotland*. Baltimore, MD: Johns Hopkins University Press.

Lauderdale, Pat. 1976. 'Deviance and moral boundaries." *American Sociological Review*, 41: 660–4.

Lea, Henry Charles. 1901. *The History of the Inquisition of the Middle Ages*, 4 vols. Franklin Square, New York: Harper.

——. 1957. *Materials Towards a History of Witchcraft*. Ed. Arthur C. Howland. New York: Lincoln Burr.

LeBon, Gustave. 1982 (1895). *The Crowd: A Study of the Popular Mind*. Marietta, GA: Larlin.

Le Goff, J. 1972. "The Town as an agent of civilization, 1200–1500." In C. M. Cipolla (ed.), *The Fontana Economic History of Europe*, vol. 1, *The Middle Ages*. New York: Fontana, pp. 71–107.

——. 1980. *Time, Work and Culture in the Middle Ages*, Chicago: University of Chicago Press.

Leff, Gordon. 1967. *Heresy in the Later Middle Ages*. Manchester: Manchester University Press.

Lemay, Rodnite H. 1978. "Some thirteenth and fourteenth century lectures on female sexuality." *International Journal of Women's Studies*, 1(4): 391–400.

Lender, Mark Edward, and James Kirby Martin. 1987. *Drinking in America: A History* (revised edn). New York: Free Press.

Lerner, Robert E. 1970. "Medieval prophecy and religious dissent." *Past and Present*, 72: 3–24.

Levack, Brian P. 1987. *The Witch-Hunt In Early Modern Europe*. London and New York: Longman.

Levin, Murray B. 1971. *Political Hysteria in America: The Democratic Capacity for Repression*. New York: Basic Books.

Levine, Harry G., and Craig Reinarman. 1987. "The monkey on the public's back." *Newsday*, January 4, Ideas Section, pp. 1, 10.

——. 1988. "The politics of America's latest drug scare." In R. Curry (ed.), *Freedom at Risk: Secrecy, Censorship, and Repression in the 1980s*. Philadelphia: Temple University Press, pp. 251–8.

Levine, Robert M. 1992. *Vale of Tears: Revisiting the Canudos Massacre in Northeastern Brazil, 1893–1897*. Berkeley: University of California Press.

Lewis, I. M. 1971. *Ecstatic Religion: An Anthropological Study of Spirit Possession*. Harmondsnorth, England: Penguin Books.

Liazos, Alexander. 1972. "The poverty of the sociology of deviance: nuts, sluts, and preverts." *Social Problems*, 20 (Summer): 103–20.

——. 1982. *People First: An Introduction to Social Problems*. Boston: Allyn & Bacon.

Lidz, Charles W., and Andrew L. Walker. 1980. *Heroin Deviance and Morality*. Beverly Hills: Sage.

Litchfield, E. Burr. 1966. "Demographic characteristics of Florentine patrician families, 16th to 19th Centuries." *Journal of Economic History*, 29: 191–205.

Lofland, John. 1969. *Deviance and Identity*. Englewood Cliffs, NJ: Prentice Hall.

Loos, Milan. 1974. *Dualist Heresy in the Middle Ages*. The Hague: Nijhoff.

Lopez, R. S. 1976. *The Commercial Revolution of the Middle Ages, 950–1350*. Cambridge: Cambridge University Press.

McCarthy, John D., and Mayer N. Zald. 1973. The *Trend of Social Movements in America: Professionalism and Resource Mobilization*. Morristown, NJ: General Learning Press.

McDonnell, E.W. 1954. *The Beguines and Beghards in Medieval Culture*. New Brunswick, NJ: Rutgers University Press.

Macfarlane, A. 1970. *Witchcraft in Tudor and Stuart England*. London: Routledge & Kegan Paul.

Mackay, Charles. 1932. *Exraordinary Delusions and the Madness of Crowds* (originally published in 1841 under the title, *Memoirs of Extraordinary Popular Delusions*; 2nd edn, published in 1852). New York: L. C. Page.

McNeill, William H. 1976. *Plagues and People*. New York, Garden City: Doubleday, Anchor Books.

McPhail, Clark. 1991. *The Myth of the Madding Crowd*. New York: Aldine de Gruyter.

McPhail, Clark, and David L. Miller. 1973. "The assembling process: a theoretical and empirical examination." *American Sociological Review*, 38 (December): 721–35.

Madaule, J. 1967. *The Albigensian Crusade: A Historical Essay*. New York: Fordham University Press.

Malawist, Marion. 1974. "Problems of growth of the national economy of Central-Eastern Europe in the late middle ages." *Journal of European Economic History*, 3(2): 319–57.

Mandonnet, P. 1944. *St Dominic and his Work*, St Louis: Herder.

Manis, Jerome. 1974. "The concept of social problems: vox populi and sociological analysis." *Social Problems*, 21 (Winter): 305–15.

——. 1976. *Analyzing Social Problems*. New York: Praeger.

Mappen, Marc. 1980. *Witches & Historians. Interpretations of Salem*. Malabar, FL: Robert E. Krieger.

Markle, Gerald E., and Ronald J. Troyer. 1979. "Smoke gets in your eyes: cigarette smoking as deviant behavior." *Social Problems*, 26 (June): 611–25.

Markson, Stephen L. 1990. "Claims-making, quasi-theories, and the social construction of the rock 'n' roll menace." In Clinton R. Sanders (ed.), *Marginal Conventions: Popular Culture, Mass Media, and Social Deviance*. Bowling Green, Ohio: Bowling Green State University Press, pp. 29–40.

Masters, Robert E. L. 1962. *Eros and Evil: The Sexual Psychopathology of Witchcraft*. New York: AMA Press.

Matalene, C. 1978. "Women as witches." *International Journal of Women's Studies*, 1: 573–87.

Mauss, Armand L. 1975. *Social Problems as Social Movements*. Philadelphia: Lippencott.

Merton, Robert K., and Robert Nisbet (eds). 1976. *Contemporary Social Problems* (4th edn). New York: Harcourt Brace Jovanovich.

Michelet, J. 1965. *Satanism and Witchcraft*, London: Tandem Books.

Midelfort, Erik H. C. 1972. *Witch Hunting in Southwestern Germany, 1562–1684*. Stanford: Stanford University Press.

——. 1981. "Heartland of the witch craze: central and northern Europe." *History Today*, February, 27–31.

Miller, David L. 1985. *An Introduction to Collective Behavior*. Belmont, CA: Wadsworth.

Molenda, Danuta. 1976. "Investments in ore mining in Poland from the 13th to the 17th centuries." *Journal of European Economic History*, 5(1): 151–69.

Monter, W. E. 1969. *European Witchcraft*. New York: Wiley.

——. 1976. *Witchcraft in France and Switzerland*. Ithaca and London: Cornell University Press.

——. 1980. "French and Italian witchcraft." *History Today*, 30: 31–5.

Morewedge, Rosemarie Thee (ed.). 1975. *The Role of Women in the Middle Ages*. Albany: State University of New York Press.

Morgan, Patricia L. 1978. "The legislation of drug laws: economic crisis and social control." *Journal of Drug Issues*, 8(1): 53–62.

Morin, Edgar. 1971. *Rumor in Orleans* (Peter Green, trans.). New York: Pantheon Books.

Mullen, Patrick B. 1972. "Modern legend and rumor theory." *Journal of the Folklore Institute*, 9(1): 95–109.

Murray, Henry A. 1962. "The personality and career of Satan." *Journal of Social Issues*, 18(4): 36–54.

Murray, M. A. 1918. "Child sacrificing among European witches." *Man*, 18: 60–2.

——. 1921. *The Witch Cult in Western Europe*. London: Clarendon Press.

Musto, David F. 1973. *The American Disease: Origins of Narcotics Control*. New Haven, CT: Yale University Press.

——. 1987. *The American Disease: Origins of Narcotic Control* (expanded edn). New York: Oxford University Press.

Nadelmann, Ethan A. 1989. "Drug prohibition in the United States: costs, consequences, and alternatives." *Science*, 245 (1 September): 939–47.

Nate, Mavis. 1975. "High prices in early fourteenth century England: causes and consequences." *Economic History Review*, 2nd series, 28(1): 1–16.

Nathan, Debbie. 1990. "The ritual sex abuse hoax." *The Village Voice*, June 12, pp. 36–44.

——. 1991. "The devil makes them do it." *In These Times*, July 24–August 6, pp. 12–3.

National Institute on Drug Abuse (NIDA). 1989. *Overview of the 1988 National Survey on Drug Abuse*. Rockville, MD: National Institute on Drug Abuse.

Nelson, Barbara J. 1984. *Making an Issue of Child Abuse: Political Agenda Setting for Social Problems*. Chicago: University of Chicago Press.

Nelson, M. 1971. "The persecution of witchcraft in Renaissance Europe: an historical and sociological discussion." Unpublished paper, University of Chicago.

——. 1975. "Why witches were women." In J. Freeman (ed.), *Women: A Feminist Perspective*. Palo Alto, CA: Mayfield, pp. 335–50.

Neuspiel, D. R., et al. 1991. "Maternal cocaine use and infant Behavior." *Neurotoxicology and Teratology*, 13 (March–April): 229–33.

Nicholas, David. 1976. "Economic Orientation and Social Change in Fourteenth Century Flanders." *Past and Present*, 70(1): 3–29.

NIDA (see National Institute on Drug Abuse).

Noonan, J. T. 1965. *Contraception: A History of its Treatment by the Catholic Theologians and Canonists*, Cambridge, MA: Harvard University Press, Belknap.

——. 1968. "Intellectual and demographic History." *Daedalus*, 97: 463–85.

O'Dea, Thomas. 1966. *The Sociology of Religion*, Englewood Cliffs, NJ: Prentice-Hall.

O'faolain, J. and L. Martines. 1973. *Not in God's Image*. New York: Harper & Row Torchbooks.

Oplinger, Jon. 1990. *The Politics of Demonology. The European witch Craze and the Mass Production of Deviance*, Selinsgrove: Susquehanna University Press. London and Toronto: Associated University Presses.

Orcutt, James D., and Blake J. Turner. 1993. "Shocking numbers and graphic accounts: quantified images of drug problems in the print media." *Social Problems*, 40 (May): 190–206.

Oreskes, Michael. 1990. "Drug war underlines fickleness of public." *New York Times*, September 6, p. A22.

Page, Ann L., and Donald A. Clelland. 1978. "The Kanawha County textbook Controversy: a study in the politics of lifestyle concern." *Social Forces*, 57 (September): 265–81.

Park, Robert E. 1972 (1904). *The Crowd and the Public and Other Essays*. Chicago: University of Chicago Press.

Parrinder, G. 1958. *Witchcraft*. Baltimore: Penguin Books.

Parsons, Talcott. 1966. *Societies, Evolutionary and Comparative Perspectives*. Englewood Cliffs, NJ: Prentice-Hall.

——. 1971. *The System of Modern Societies*. Englewood Cliffs, NJ: Prentice Hall.

Payer, Pierre J. 1980. "Early medieval regulations concerning marital sexual relations." *Journal of Medieval History*, 6(4): 353–76.

Peled, Tziona. 1971. *Attitudes of Youth in School Towards Drugs: Selective Findings from the Study on Values. Plans and Youth Behavior*. Jerusalem: The Institute for Applied Social Research (Hebrew).

Peled, Tziona and Haviva Schimmerling. 1972. "The drug culture among youth of Israel: the case of high school students." In S. Shoham (ed.), *Israel*

Studies in Criminology, vol. 2. Jerusalem: Jerusalem Academic Press, pp. 125–52.

Penrose, Bois. 1962. *Travel and Discovery in the Renaissance, 1420–1620*. New York: Atheneum.

Perrow, Charles. 1984. *Normal Accidents: Living with High-Risk Technologies*. New York: Basic Books.

Peyrot, Mark. 1984. "Cycles of social problem development: the case of drug abuse." *The Sociological Quarterly*, 25 (Winter): 83–96.

Pfohl, Stephen J. 1977. "The 'discovery' of child abuse." *Social Problems*, 24 (February): 310–22.

Piers, Maria W. 1978. *Infanticide*. New York: W. W. Norton.

Pirenne, Henry. 1937. *Economic and Social History of Medieval Europe*. New York: Harcourt Brace.

Plummer, Kenneth. 1979. "Misunderstanding labelling perspectives." In David Downes and Paul Rock (eds), *Deviant Interpretations*. London: Martin Robertson, pp. 85–121.

Policelli, Eugene F. 1978. "Medieval women: a preacher's point of view." *International Journal of Women Studies*, 1(3): 281–96.

Postan, M. M. 1950. "Some economic evidence of declining population in the later Middle Ages." *Economic History Review*, 2nd series 2(3): 221–46.

Postan, M. M. and E. R. Rich (eds). 1952. *The Cambridge Economic History of Europe*, vol. 2, *Trade and Industry in the Middle Ages*. Cambridge: Cambridge University Press.

Pounds, N. J. C. 1979. *A Historical Geography of Europe*. New York and London: Cambridge University Press.

Power, Eileen. 1926. "The position of women." In C. G. Crump and E. F. Jacob (eds), *The Legacy of the Middle Ages*. Oxford: Clarendon, pp. 401–37.
——. 1975. *Medieval Women*, ed. M. M. Postan. Cambridge: Cambridge University Press.

Puech, Henry-Charles. 1974. "Manicheism." *Encyclopedia Britannica*, vol. 11, Chicago: Encyclopedia Britannica.

Quindlen, Anna. 1990. "Hearing the cries of crack." *New York Times*, October 7, p. E19.

Quinney, Richard. 1970. *The Social Reality of Crime*. Boston: Little, Brown.

Radbill, S. X. 1974. "A history of child abuse and infanticide." In S. L. Steinmets and L. A. Strauss (eds), *Violence in the Family*. New York: Dodd, Mead, pp. 173–9.

Rahav, Giora, Meir Teichman, and Zippora Barnea. 1985. *Drugs and Alcohol among Adolescents*. First scientific report. Tel Aviv: Institute of Criminology, Tel Aviv University (Hebrew).

Rattansi, P. M. 1972. "The social interpretation of science in the 17th century." In P. Mathias (ed.), *Science and Society, 1600–1900*. Cambridge: Cambridge University Press, pp. 1–32.

Ray, Oakley. 1978. *Drugs, Society, and Human Behavior* (2nd edn). St Louis: Mosby.

Reicher, Gideon, and Israel Tommer. 1982a. "High school principals do not cooperate in the war against drugs." *Yedioth Ahronoth*, May, 19, p. 4 (Hebrew).

——. 1982b. "Drug abuse is prevalent among religious youth too." *Yedioth Ahronot*, June 3, p. 4 (Hebrew).

Reinarman, Craig. 1988. "The social construction of an alcohol problem: the case of mothers against drunk drivers and social control in the 1980s." *Theory and Society*, 17(1): 91–120.

Reinarman, Craig, and Harry G. Levine. 1989. "The crack attack: politics and media in America's latest drug scare." In Joel Best (ed.), *Images of Issues: Typifying Contemporary Social Problems*. New York: Aldine de Gruyter, pp. 115–37.

Richardson, Gale A. 1992. "Prenatal Cocaine Exposure." Unpublished paper, Western Psychiatric Institute and Clinic, Pittsburgh, PA.

Richardson, Gale A., and Nancy L. Day. 1991. "Maternal and neonatal effects of moderate cocaine use during pregnancy." *Neurotoxicology and Teratology*, 13 (July–August): 455–60.

Richardson, James T., Joel Best, and David Bromley (eds). 1991. *The Satanism Scare*. New York: Aldine de Gruyter.

Ridley, Florence H. 1967. "A tale told too often." *Western Folklore*, 26(2): 153–6.

Robbins, Russell Hope. 1959. *The Encyclopedia of Witchcraft and Demonology*. New York: Crown Publishers.

——. 1978. *Witchcraft: An Introduction to the Literature of Witchcraft*. New York: Kta Press.

Robock, Alan. 1979. "The Little Ice Age: Northern Hemisphere average observations and model calculations." *Science*, 206(4425): 1402–4.

Rose, Elizabeth. 1993. "Surviving the unbelievable." *Ms.*, January/February, pp. 40–5.

Rose, Elliot E. 1962. *A Razor for a Goat*, Toronto: Toronto University Press.

Rose, Jerry D. 1982. *Outbreaks: The Sociology of Collective Behavior*. New York: Free Press.

Rosen, George. 1969. *Madness in Society*. New York: Harper Torchbooks.

Rosenthal, Marilynn. 1971. "Where rumor raged." *Trans-action*, 8 (February): 34–43.

Rosnow, Ralph L. 1988. "Rumor as communication: a contextualist approach." *Journal of Communication*, 38 (winter): 12–28.

——. 1991. "Inside rumor: a personal journey." *American Psychologist*, 46 (May): 484–96.

Rosnow, Ralph L., and Gary Alan Fine. 1976. *Rumor and Gossip: The Social Psychology of Hearsay*. New York: Elsevier.

Roth, Cecil. 1971. "Inquisition." *Encyclopedia Judaica*: 1379–1407.

Rothman, Robert A. 1993. *Inequality and Stratification: Class, Color, and Gender* (2nd edn). Englewood Cliffs, NJ: Prentice-Hall.

Rubington, Earl, and Martin S. Weinberg (eds). 1987. *Deviance: The Interactionist Perspective* (5th edn). New York: Macmillan.

Runciman, Steven. 1955. *The Medieval Manichee*, London: Cambridge University Press.

Russell, Diana E. H. 1986. *The Secret Trauma: Incest in the Lives of Girls and Women*. New York: Basic Books.

Russell, Jeffrey Burton. 1971. *Religious Dissent in the Middle Ages*. New York: Wiley.

——. 1972. *Witchcraft in the Middle Ages*. Ithaca, NY: Cornell University Press.

——. 1977. *The Devil*. Ithaca, NY: Cornell University Press.

Sanger, William W. 1937. *The History of Prostitution*. New York: Eugenics.

Scheingold, Stuart A. 1984. *The Politics of Law and Order: Street Crime and Public Policy*. New York: Longman.

——. 1991. *The Politics of Street Crime: Criminal Process and Cultural Obsession*. Philadelphia: Temple University Press.

Schneider, Andrew. 1993. "Latin America senses retreat as Clinton administration muzzles drug war." *Indianapolis Star*, February 13, p. 1.

Schneider, Joseph W. 1985. "Social problems theory." *Annual Review of Sociology*, 11: 209–29.

Schneider, Joseph W., and John I. Kitsuse (eds). 1984. *Studies in the Sociology of Social Problems*. Norwood, NJ: Ablex.

Schur, Edwin M. 1979. *Interpreting Deviance: A Sociological Introduction*. New York: Harper & Row.

——. 1980. *The Politics of Deviance: Stigma Contests and the Uses of Power*. Englewood Cliffs, NJ: Prentice-Hall/Spectrum.

Scott, George Ryley. 1936. *A History of Prostitution*. London: Laurie.

Seligmann, Jean, et al. 1992. "The new age of Aquarius." *Newsweek*, February 3, pp. 65–7.

Shamir, Aharon. 1982. "The death drug." *Yedioth Ahronoth*, May 21, supplement, p. 11 (Hebrew).

Shenon, Philip. 1990. "War on drugs remains top priority, Bush says." *New York Times*, September 6, p. A22.

Shibutani, Tamotsu. 1966. *Improvised News: A Sociological Study of Rumor*. Indianapolis, IN: Bobbs-Merrill.

Shils, Edward. 1970. "Centre and periphery." In *Selected Papers by E. Shils*, Chicago, Department of Sociology, University of Chicago Student Edition.

Shoham, Giora S., Nili Geva, P. Kliger, and T. Chai. 1974. "Drug abuse among Israeli youth: epidemiological pilot study." *U.N. Bulletin on Narcotics*, 20(2): 9–28.

Shoham, Giora S., Giora Rahav, Y. Esformer, Joanna Blau, Nava Kaplinsky, R. Markovsky, and B. Wolf. 1979. "Differential patterns of drug involvement among Israeli youth." *U.N. Bulletin on Narcotics*, 30(4): 17–34.

——. 1981. "Polar types of reported drug involvement among Israeli youth." *The International Journal of the Addictions*, 16(7): 1161–7.

Shumaker, Wayne. 1972. *The Occult Sciences in the Renaissance*. Berkeley, Los Angeles, London: University of California Press.

Sinclair, Andrew. 1962. *Prohibition: The Era of Excess*. London: Faber & Faber.

Sirois, Francois. 1974. *Epidemic Hysteria*. Copenhagen: Munsgaard.

Slovic, Paul, Baruch Fischoff, and Sara Lichtenstein. 1980a. "Facts and fears: understanding perceived risk." In Richard C. Schwing and Walter A. Albers (eds), *Societal Risk Assessment: How Safe Is Enough?* New York: Plenum Press, pp. 181–212.

——. 1980b. "Risky assumptions." *Psychology Today*, June, pp. 44–8.

——. 1981. "Perceived risk: psychological factors and social implications." *Proceedings of the Royal Society of London*, A376(1): 17–34.

Slovic, Paul, Mark Layman, and James H. Flynn. 1991. "Risk, perception, trust, and nuclear waste: lessons from Yucca Mountain." *Environment*, 33 (April): 7–11, 28–30.

Solzhenitsyn, A. I. 1975. *The Gulag Archipelago*. New York: Harper & Row.

Spector, Malcolm, and John I. Kitsuse. 1973. "Social problems: a re-formulation." *Social Problems*, 21 (fall): 145–59.

——. 1977. *Constructing Social Problems*. Menlo Park, CA: Cummings.

——. 1987. "Preface to the Japanese edition: constructing social problems." *SSSP Newsletter*, 18 (fall): 13–15.

Spengler, J. J. 1968. "Demographic factors and early modern economic development." *Daedalus*, 97: 433–43.

Sprenger, J. and H. Kramer. [1487–1489] 1968. *Malleus Maleficarum* (trans., Montague Summers). London: Folio Society.

Stolz, Barbara Ann. 1990. "Congress and the War on Drugs: An Exercise in Symbolic Politics." Paper for presentation at the American Society of Criminology, Baltimore, November 9.

Stromer, Wolfgang von. 1970. "Nuremberg in the international economics of the Middle Ages." *Business History Review*, 44(2): 210–21.

Stuard, Susan M. (ed.). 1976. *Women in Medieval Society*. Philadelphia: University of Philadelphia Press.

Sumption, Jonathan. 1978. *The Albigensian Crusade*. London: Faber & Faber.

Sutherland, Edwin H. 1950a. "The sexual psychopath laws." *Journal of Criminal Law and Criminology*, 40 (January–February): 534–54.

——. 1950b. "The diffusion of sexual psychopath laws." *American Journal of Sociology*, 56 (September): 142–8.

Szasz, Thomas S. 1970. *The Manufacture of Madness*. New York: Harper & Row.

——. 1975. *Ceremonial Chemistry: The Ritual Persecution of Drug Addicts and Pushers*. Garden City, New York: Doubleday Books.

Taylor, Shelley E. 1982. "The availability Bias in social perception and interaction." In Daniel Kahneman, Paul Slovic, and Amos Tversky (eds), *Judgment Under Uncertainty; Heuristics and Biases*. Cambridge, England: Cambridge University Press, pp. 190–200.

Thomas, Keith. 1971. *Religion and the Decline of Magic*. New York: Scribners.

Thompson, William. 1990a. "Moral Panics, Pornography, and Social Policy." Paper presented to the annual meeting of the American Society of Criminology, Chicago.

——. 1990b. "Moral crusades and media censorship." *Franco-British Studies*, no. 9 (spring): 30–41.

Thompson, William, Alison King, and Jason Annetts. 1990. "Snuff, Sex, and Satan: Contemporary Legends and Moral Politics." Paper presented to the International Society of Urban Legends, Sheffield, England.

Thorndike, L. 1941. *History of Magic and Experimental Science*. New York: Columbia University Press.

Thrupp, S. L. 1972. "Medieval industry, 1000–1500." In Cipolla, C. M. (ed.), *The Fontana Economic History of Europe*, vol. 1, *The Middle Ages*. New York: Fontana, pp. 221–74.

Toufexis, Anastasia. 1991. "Innocent victims." *Time*, May 13, pp. 56–60.

Trebach, Arnold S. 1982. *The Heroin Solution*. New Haven, CT: Yale University Press.

Trevor-Roper, H. R. 1967. *The European Witch Craze of the Sixteenth and Seventeenth Centuries and Other Essays*. New York: Harper Torchbooks.

Trexler, Richard C. 1973. "Infanticide in Florence: new sources and first results." *History of Childhood Quarterly*, 1(1): 98–116.

Troyer, Ronald J. 1989. "The surprising resurgence of the smoking problem." In Joel Best (ed.), *Images of Issues: Typifying Contemporary Social Problems*. New York: Aldine de Gruyter, pp. 159–76.

Troyer, Ronald J., and Gerald E. Markle. 1983. *Cigarettes*. New Brunswick, NJ: Rutgers University Press.

Tucker, E. 1980. "Antecedents of contemporary witchcraft in the Middle Ages." *Journal of Popular Culture*, 14(1): 70–8.

Turberville, A. S. 1964. *Medieval Heresy and the Inquisition*. London: Archon.

Turner, Patricia A. 1993. *I Heard It Through the Grape-Vine: Rumor in African-American Culture*. Berkeley: University of California Press.

Turner, Ralph H., and Samuel J. Surace. 1956. "Zoot-suiters and Mexicans: symbols in crowd behavior." *American Journal of Sociology*, 62 (July): 14–20.

Tversky, Amos, and Daniel Kahneman. 1982. "Availability: a heuristic for judging frequency and probability." In Daniel Kahneman, Paul Slovic, and Amos Tversky (eds), *Judgment Under Uncertainty: Heuristics and Biases*. Cambridge, England: Cambridge University Press, pp. 163–78.

Ungar, Sheldon. 1990. "Moral Panics, the Military-Industrial Compex, and the arms race." *The Sociological Quarterly*, 31(2): 165–85.

——. 1992. "The rise and (relative) decline of global warming as a social problem." *The Sociological Quarterly*, 33(4): 483–501.

Useem, Bert, and Mayer N. Zald. 1982. "From pressure group to social movement." *Social Problems*, 30: 144–56.

Usher, A. D. 1956. "The history of population and settlement in Euro-Asia." In J. J. Spengler and D. D. Duncan (eds), *Demographic Analysis*. Glencoe, IL: Free Press.

Vanderford, Marsha L. 1989. "Vilification and social movements: a case study of pro-life and pro-choice rhetoric." *Quarterly Journal of Speech*, 75 (May): 166–82.

Van der Wee, Herman. 1975. "Structural changes and specialization in the industry of the southern Netherlands." *Economic History Review*, 2nd series, 28(2): 203–21.

Victor, Jeffrey S. 1989. "A rumor-panic about a dangerous satanic cult in western New York." *New York Folklore*, 15(1–2): 23–49.

——. 1990. "Satanic cult legends as contemporary legend." *Western Folklore*, 49 (February): 51–81.

——. 1991. "The dynamics of rumor-panics about satanic cults." In James T. Richardson, Joel Best, and David Bromley (eds), *The Satanic Scare*. New York: Aldine de Gruyter, pp. 221–36.

——. 1993. *Satanic Panic: The Creation of a Contemporary Legend*. Chicago, IL: Open Court Publishing.

Waddington, P. A. J. 1986. "Mugging as a moral panic: a question of proportion." *The British Journal of Sociology*, 37(2): 245–59.

Wakefield, W. and A. Evans (eds). 1969. *Heresies of the High Middle Ages*. New York: Columbia University Press.

Warner, M. 1976. *Alone of All Her Sex: The Myth and Cult of the Virgin Mary*. New York: Knopf.

Weber, M. 1964. *The Sociology of Religion*. Boston: Beacon Press.

——. 1968a. *Economy and Society: An Outline of Interpretive Sociology*. Ed. Guenther Roth and Claus Vittich; trans. Ephraim Fischoff et al. Totawa, NJ: Bedminster Press.

——. 1968b, *Max Weber on Charisma and Institution Building*. Edited with an introduction by S. N. Eisenstadt. Chicago: University of Chicago Press.

Webster, Charles (ed.). 1979. *Health, Medicine and Mortality in the Sixteenth Century*. Cambridge: Cambridge University Press.

Weisburd, David, Stanton Wheeler, Elin Waring, and Nancy Bode. 1991. *Crimes of the Middle Classes: White-Collar Offenders in the Federal Courts*. New Haven, CT: Yale University Press.

Weisman, Richard. 1984. *Witchcraft Magic and Religion in 17th Century Massachusetts*. Amherst: University of Massachusetts Press.

Wellford, Charles. 1975. "Labelling theory and criminology: an assessment." *Social Problems*, 22(3): 332–45.

White, Andrew Dickson. 1913. *A History of the Warfare of Science with Theology*. New York: D. Appleton.

Whitlock, F. A. 1979. "Witch crazes and drug crazes: a contribution to the social pathology of credulity and scapegoating." *Australian Journal of Social Issues*, 14(1): 43–54.

Williams, Charles. 1959. *Witchcraft*. New York: Meridian Books.

Williams, Hubert. 1986. "Every Narcotics User Is a Scourge and a Bum." *Newsday*, November 9, Ideas Section, p. 11.

Wolanski, Ami. 1981. *National Survey on the Progress of Youth – 1980*. Jerusalem: Ministry of Education, Youth Branch (Hebrew).

Wolanski, Ami, and David Kfir. 1982. *Characteristics, Functions and Treatment of Disconnected Youth and Those in Street Groups. Data from the Second National Survey of the Units for Progress of Youth – 1981*. Jerusalem: Ministry of Education, Youth Branch (Hebrew).

Woolgar, Steve, and Dorothy Pawluch. 1985. "Ontological gerrymandering: the anatomy of social problems explanations." *Social Problems*, 32 (February): 213–27.

Wrigley, E. A. 1969. *Population and History*, London: Weidenfeld & Nicolson.

Wright, Lawrence. 1993a. "Remembering Satan – Part I." *The New Yorker*, May 17, pp. 60–81.

——. 1993b. "Remembering Satan – Part II." *The New Yorker*, May 24, pp. 54–76.

Yin, Peter. 1980. "Fear of crime among the elderly: some issues and suggestions." *Social Problems*, 27 (April): 492–504.

Young, Jock. 1971a. *The Drugtakers*. London: MacGibbon & Kee.

——. 1971b. "The Role of the police as amplifiers of deviance, negotiators of of drug control as seen in Notting Hill." In Stanley Cohen (ed.), *Images of Deviance*. Harmondsworth, England: Penguin Books, pp. 27–61.

——. 1987. "The task facing a realist criminology." *Contemporary Crises*, 11: 337–56.

Zald, Mayer N., and John D. McCarthy (eds). 1987. *Social Movements in Organization Society: Collected Essays*. New Brunswick, NJ: Transaction Books.

Zatz, Marjorie S. 1987. "Chicano youth gangs and crime: the creation of a moral panic." *Contemporary Crises*, 11(2): 129–58.

Zguta, Russell. 1977. "Witchcraft trials in seventeenth century Russia." *American Historical Review*, 82(5): 1187–207.

Ziegler, Philip. 1971. *The Black Death*. New York: Harper & Row.

Zilboorg, G. with Henry, G. W. 1941. *A History of Medical Psychology*. New York: Norton.

Zurcher, Louis A., Jr, and George R. Kirkpatrick. 1976. *Citizens for Decency: Anti-Pornography Crusades as Status Defense*. Austin: University of Texas Press.

Zurcher, Louis, Jr, George R. Kirkpatrick, Robert G. Cushing, and Charles K. Bowman. 1971. "The anti-pornography campaign: a symbolic crusade." *Social Problems*, 19(2): 217–38.

INDEX OF AUTHORS

INDEX OF SUBJECTS